YOUNG HITLER

THE MAKING OF THE FÜHRER

PAUL HAM

PEGASUS BOOKS
NEW YORK LONDON

Young Hitler

Pegasus Books Ltd
148 West 37th Street, 13th Floor
New York, NY 10018

ISBN: 978-1-68177-747-4

10 9 8 7 6 5 4 3 2 1

Printed in the United States of America
Distributed by W. W. Norton & Company, Inc.

'What good fortune for governments that
the people do not think'
Adolf Hitler

'Nothing in all the world is more dangerous than
sheer ignorance and conscientious stupidity'
Martin Luther King

Contents

A little context . . .

No other leader or political movement has relied so heavily on catastrophic events for their rise to power as Adolf Hitler and the Nazi Party.

Hitler could not have travelled from 'Viennese bum' (as his once trusted colleague Hermann Göring later damned him) to 'Führer' without the apocalyptic conditions created by the First World War (1914–18) and its aftermath. Dismissed as a homeless crank before the war, Hitler was hailed as a messiah-like figure after it. 'What happened under Hitler,' writes the historian Ian Kershaw, 'is unimaginable without the experience of the First World War and what followed it.'[1]

Far less clear is *how* the experiences of Hitler's youth, especially during the First World War, wrought the conqueror of Europe out of this unpromising human clay. What mysterious alignment of nature, nurture, accident and opportunity created one of the most murderous dictators of the twentieth century? What, in short, *made* the Führer?

Every individual is powerfully shaped by extreme experiences in their childhood and youth, and Hitler was no exception. His memory of the Western Front was a constant companion in his life, a brooding passenger on the path to power, shaping his every thought and action. And he had a formidable recollection of it. Unlike most of his fellow soldiers, who were relieved when it was over and longed to go home, Hitler thrilled to battle, refused to accept defeat and fell into the darkest slough of despond at the Armistice. The war was a red-hot brand on his personality, a scorching reverie, an unforgettable dance with death.

Yet Hitler's Great War hasn't received the attention it deserves. Biographers tend to consign it to the sidelines, as a rite of passage, a youthful diversion; or they describe how he performed as a soldier. Yet, as Hitler himself often stated, that war and its immediate consequences were the most formative personal experiences of his life, with an immense impact on everything that followed.[2] Indeed, Hitler's 'first war' cries out for reassessment as *the* causative factor in his rise to power. But for most people, his role in it, and its aftermath, remains curiously obscure.

Nazi censors and myth-makers haven't helped. After he was elected chancellor, Hitler went to extraordinary lengths to suppress the facts about his youth – even ordering the execution of an 'art dealer' who had befriended him as a young man and who threatened to reveal unsavoury details of his early life in Vienna. So extreme were the measures Hitler and the Nazi propagandists took to preserve the myth of the 'Führer', that they beg the question: how much were they hiding, and why?

A little context may help to set the scene for the story that follows. The world Hitler was born into, in 1889, was at the flood tide of a period of immense economic development, colonial expansion and social upheaval. The 1890s were the fag ends of the 'Gilded Age', and for a few people it was exceptionally gilded. In Europe, in 1890, the wealthiest decile (top tenth) owned almost 90 per cent of total wealth (and would do so up until 1914), as the economist Thomas Piketty has shown.[3] Most of the rest lived in a state of grinding poverty, short life expectancy and constant anxiety.

The European powers were animated less by the social injustices at home than by the lure of the 'New Imperialism' abroad, chiefly the race to possess the world's remaining resource-rich territories in Africa. The 'Scramble for Africa', which took place between 1870 and 1913, resulted in a virtual free-for-all as European nations raced to seize and carve up this ancient patchwork of tribal lands. As *The Scramble for Africa*, the classic work by Thomas Pakenham, has shown, 'Africa was sliced up like a cake, and the pieces swallowed by five rival nations. By the end of the century the passions generated by the Scramble had helped to poison the political climate in Europe, brought Britain to the brink of war with France, and precipitated a struggle with the Boers, the costliest, longest and bloodiest war since 1815.'[4]

The Scramble left the two leading imperialists, France and Britain, feuding over the richest spoils, with Germany holding a few scraps, the dangerously embittered loser. These fresh colonial seizures would not reverse the slow decline of the chief imperial powers. The British and French were already feeling premonitions of eclipse. The German and American economies were growing at a faster rate, and would soon be strong enough to challenge the dominance of Britain and France over a world swaddled in the bright pink and blue of their colonial rule.

Workers, too, wanted a share in the wealth of the world. Rumblings from within were threatening to check the greed and power of the capital-owning classes. Throughout Europe, workers' movements were in full-throated roar, with new socialist or 'labour' parties forming: the Sozialistische Arbeiterpartei (SAPD) in Germany in 1875; the Labour Party in Britain in 1900; and the Parti socialiste de France in 1902. The American Populist (or People's) Party, an agrarian workers' party, enjoyed its greatest success during the financial panic of the mid-1890s (before it folded into the Democrats).

In tandem, rising economic nationalism spawned a mood of aggressive patriotism and racial rivalry. Whole peoples – nations, religions, tribes – were deemed 'superior' or 'inferior' according to the widely accepted theory of 'Social Darwinism'. Put simply, this bastardized application of the science of evolution to human society decreed that the 'fittest race' would one day rule the earth.

As the world spilled into the twentieth century, a new social conservatism arose among European youth, characterized by a resurgent faith in God, King (or Kaiser or Tsar) and Country. Many French and German students in particular shunned the decadence of their parents' generation and yearned for a return to the Old Certainties.[5] Militant nationalism inflamed European prejudice against ethnic minorities. The Jews, in particular, were widely reviled and routinely persecuted. In the late nineteenth century, the Russians launched massive 'pogroms', or violent attacks, against Jewish communities. In response, hundreds of thousands of Eastern European Jews fled to Western Europe, with many settling in Germany and Austria–Hungary, chiefly Vienna.

The French demonstrated a less bloody but no less pernicious brand of Jewish vilification. The Dreyfus Affair of 1894–1906, in which an innocent Jewish officer was wrongly accused of treason, split the nation and exposed the depths of French anti-Semitism.

The masses were less interested in the cruelty played out in a distant colony or the state of a persecuted minority than in the dazzling inventions of the Machine Age, which reached its height between 1890 and 1920: soaring buildings, fabulous flying machines, sparkling auto-mobiles and weapons of unprecedented destructive power, alongside tinned soup, radioactivity, the cinematograph (forerunner of the movie projector) and the first scientific evidence that CO_2 produces global warming. The astonishing array of discoveries prefigured the way people would live for the next hundred years.

Bliss it was to be alive at the dawn of the twentieth century, for those with the power and wealth to enjoy it. And one of the brightest suns on the horizon was a young political entity, recently unified and bursting with self-confidence: 'Deutschland'.

Hitler's life cannot be understood without comprehending his devo-tion to the German state, the 'Fatherland' of his youthful dreams. This went beyond mere patriotism. It was a visceral longing for a future ruled by a Greater Germany, a 'Pan-Germany'. In the years before the First World War, this seemed realizable, even inevitable, in the eyes of the few German supremacists and Prussian militarists Hitler so admired.

The historical roots of Hitler's passion lay in the creation of Imperial Germany in 1871 – the result of the unification of twenty-six kingdoms, duchies and principalities that had dominated Central Europe since the defeat of Napoleon in 1815. The stern hand of Otto von Bismarck, the 'Iron Chancellor', moulded these constituents into a unified state, over which the Prussians and the Hohenzollern Kaisers assumed leadership after their emphatic victory in the Franco-Prussian War of 1870–71.

The new German Reich stood to benefit from political unity and an internal free trade zone (the *Zollverein*), which would spread the harvest of economic success from Prussia to Bavaria. And yet 'race' and 'culture' were equally powerful incentives towards unification. Deutschland drew on Pan-Germanism – the recognition of a shared polity, bound by a common language (92 per cent spoke German); religion (most called themselves Lutheran); and a palpable sense of national destiny, borne on a belief in the supremacy of German culture and an acute consciousness of what it meant to be 'German': a sensation or spirit rather than a nationality, traceable to the distant past – beyond the Holy Roman Empire to the ancient world of the Teutonic tribes and Wagnerian mythology.

Four decades (1871–1913) of awesome economic growth followed German unification, fuelled by a surging population that rose from 41 million to 68 million in that time. By 1900 Germany had outgrown Britain as the largest economy in Europe, with the second largest rail network in the world after the United States.[6] By 1913, Germany had replaced Britain as Europe's biggest exporter of steel. The new Germany also offered the most progressive social policies in Europe. Bismarck had introduced, in the 1880s, Europe's first welfare system, and enacted laws that gave workers health and accident insurance, maternity benefits and a national pension scheme, well ahead of any other developed nation.[7] From 1871 every German man was eligible to vote, a freedom not extended to all British men until 1918 (German women were granted universal suffrage in 1918, ten years ahead of British women).

In short, in contrast to what Britain, France and Russia (known as the Triple Entente) deceitfully portrayed as a menacing tyranny in the decade before the outbreak of the First World War – some historians still compare pre-1914 Germany with the Nazi regime[8] – Germany was in fact the most liberal state in Europe, with a vibrant Social Democratic Party.

In Prussia, however, lurked the authoritarian underbelly to this state of progressive liberalism. The Prussian military class hankered to expand Germany's borders, to secure the Reich from the threat of Russia and acquire a colonial empire in the British and French mould. In the early 1900s, their pickelhaubed commanders lacked the political clout to realize this goal. Yet the Prussians looked and sounded aggressive enough to inflame the Triple Entente's war-mongering, which had the perverse effect of weakening Berlin's civilian government and reinforcing the Prussian generals, hastening the march to war.

Feeling squeezed in a three-way vice by Russia, France and Britain, Germany's military rulers drew up a fantastic plan for a 'preventative' war, a 'charge out of the fortress', to pre-empt an attack by their perceived enemies and secure the young Reich.

In July 1914, Berlin activated it. After Chancellor Theobald von Bethmann-Hollweg effectively ceded control of the nation to the military, the Prussian warlords *manufactured* a case for war out of a manageable crisis in the Balkans. The assassination of Archduke Franz Ferdinand did not, in itself, *cause* the First World War any more than the flutter of butterfly wings: the murder of the heir to the Austro-Hungarian throne merely provided the tinder to those in Berlin and Vienna who were already determined to start one.[9]

No group was keener on war with the Serbs than the German-speaking minority in Austria, the fiercely loyal 'Pan-Germans', including the Hitler family, who found themselves part of a restless minority in the polyglot Austro-Hungarian Empire, a curious ethnic relic of the historical convulsions of the nineteenth century.

A brief summary of those upheavals will help us to understand why young Hitler, an Austrian, grew up in thrall to the German nation and felt contempt for the Austro-Hungarian regime. In 1815 the Congress of Vienna, convened to negotiate the peaceful reconstruction of Europe after the defeat of Napoleon, created a loose association of thirty-nine German states, or principalities, known as the German Confederation, the majority of which would later be unified by Bismarck (see above). It was conceived as the prelude to a modern state that would replace the ailing Holy Roman Empire.

Riven by internal disputes and competing power claims, the Confederation failed to consolidate, ruptured under the democratic revolutions that swept Europe in 1848, and was eventually torn apart when its two most powerful members, Prussia and Austria, and their allies, went to war in 1866. This climax of old hostilities, traceable to the invasion of Austrian-controlled Silesia in 1740 by Prussia's Frederick the Great, ended with Austria's defeat.

Excluded from the new German sphere, Vienna's ruling Habsburg dynasty scrabbled together a 'dual monarchy' with Hungary, under the Austro-Hungarian Compromise of 1867. Meanwhile Prussia, under the firm guidance of Bismarck, confirmed its ascendancy over the German principalities and, with the defeat of France in the Franco-Prussian War in 1871, forged ahead with the creation of the unified German state.

A pervasive feature of Bismarck's Germany, as we have seen, was the citizens' rich conception of themselves as 'German', in the sense of sharing a national – and racial – affinity. Hitler's family, along with millions of fellow German-speaking Austrians, shared this palpable German identity, regardless of the fact that they lived in a different country. It was a near-mystical connection that transcended politics and geography.[10] And yet, they were excluded from the newly formed German Reich and felt like outcasts, exiled from the land of their origins.

Of the eleven different nationalities in Austria–Hungary, the German Austrians formed the most powerful ethnic bloc, numbering 12.7 million, almost a quarter of the empire's 52.8 million total, followed by Hungarians (20 per cent), Czechs (13 per cent) and Poles (10 per cent). The ethnic Germans would never cease to yearn for a return to the Fatherland, dreaming of the day that a Greater Germany would subsume all Austria (a dream Hitler would fulfil with the Anschluss of March 1938, when he annexed Austria to the Third Reich). The flip-side of their Germanophilia was their contempt for the multi-racial composition of the Austrian realm, chiefly its multi-tongued Parliament in Vienna – feelings the young Hitler would fully absorb.

In the 1880s and 1890s, these Pan-Germans were solidly represented in the Linz area where Hitler grew up. Indeed, the Linz Programme, a political manifesto published in 1882 and named after the capital of Upper Austria, called for the 'Germanicization' of the Austro-Hungarian Empire and the occupation of the Slavic lands.[11] But it was in Vienna that, as we shall see, they found their most emphatic voice, among a group of far-right politicians, hack journalists and soap-box preachers seized by a vision of the German people rising up to take control of the senescent Habsburg Empire.

On 11 November 1918, after four years of a world war in which 37 million people were killed or wounded, Germany surrendered.

With their currency worthless, their nation humiliated, their monarchy finished and their lives touched by the death of their fathers, sons and husbands, the German people turned in despair to an unlikely 'saviour': an unknown Austrian war hero with unusual charisma, a voice like a bludgeon and a will of iron, whose refusal to accept the peace settlement and thunderous pledge to make Germany great again seized the imagination of a nation broken by the bloodiest conflict the world had known.

Young Hitler: The Making of the Führer is more than the story of his early years. It aims to show how his personal experiences of war wrenched an already disturbed mind in the direction of a programme of genocidal revenge. It seeks to demonstrate how the 'Führer' – in the sense of what Hitler would *personally* become – could not have been possible without his immersion in the First World War and its aftermath, experiences he would remember as the most formative of his life. In a broader sense, *Young Hitler* describes how the brutalized society of post-war Germany performed the role of Dr Frankenstein to any number of cranks, extremists and criminals, and gave a man like Adolf Hitler a launch pad and a breeding ground.

A word of caution: writing about this man is notoriously difficult because Hitler and the Nazis tried to erase or amend his past in order to remake his life as legend. The biographer is thus drawn into a net cast by the subject to preserve a myth. To survive entrapment we must unpick the net. Hindsight threatens to overwhelm the task, because everything written about Hitler is, consciously or not, conditioned by the fact of the Holocaust. Aspects of his early life that would humanize him – his love for his mother, his friendships with Jews in Vienna – only seem unusual or surprising in light of what followed.

Should one attempt to humanize him? Some people think it morally obscene to try to imagine Hitler as a boy, a youth, a soldier, with thoughts and feelings; for them, he will always be the monster who ordered the Holocaust (witness their reaction to the perceived 'humanizing' of the Führer in the film *Downfall*). We learn nothing from this kind of thinking. As the resurgent neo-Nazism in our own time makes painfully clear, Hitler was not unusual: his baggage of hatred weighs down many people today. His mind was an extreme manifestation of how many people thought – then and now.

To brand Hitler a monster, a psychotic killer, the incarnation of evil, and then walk away as if our job is done, suggests that he was a rare and inexplicable phenomenon, a freak of history whom we're unlikely to meet again. No doubt he had freakish abilities: exceptional skills as a public speaker, a formidable memory and a frigid charm. The unsettling truth, however, is that Hitler was all too human: he personified the feelings of millions, and still does.

And yet, Hitler's murderous hatred of, and determination to destroy, the Jewish people, as well as his racial theories that condemned other defenceless minorities (homosexuals, the Roma and Sinti, the mentally and physically disabled) to the death camps continue to defy conventional understanding.

Young Hitler: The Making of the Führer seeks the answers in his youth, by retracing the events that compelled him to flee his family and the country of his birth, and fling himself on to the battlefield, only to find his life's dream in ruins on his return to war-ravaged Germany.

Note: The chapter titles that follow are Hitler's own words, taken from Mein Kampf *or his later* Table Talk.

Chapter One

'At the time I thought everything should be blown up'

On Easter Saturday, 20 April 1889, in the small Upper Austrian town of Braunau am Inn, where they lived in a rented apartment above a tavern, a child whom they named Adolf was born to Alois and Klara Hitler. The couple had already had two children, a boy, Gustav, and a girl, Ida, both of whom had died very young, bringing their parents immeasurable grief. And so, on her surviving son Klara resolved to devote all her love and maternal care.

It is impossible to imagine Hitler's rise to power had he retained his father's original surname of Schicklgruber. The image of hundreds of thousands of Germans raising their right arms and shouting *'Heil Schicklgruber!'* is not only laughable, it is impossible. Such is the power of a name.

Alois was born in Döllersheim, Lower Austria, in 1837 to an unmarried farmer's daughter called Maria (or Marie) Anna Schicklgruber; the identity of his father remains unknown. Five years after Alois's mysterious birth, Maria Anna married a poor, fifty-year-old miller's assistant called Johann Georg Hiedler. After her untimely death in 1847, the care of Alois was entrusted to Georg's wealthy younger brother, a farmer in the nearby village of Spital called Johann Nepomuk, who spelled his surname Hüttler (it was commonplace at the time to find different spellings of the same family name).

In 1876, when Alois was thirty-nine, and with his family's support, he discarded his unfortunate surname and replaced it with a variant of his foster father's. He would henceforth be known as Alois 'Hitler', a name of fourteenth-century Germanic-Czech origins meaning 'small-holder'. Alois's decision had little to do with his career ambitions: to that point, 'Schicklgruber' had not hindered his progress as a respected customs official. More likely, he adopted the surname to secure his legitimacy – and thus his inheritance – and to distance himself and his family from their impoverished past. The Schicklgrubers had been poor farmers and his mother and Georg so short of money that they were forced, at times, to sleep in a cattle trough.

In early 1879 Nepomuk and three other witnesses made official the lie that Alois Hitler was the legitimate son of 'Georg Hitler', as inscribed in the entry in the parish registry at Döllersheim. And so the greatest impediment to Adolf's future prospects as a politician was struck from the record and the boy's father pronounced 'legitimate'.

The identity of Alois's true father (and Adolf's paternal grandfather) remains a mystery. Some believe Alois was the product of a love affair between Maria Anna and Johann Nepomuk, who, just to complicate matters, happened to be Klara's grandfather. If true, that would have made Hitler's mother a blood relation to Alois, and Hitler the offspring of an incestuous relationship. Another widespread belief is that Alois's father was an itinerant Jew who had slept with Maria Anna on his way through town. Despite there being no evidence, Hitler's 'Jewish grand-father' remains a popular myth, wrongly believed to this day.

Alois Hitler, a dutiful government functionary, was among those German-speaking Austrians who tended to feel 'more German than the Germans' in the ethnic chaos of the Austro-Hungarian Empire, with its eleven nationalities, nine different languages and several religions. He was respectable, even charming, in public, but in private he turned into a humourless boor, absorbed in ruling his domestic dictatorship when he wasn't visiting the local tavern. He was 'an authoritarian, domineering, overbearing husband,' writes Kershaw, 'and a stern, distant, masterful and often irritable father.'[1] If he seems a domestic tyrant by today's standards, however, back then he was fairly typical of his time. He was also a responsible, status-proud provider, with a passion for beekeeping.

Restless and itinerant, Alois was often on the move, changing homes and villages and dragging his family with him. In 1892, when Adolf was three years old, Alois was promoted to Higher Collector of Customs, a position of some prestige, and the family moved to Passau in Bavaria, on the German side of the border, imbuing Adolf's speech with a German accent. In the same year, the family suffered a further tragedy: another son, Otto, was born, and died after only seven days. Klara, a devoted mother, felt the blow especially hard.

Klara Hitler (*née* Pölzl) was twenty-three years younger than Alois and his third wife. He had two children from his second marriage, Alois Jr and Angela, who lived with the family in the 1890s after the death of their mother. While Klara did her best to involve them, they felt excluded and neglected as young Adolf received the lion's share of her affection. In 1943, Alois Jr's son Patrick complained that Adolf had been 'spoiled from early in the morning until late at night, and the stepchildren had to listen to endless stories about how wonderful Adolf was.'[2] Alois Jr left the family home at fourteen, and Angela married when she was twenty.

Alois and Klara had met when she worked as his housemaid. A modest village girl, she was a soft, put-upon woman, with neatly plaited brown hair, 'beautifully expressive grey-blue eyes',[3] and a quiet, if ineffectual, persistence. She would try to defend her son from her husband's rages, and took Adolf's side when he disobeyed Alois's edicts, as he would increasingly do as he grew older, provoking occasional beatings and stormy scenes. Much has been made of Hitler's father's violence, but there is no evidence that his beatings were any harsher than most little boys received at the time.

In this atmosphere, the mother's protective love offered a warm and smothering refuge for her son. Hitler himself would recall, in *Mein Kampf,* being his 'mother's darling' and living in a 'soft downy bed'.[4]

He more than reciprocated her love, according to the family's Jewish doctor, Eduard Bloch. 'Outwardly his love for his mother was his most striking feature,' Dr Bloch later wrote. 'I have never witnessed a closer attachment.'[5] August Kubizek, the only friend of Hitler's youth, would similarly observe: 'Adolf really loved his mother . . . I remember many occasions when he showed this love for his mother, most deeply and movingly during her last illness; he never spoke of his mother but with ·deep affection . . . When we lived together in Vienna he always carried his mother's portrait with him.'[6]

In 1894, when Adolf was five, Klara gave birth to another son, Edmund, and in 1896 to a girl, Paula. Deprived of his status as his mother's favourite, young Adolf grew sullen and resentful. He absorbed himself in the western novels of Karl May. He adored Old Shatterhand, May's greatest hero, and the American Indian leader Winnetou. He flung himself into games of cowboys and Indians, an activity that he kept up well into adolescence, long after his peers had turned their minds to sport or girls. Bereft of friends his own age, Adolf would recruit younger boys into his 'tribe' and impel them to play.

Hitler would invoke the memory of May throughout his life. The popular storyteller was a kind of mentor: '[W]hen faced by seemingly hopeless situations,' Albert Speer later wrote, '[the adult Hitler] would still reach for these stories [because] they gave him courage like works of philosophy for others or the Bible for elderly people.'[7]

In late 1898 the family moved into a small house next to the cemetery in the village of Leonding, just outside Linz (destined to be a Nazi shrine in years to come). One of his earliest sketches, 'Our Bedroom', suggests in its title that the entire family crowded into two single beds. In fact, this was Adolf and Paula's room, where each morning he dreaded the prospect of his sister kissing him, as their mother had urged her to do. His brother, Edmund, slept with his parents. The boy died of measles in 1900, aged six, restoring Adolf's status as his mother's only son.

By the age of twelve Hitler had grown into an emotionally indulged, self-absorbed boy with a marked contempt for authority and the temper of a bully. One witness remembered an 'imperious' child, 'quick to anger', who 'wouldn't listen' to anyone: 'He would get the craziest notions and get away with it. If he didn't have his way he got very angry . . . [H]e had no friends, took to no one and could be very heartless. He could fly into a rage over any triviality.'[8]

Hitler's high-schooling involved two institutions, neither of which was able to help this stubbornly indolent lad who seemed determined to remain impervious to instruction. While he had done well at his *Volkschule*, or elementary school, in the village of Fischlham near Linz, his happy days there had ended abruptly in 1900 when his father decided to send him to the *Realschule* in the city, which emphasized technical subjects, rather than to the classically orientated *Gymnasium*, or grammar school. Here, Hitler failed to perform adequately in any discipline except drawing. Mocked as a country yokel, he neither made friends nor sought any. He dragged himself sullenly to classes. He ridiculed authority. He failed mathematics and natural history, and in 1901–2 had to repeat Year 1.

Hitler admired only one teacher, Dr Leopold Poetsch, a German who taught history and filled the boy's head with stirring tales of Germany's heroic past: '[Poetsch] penetrated through the dim mist of thousands of years,' Hitler later wrote. 'When we listened to him we became afire with enthusiasm and we were sometimes moved even to tears.'[9] Hitler would later attribute his transformation into a young nationalist 'revolutionary' to Poetsch's lessons, a classic example of retroactively imbuing a past relationship with fateful power. Hitler loaded up Georg Ritter von Schönerer, the then popular leader of the Pan-German movement, with similar influence over his juvenile mind. Yet Schönerer's thundering German supremacism and anti-Semitism were in far-away Vienna.

Here in Linz, it was Hitler's schoolboy impressionability and intimacy with Poetsch, whom he fondly recalled as a 'gray haired, eloquent old gentleman' and father-figure, that activated his nascent pride in a Greater Germany and seeded the idea of Jews and Slavs as not only undesirable aliens but also as inferior *races*. Poetsch came from the southern German-language region bordering the South Slavs, where his experience of the racial struggle 'made him a fanatical German nationalist', writes William Shirer.[10] Certainly Hitler never forgot his favourite teacher. Many years later, on a tour of occupied Austria as Führer in 1938, he visited Poetsch in Klagenfurt and was delighted to find that his childhood mentor had been a member of the underground Nazi SS in Austria, which had been banned in the years before the country capitulated to German occupation.

At school, Hitler's only real interest was 'art', not history as he later claimed, despite failing to achieve 'Excellent' for any of his drawings; 'Good' was his highest grade in the subject in four years at the *Realschule*. One of his surviving sketches (presumably not a piece of course work) depicts his then art teacher masturbating, an image that psycho-historians would probably do well to ignore: how many schoolboys, none of them future dictators, have similarly mocked their teachers?[11]

Despite his inauspicious sallies with a pencil, from a young age Adolf declared that he wanted to be a 'great artist'. Alois took it as a personal affront, dismissing his son's dream as preposterous. Furious at the boy's indolence, he urged Adolf to follow his example and enter the civil service, and in this dispute over his future the threads of Hitler's tense relationship with his father snapped. 'It was simply inconceivable to him,' he would later say of Alois, 'that I might reject what had become the content of his whole life . . . Then barely eleven years old, I was forced into opposition for the first time in my life.' He concluded: 'I did not want to become a civil servant.'[12]

When, aged thirteen, Hitler again informed his father of his ambitions, Alois was 'struck speechless': 'Painter? Artist?' he cried scornfully, Hitler later related. 'He doubted my sanity, or perhaps he thought he had heard wrong or misunderstood me.'[13] The boy's dreams conjured everything Alois most loathed and feared: the worthless future and chronic poverty of a lazy bohemian – the very opposite of the provincial, respectable civil servant Alois had striven to be. 'Artist, no, never as long as I live!' Hitler would remember his father shouting. Father and son would never be reconciled on the point. 'And thus the situation remained on both sides,' Hitler wrote in *Mein Kampf.* 'My father did not depart from his "Never!" And I intensified my "Oh, yes!"'[14]

Adolf's defiance was 'a rejection of everything that his father stood for, and hence a rejection of his father himself.'[15] 'To become a painter would have been the worst possible insult to his father,' August Kubizek, Hitler's teenage friend, would recall.[16] From that point on, the boy received a 'sound thrashing every day', his sister Paula would remember, though in fact the beatings were probably less frequent than that.

In trying to protect her son, Klara hoped to 'obtain with her kindness' what his father had failed to achieve with cruelty.[17] Hitler's childhood henceforth oscillated between feelings of deep affection for his mother and fear of, and often hatred for, his father, which helps to explain the insufferable tantrums that began around this time, recurring with terrifying intensity into adulthood.

On the morning of 3 January 1903, sixty-five-year-old Alois collapsed in his chair at his local café in Leonding and was soon pronounced dead, of internal bleeding. Hitler's immediate reactions were grief and tears at the loss of the father he had probably feared more than hated; certainly Kubizek believed that Hitler grudgingly respected Alois and, much later, in *Mein Kampf* Hitler himself would write of his respect for his father. However, a measure of relief tempered the family's mourning. They were now well cared for financially, with Klara's widow's pension, and freed from the stifling presence of a man who had exhausted any capacity for love his son might once have felt.

Some boys feel inspired to honour through imitation their father's memory. Not young Hitler, who, as if in defiance of his late father, continued to fulfil his family's low expectations of him. If he had hidden talents, as some of his teachers believed, he kept them well disguised under an affectation of careless indifference. Young Adolf was irremediably lazy when it suited him. His sliding academic performance accentuated his moroseness and strong temper, and dulled his self-esteem. In 1903–4, so bad were his Year 3 reports that he was allowed to advance to the fourth form only by leaving the *Realschule* in Linz and continuing his education at one of the outlying provincial schools. He was being effectively expelled. 'For the moment only one thing was certain: my obvious lack of success at school,' Hitler later admitted. 'What gave me pleasure I learned, especially everything which, in my opinion, I should later need as a painter. What seemed to me unimportant . . . or was otherwise unattractive to me, I sabotaged completely.'[18] A former teacher, Dr Eduard Huemer, would remember him as stubborn, high-handed, dogmatic and hot-tempered, prone to playing pranks on other boys.[19]

At his new school in Steyr, near Linz, his grades plummeted further, perhaps partly a result of his leaving home for the first time to lodge with a foster family. He missed his mother's quiet affection, and later admitted that he felt acute homesickness: '. . . he had been filled with yearning and resentment when his mother sent him to Steyr,' Dr Josef Goebbels would later note.[20] In 1904–5 he failed German language and mathematics, subjects that were critical to his advancement.

This time, he avoided the humiliation of the school rejecting him by deciding to abandon formal education altogether. In the summer of 1905, at the age of sixteen, he dropped out. On his last day at Steyr, Hitler went out to celebrate, apparently alone. He later claimed to have lost his final school report, telling his mother that it had blown out of the window of his train. In fact, the school director later discovered it, soiled and crumpled: young Adolf had used his report as toilet paper.

Hitler left the *Realschule* feeling nothing but hatred for the school, his schoolmates and his teachers. They were to blame for his failure, not him. His loathing of authority also embraced the Catholic Church in which he was raised, probably the result of the fury he felt towards a school priest who had offended him. Of Hitler's confirmation in Linz Cathedral in 1904, his godfather, Johann Prinz, would recall the most 'gruff and obstinate' of boys: 'I had the impression that he found the whole confirmation disgusting.'[21] In 1942 Hitler reflected on his adolescence: 'At thirteen, fourteen, fifteen, I no longer believed in anything, certainly none of my friends believed in the so-called communion . . . [A]t the time I thought everything should be blown up.'[22]

Whence arose his juvenile rage at the world? Hitler had not had a 'difficult childhood'. He was not born into poverty, or a loveless or broken family. The answer has eluded the powers of psychiatrists. 'For all we know,' Volker Ullrich, Hitler's most recent biographer, concludes, 'Hitler seems to have had a fairly normal childhood . . . [T]here are no obvious indications of an abnormal personality development to which Hitler's later crimes may be attributed. If Hitler had a problem it was an over-abundance rather than a paucity of motherly love.'[23]

Hitler justified the decision to end his education by claiming he was sick. He persuaded his mother to hope that, as the only 'man' in the family, he would be able to help her around the house. Klara relented, but in both respects he deceived her: he was not ill enough to terminate his education; and in the ensuing two years he would prove a useless 'man about the house', given to loafing, drawing, long walks and little housework. Household tasks he thought beneath the dignity of the radical bohemian he aspired to be, and he simply refused to do any.

At this time, the Hitlers were living in a small apartment on the third floor of a tenement building at Humboldtstrasse 31 in Linz. To augment her pension, Klara let out the main bedroom to lodgers, so she and Paula slept in the living room while Adolf occupied the spare room (or closet). His late father's grim portrait stared down from the walls and several of Alois's pipes were carefully laid out on the shelves. The ghost of the petty tyrant lived on, distilling a drip of defiance in the mind of his son. Hitler continued to pursue a 'life of leisure', as he called it, with painting, writing and reading – chiefly stories from German mythology about the heroic feats of Teutonic tribes – and affecting a dandyish indifference to his future prospects.

Everyone who knew him at the time would recall how the sixteen-year-old threw himself at drawing, usually buildings, museums or bridges, with a manic fervour, late into the night, to the exclusion of any other person or concern. During these creative bursts, Hitler would retreat into a fantasy in which he would redesign Linz and fashion new cities, imagining himself a genius with the power to change the world (thirty-five years later, he would in fact order a new bridge over the Danube based on his youthful designs).[24] The slightest knock to this dream-made-real threw him into fits of rage and despair, such as when he failed to win a lottery in which he had convinced himself he was destined to triumph. His winnings were supposed to finance his design of a grand house on the Danube. In Hitler's mind, bad luck had nothing to do with it. Dark forces were to blame. He denounced the lottery organizers and the government, whom he accused of rigging the outcome against him.[25] He raged at the credulity of the poor lottery players, doomed forever to lose their savings. Everyone was to blame for Hitler's failure to win the jackpot except the angry adolescent whose numbers had not come up.

Chapter Two

'At home I do not remember having heard the word Jew'

In 1904, behind the colonnades inside the Linz opera house, from where it was possible to watch the performance with a cheap 'standing-room' ticket, Hitler, then aged fifteen and still at the *Realschule* in Steyr, first met August Kubizek ('Gustl'), who was nine months older and destined to become his only boyhood friend. Gustl was a shy, thoughtful young man and a talented musician. His first impression of Adolf was of 'a remarkably pale, skinny youth . . . who was following the performance with glistening eyes. I surmised that he came from a better-class home, for he was always dressed with meticulous care and was very reserved.'[1]

Thus began their odd friendship, as described in Kubizek's 1951 recollections *The Young Hitler I Knew*, an authentic memoir of Hitler's boyhood.[2] No doubt it contains errors of emphasis and fact, skewed by distance and hindsight, yet it accurately portrays this strangely lopsided relationship, in which Hitler always ran the show, berating Gustl for his lack of punctuality, shouting down his friend's conventional middle-class ideas, and generally dominating the quiet and inoffensive music-lover, who patiently acceded to the will of his overbearing companion.

The relationship worked because each young man found his role and stuck to it: Hitler the braggart and poseur; Kubizek the self-effacing acolyte and patient listener. Gustl's passivity and wry sense of humour proved perfect foils to Hitler's bossiness, self-importance and aggression. They performed a sort of double act. And while Hitler's braggadocio compensated for his academic inadequacy, Kubizek's quiet confidence reflected a genuine ability; when they met he was working in his father's upholstery business and studying music, and he would later become an accomplished musician and minor conductor.

Kubizek saw Hitler as a curiosity, a character to be studied, as well as a friend; Hitler revelled in Kubizek's deference and admiration. Neither youth showed much interest in girls, though Hitler's swagger seems to have drawn the eyes of some of the opera-going ladies. Their relationship was not homosexual, as has been suggested. They shared a love of opera, chiefly the works of Richard Wagner, and regularly attended performances.

At the time, Hitler was of average height, skinny, with sunken cheeks. He already wore his black hair straight down over his forehead. He dressed in the pointedly bohemian style his father would have loathed: a broad-brimmed hat, black kid gloves, white shirts and black, silk-lined overcoats. He neither played nor took any interest in sport (though he occasionally skied). He roamed the streets of Linz dreaming of how he would rebuild the city.

Those who met him often remarked on Hitler's extraordinary eyes. They were 'shining', 'blank' and 'cruel', Kubizek's mother would recall.[3] 'Never in my life,' Kubizek wrote, 'have I seen any other person whose appearance was so completely dominated by the eyes . . . In fact, Adolf spoke with his eyes, and even when his lips were silent one knew what he wanted to say.'[4] Sharp and defiant, Hitler's eyes outshone his unappealing facial features – a thin-lipped mouth, straight nose with fleshy nostrils, and faint suggestions of facial hair (his toothbrush moustache would not appear until after the war).

Communication between Hitler and Kubizek was entirely one-sided. Hitler showed little interest in anyone but himself and his own ambitions, and furiously attacked those who, he believed, failed to understand him or obstructed his plans. In fact, he had an audience of one: Kubizek listened and nodded, later observing with a weary shrug, 'My work was to [Hitler] nothing but a tiresome hindrance to our personal relationship. Impatiently he would twirl the small black cane which he always carried' (a precursor to the whip he would wield in Munich after the First World War). When Adolf dropped out of education and Gustl innocently asked whether he would get a job, Hitler gruffly replied, 'Of course not,' as if jobs were for lesser beings.[5]

On their daily walks around Linz, Hitler would launch into long, angry speeches on any subject that seized him. He delivered these tempestuous bursts with a verbal dexterity that astonished Kubizek: great gusts of unbroken verbiage issued forth, about art, the city's design, the bridge over the Danube, a new underground railway system and, of course, the latest Wagner performance. He would swamp his companion with waves of rising fury, as if imagining he were addressing a great crowd and not his only friend. Spellbound, Gustl decided that Adolf had a primal need to shout:

These speeches, usually delivered somewhere in the open, seemed to be like a volcano erupting. It was as though something quite apart from him was bursting out of him. Such rapture I had only witnessed so far in the theatre, when an actor had to express some violent emotions, and at first, confronted by such eruptions, I could only stand gaping and passive, forgetting to applaud. But soon I realised that this was not play-acting. No, this was not acting, not exaggeration, this was really felt, and I saw that he was in dead earnest . . . Not what he said impressed me first, but how he said it. This to me was something new, magnificent. I had never imagined that a man could produce such an effect with mere words. All he wanted from me, however, was one thing – agreement.[6]

And if he dissented? 'Harmless things, like a couple of hasty words, could make him explode with anger.'[7]

Hitler's chief topics were architecture, the Habsburgs and German greatness. He would bang on for hours about the flaws in the urban design of Linz and sketch how the city should be rebuilt (many years later, the fifty-year-old would ruthlessly try to execute what the fifteen-year-old had so precociously conceived). Echoing the standard Pan-German line of the time, he disdained what he knew of the Habsburg rule as ineffectual, and dismissed as unworkable the racial melting pot of the Viennese Parliament, which, at any time, consisted of representatives of many of the empire's different nationalities, including Germans, Czechs, Poles, Hungarians and Italians. He yearned for the day when Austria's German minority would merge with their kinsmen to create a new German Reich that would dominate Europe. Kubizek, who had little interest in politics, would never forget his friend's incessant use of the word 'Reich'. Hitler's contempt for the Austrian regime deepened in direct proportion to his admiration for all things German, an infatuation ingrained in him by growing up in the German-speaking community in Austria, and by the rich tales of German conquest he'd read about at school.

Of the greatest Germans on whom he would lavish admiration – Martin Luther, Frederick the Great, Bismarck and Friedrich Nietzsche – none was dearer to him than his beloved Wagner. Hitler immersed himself in Wagner, reading everything he could find on the composer. On their long walks, he would suddenly seize Kubizek and recite a passage from one of his idol's letters, or hum an aria. His special favourite was *Lohengrin*, a tale from heroic German legend. He hoped one day to attend the concert hall in Bayreuth, the composer's former home.

During these garrulous outbursts Hitler showed no compassion, humility or wit – a characteristic he would carry into manhood. Other people seemed to exist for him only insofar as they could help him to realize his plans. And if the residents of Linz considered him a loudmouth and a misfit, Kubizek patiently suspended disbelief in his friend's soaring ambition, of which Hitler talked as if its accomplishment were not merely feasible but also a *fait accompli*.

Of course, there was nothing unusual or especially ominous about this gormless, self-absorbed young man, prone to rages if he didn't get his way. At this point in his life, however, when a firm and loving hand might have guided him in a more promising direction, a series of misfortunes, which had already started with the death of his father, would cast him into the world as an unloved and homeless failure.

Hitler showed few signs of anti-Semitism or racial hatred at this time, partly because he simply gave the matter little thought. His speeches to Gustl barely mentioned the Jews. Despite the fact that the leading Pan-Germans, as we shall see, were ferocious anti-Semites, Hitler's upbringing was remarkably racially tolerant for the times and distinctly not 'anti-Semitic'. His father had not tolerated racial prejudice at home, as Hitler would recall in *Mein Kampf*:

Today it is difficult, if not impossible, for me to say when the word 'Jew' first gave me ground for special thought. At home I do not remember having heard the word during my father's lifetime. I believe that the old gentleman would have regarded any special emphasis on this term as cultural backwardness. In the course of his life he had arrived at more or less cosmopolitan views which, despite his pronounced national sentiments, not only remained intact, but also affected me to some extent.[8]

This must be set beside the fact that Hitler's father associated with extreme German nationalists, who were well known for their anti-Jewish feelings. The whole tenor of the Pan-German mind was casually anti-Semitic, just as it was anti-Slavic. Kubizek recalled Hitler remarking one day, as they passed a synagogue, 'That doesn't belong in Linz'. Not too much should be made of this: in any case, there were few Jews in Linz and only one Jewish boy at the *Realschule* – Ludwig Wittgenstein, the future philosopher, and a year ahead of his age group (Hitler was a year behind). It seems they barely knew each other.[9]

'Not until my fourteenth or fifteenth year did I begin to come across the word "Jew" with any frequency,' Hitler wrote in *Mein Kampf*, 'partly in connection with political discussions. This filled me with mild distaste, and I could not rid myself of an unpleasant feeling that always came over me whenever religious quarrels occurred in my presence. At that time I did not think anything else of the [Jewish] question.'[10]

In the spring of 1906 Hitler announced to Gustl that he was in love. The object of his desire was a girl, slightly older than him, tall and blonde, called Stefanie Isak, whom he would see walking with her mother on the Landstrasse, the main street in Linz. Her Jewish surname compounds the evidence that Hitler felt little, or only passing, hostility to the Jewish residents of Linz. Love would conquer all.[11] Yet Hitler's presumption that Stefanie reciprocated his feelings faced an immediate hurdle: he failed to make them known to her. The relationship existed purely in his mind. Of his existence, she was virtually unaware. If Stefanie deigned to bestow a fleeting glance on him during her daily outings, however, Hitler excitedly imagined that she adored him.

Every day, with Gustl wearily in tow, Adolf would position himself across the street and gaze longingly at the passing target of his affection. He fell into raptures at her approach, and his infatuation soon became an obsession. According to Gustl, he wrote poems and letters to her (never sent); he constructed elaborate stories about their future together; he even seemed to think he had a telepathic connection with her. Stefanie became, for him, the classic Wagnerian heroine: she was Elsa and he Lohengrin, borne along on a swan to rescue her. In response to these delusions, Kubizek maintained a diplomatic silence. If he dared to suggest that Stefanie might not feel the same way, Hitler shouted, '. . . you can't understand the true meaning of extraordinary love!'[12]

Too shy to introduce himself, Adolf dispatched Gustl to spy on his beloved. Kubizek unearthed disturbing facts that threatened to derail Hitler's hope of marrying Stefanie: apparently she loved waltzing and had several suitors. 'You must take dancing lessons, Adolf,' Kubizek suggested slyly. This enraged Hitler, who loathed dancing and refused throughout his life to engage in it ('Dancing is an occupation unworthy of a statesman!' he would later declare, describing the waltz as 'much too effeminate for a man'[13]). 'I shall never dance!' he fumed at Gustl. 'Do you understand! Stefanie only dances because she is forced to by society on which she unfortunately depends. Once she is my wife, she won't have the slightest desire to dance!'[14]

A more serious impediment to Hitler's love were Stefanie's suitors. Intensely jealous of these young men, who reportedly surrounded her, Hitler contemplated suicide by jumping into the Danube. Either that, or he would kidnap her and force her to marry him.

For nearly four years Hitler would cherish his love for this blameless girl as 'the purest dream of his life' – years during which the couple scarcely exchanged glances and never spoke a word. From Vienna, where he would soon move to pursue a career as an artist, he sent her a single, unsigned postcard declaring his love for her. 'Once I received a letter,' she would recall, 'from someone telling me he was now attending the Art Academy, but I should wait for him, he was going to return and marry me.'[15] It was not until decades later that she discovered the sender's identity.

In 1908 Hitler's fantasy came to an abrupt end. Stefanie became engaged to Maximilian Rabatsch, an officer garrisoned in Linz, and married him in 1910.

Chapter Three

'I had honoured my father, but my mother I had loved'

Hitler first visited Vienna in May 1906, aged seventeen, ostensibly to study the paintings in the Kunsthistorisches Museum (Museum of Fine Arts). He stayed a fortnight, agog before the Opera House, the Parliament building, the great mansions around the Ringstrasse and the glittering omnipotence of the House of Habsburg, the architecture of which he would study and imitate. The great stamp of imperial power awed but did little to diminish Hitler's scorn for the Austro-Hungarian regime; he continued to despise the Habsburgs as weak and decadent, incapable of ruling their racially polyglot realm.

That was the curious thing about this young man: he seemed barely aware of his status as just one of millions of disenfranchised 'non-people', whose lives sloshed around in the dregs of empire. Hitler spoke as if he'd already acquired the power to rebuild cities and challenge Austrian might: the grandeur of Habsburg Vienna, even in the festering twilight of the emperor's reign, was merely another problem that he, the dawdling nonentity from Linz, would one day fix.

The opera was the high point of Hitler's brief visit. He attended two performances, of Wagner's *Tristan and Isolde* and *The Flying Dutchman*, conducted by Gustav Mahler and designed by Alfred Roller, two of the greatest names in operatic performance. Hitler deeply admired them both, and in these early years would defend Mahler whenever he heard anyone making anti-Semitic comments about the composer. Though born a Jew, Mahler had converted to Catholicism, but that did little to disguise his 'race' in the eyes of Austrian anti-Semites. (The Nazis would not recognize converts; because Mahler had 'Jewish blood', they would later ban his music.)

On his return to Linz, Adolf regaled Gustl with the aesthetic splendours of Vienna and the magnificence of Wagner's operas. His passion for Wagner knew no bounds and would never abate. While his youthful favourite remained *Lohengrin*, a lesser-known work made a deep impression: *Rienzi: The Last of the Tribunes*, a claustrophobic opera the composer had disowned. In the story, set in fourteenth-century Rome, Rienzi is portrayed as the victim of the malicious plotting of 'the superpowers, the Church and the German Emperor'.[1]

Hitler first saw *Rienzi* in Linz in 1906, with Kubizek. He closely identified with the besieged hero and emerged from the opera in raptures, transported to another time and place. Gustl found himself being led to the top of the city's Freinberg Hill, where Hitler unleashed a speech of dazzling self-aggrandizement, addressed more to himself than to his baffled friend. 'In grand, captivating images,' Gustl wrote, 'he told me about his future and the future of his people. He spoke of a special mission that would one day be his.' Entranced by his plans for the German people, Hitler pleaded tearfully with Gustl that he needed to be left alone and sauntered off into the night. Gustl would take decades 'to understand what these hours of otherworldly rapture had meant to my friend . . . It was an unknown youth who spoke to me in that strange hour.'[2]

Hitler would never forget that night at the opera, confiding in Winifred Wagner, the composer's daughter-in-law, in 1939, 'That was the hour everything started'. He meant the start of his life's mission, to avenge the German people against their oppressors. It was a backward projection on to a time in which he had no identifiable mission, no schooling and no job, but the episode would sit well in the heroic pantheon that Nazi propagandists would construct of his life.

Rienzi certainly had a profound impact on Hitler, even if we overlook Kubizek's embellishments and the Nazis' myth-making. It was almost as if he believed Rienzi had sent him a psychic message, to lead the German people out of darkness. Hitler would refer to the opera throughout his life and cast himself, like Rienzi, as the avenging hero of his nation. The opera's overture even became the unofficial anthem of the Third Reich.[3]

Aware of his love of the opera, Frau Wagner later gave the Führer the original score. Her devotion to him would never diminish throughout her long life, provoking rumours that they were lovers. Fittingly, the manuscript would accompany the Führer into his Berlin bunker in 1945 and disappear into the flames of his personal *Götterdämmerung.*[4]

Vienna was all Hitler could talk about, for now. 'In his mind,' wrote Kubizek, 'he was no longer in Linz, but lived at the centre of Vienna.'[5] At the end of 1906 he resolved to return to the city to study drawing. He had every confidence that the famous Academy of Fine Arts would accept him. His mother, Klara, approved of the scheme, hoping it would give her aimless son a direction. His aunt Johanna Pölzl ('Hanitante'), Klara's handicapped younger sister, offered to finance his studies, contingent on him passing the academy's entry exams, to be held in October 1907.

Early that year the life of the one person who truly loved him was at risk. In January 1907 Klara Hitler complained of a severe chest pain and Dr Bloch diagnosed breast cancer. She probably wouldn't survive, he told the family. Hitler wept. 'His long, pale face twisted,' Bloch would recall. 'Tears flowed from his eyes. Did his mother have no chance, he asked.'[6]

Hitler devoted himself at once to his mother's care. He sat by her bedside as she recovered in Linz's Barmherzige Schwestern Hospital from a double mastectomy. According to the hospital's invoice, 'the son' paid the medical bill, of 100 crowns (the family had had no medical insurance), presumably with his aunt's assistance.[7] Her condition improved, but she was not strong enough to climb the three floors to the Humboldstrasse flat, so in May the family moved to an elegant apartment in the small town of Urfahr, across the Danube from Linz. Though expensive – the rent consumed half of Klara's pension – the first-floor flat was easier on the weak woman, and she enjoyed striking views of Mount Postling.

In September that year Hitler resumed his plan to return to Vienna and sit the entrance exams for the Viennese Academy. He rented a small room off a sunken courtyard, with a shared toilet, in a nondescript block at Stumpergasse 31 in Mariahilf, an impoverished district, home of the 'little people' of the Austrian capital: students, the unemployed, tramps and vagrants. His landlady was a Czech seamstress named Maria Zakreys.

About 2 million people lived in Vienna at the time, making it the fourth largest city in Europe and the sixth largest in the world, host to the usual excesses of the fabulously rich and privations of the wretchedly poor. Electric streetlighting had reached most of the centre, but not here: gas lamps shed pools of dreary light on the streets and kerosene flickered in the little flats.

Supremely confident of his success, Hitler convinced himself that passing his exams would be child's play: 'Now I was in the fair city for the second time, waiting with burning impatience, but also with confident self-assurance, for the result of the entrance examination.'[8] Of the 112 candidates, 33 (including Hitler) made it through the first round. He failed the second, from which 28 were accepted. 'Drawing exam unsatisfactory' was the abrupt assessment of his six rudimentary sketches on the set themes: 'Expulsion from Paradise', 'Hunting', 'Spring', 'Construction Workers', 'Death' and 'Rain'.

Hitler was mortified: '. . . when I received my rejection, it struck me as a bolt from the blue.'[9] He complained to the rector of the academy, who advised him to apply to the School of Architecture, as his drawings showed an aptitude for urban design. For this, though, he was ineligible, as he lacked his school leaving certificate. It is untrue that Hitler's extreme anti-Semitism grew out of his rejection from the

Academy of Fine Arts; none of the five faculty professors who selected the successful candidates was Jewish, debunking this idea.

Every young person experiences rejection at some point, but for Hitler this was a mortal wound. In *Mein Kampf* he endows this episode with extraordinary portent, a revelation of his mysterious 'dual' character:

> Downcast, I left von Hansen's magnificent building [where the Academy of Fine Arts is housed] . . . for the first time in my life at odds with myself. For what I had just heard about my abilities seemed like a lightning flash, suddenly revealing a conflict with which I had long been afflicted . . . In a few days I myself knew that I should some day become an architect. To be sure, it was an incredibly hard road; for the studies I had neglected out of spite at the *Realschule* were sorely needed.

So he simply gave up: 'The fulfilment of my artistic dream seemed physically impossible.'[10]

Shortly after this humiliation, Hitler heard that his mother's condition was grave. In fact, the situation was hopeless, Dr Bloch informed the eighteen-year-old on his return to Linz that October. Klara was dying. In despair at the imminent loss of the only person he loved, Hitler did everything he could to ease her last weeks. His devotion was 'indefatigable', as both Dr Bloch and his sister Paula later testified.[11] Kubizek wrote: 'Adolf read her every wish from her eyes and showed her the tenderest sort of care. I had never seen him be so solicitous and gentle.'[12]

Little was known of breast cancer at the time. There were no mammograms, chemotherapy or adequate painkillers. Surgery was the only way of controlling the disease, but that was a very blunt tool. The cancer often returned in a fungating form, as it did to Klara Hitler: the cancerous mass was eating through the skin of her chest.

Dr Bloch's treatment, customary at the time, was excruciatingly painful: iodoform, then a widely used antiseptic, was poured into the open wound. 'The suffering of such patients from the bleeding, sometimes rotting, sometimes painful tumour deposits can be horrible to see,' according to Professor Sandy Macleod, a cancer specialist, in a 2005 article on the treatment.[13] Klara endured this pain for six weeks. 'Her son agonized over every moment of her suffering.'[14]

Mercifully, Klara died on 21 December 1907, aged forty-seven, in the house at Blütenstrasse 9, Urfahr. Hitler was found by her bedside the next morning, distraught. 'It was a dreadful blow,' he later wrote, 'particularly for me. I had honoured my father, but my mother I had loved.'[15] Recalling the impact on the boy, Dr Bloch would write, in 1941: 'In all my career I have never seen anyone so prostrate with grief as Adolf Hitler.'[16]

The funeral procession made its melancholy way through Linz on 23 December to the churchyard at Leonding where Alois was buried, the proximity to the festivities of Christmas intensifying the family's loss: 'The black-clad Hitler, pale and gaunt, carrying a top hat under his arm stalked solemnly through the streets . . . leading a small band of mourners.'[17] When the cortège wound past Stefanie's house, she herself paused at the window, leading Hitler to think she was paying her respects; in fact, she had no idea for whom the church bells tolled.

Later claims that Dr Bloch's failure to save Klara produced in Hitler the violent anti-Semitism that led to the Holocaust are groundless.[18] There is no evidence that Bloch poisoned Hitler's mother by applying massive doses of iodoform, as Rudolph Binion and other historians have claimed.[19] At the time, Hitler profusely thanked Bloch for trying to help her: 'I will be forever grateful to you, Doctor,' he told the Jewish surgeon on the day of Klara's funeral.[20] He later sent the doctor self-painted postcards from Vienna and in 1940, in what may be seen, in the circumstances, as a tyrant's concession, put Bloch under special protection of the Gestapo and approved the doctor's and his family's safe passage to America.[21]

On 1 January 1908 Hitler visited his parents' graves in Leonding. With his mother's death, he had lost the only person he loved. There was nobody left for him in Linz. He was not in touch with his older half-siblings; meanwhile, Paula, whom he would not see again for many years, went to live with their half-sister, Angela Raubal. Young Hitler resolved to leave his childhood home at once and return to Vienna.

CHAPTER FOUR

'The whole academy should be dynamited'

In receipt of an orphan's pension of 25 crowns a month and his share of his mother's small estate, Hitler left for Vienna on 12 February 1908, with no plans to return to Linz. He was to live in the Austrian capital for the next five years, tossed about, in his later telling, in a world of misery and poverty, 'the hardest, though most thorough, school of my life'.[1]

This image of himself – an echo of Rienzi, rising out of the darkest depths to lead the German people into light – would prove useful to Nazi mythologists. But it was wide of the mark. No doubt he lived modestly, like most students, and for nearly a year, as we shall see, in wretched poverty. And yet his circumstances were initially far better than he later claimed. He and his sister had inherited 2,000 crowns (the equivalent, in relative terms today, of about £74,000 or US$94,400), to be shared between them – enough to allow him to live in Vienna without work for a year at the time – and he would come into their father's trust fund, worth 625 crowns, when he turned twenty-four.

On his return to the city, he moved back into the flat in which he'd stayed on his previous visit, with the seamstress Maria Zakreys, in the sunken courtyard of Stumpergasse 31, Mariahilf, and promptly wrote to Kubizek: 'All of Vienna is waiting. So come soon.' To Hitler's delight, Gustl replied that he would arrive in April: his parents had agreed to let him continue his musical studies at the Vienna Conservatory (where he had been accepted to play in the orchestra). He would bring his viola, Gustl warned. Hitler's cheerful reply, sent on 19 April 1908, offers a glimpse of his belittling sense of humour and a hint of sensitivity to Gustl's success:

> Dear Gustl . . . I am delighted that you are bringing a viola. On Thursday I shall buy two Kronen's worth of cotton wool and 20 Kreuzer's worth of sticking plaster, for my ears naturally. That, on top of all this, you are growing blind, has plunged me into a profound depression: you will play even more wrong notes than before. Then you will go blind and I will eventually go deaf. Alas! Meanwhile I wish you and your esteemed parents at least a happy Easter, and I send them my hearty greetings, and to you, too. Your Friend.[2]

When Gustl arrived, the friends shared the room with a large piano and little else in the way of furniture. They lived in the city amidst everything they admired: fine musicians, classical architecture, grand opera. They were two young men in their prime, with the money and freedom to enjoy themselves in the heart of Europe. They attended the opera and concerts, and Hitler frequently visited Parliament, where the motley array of races, languages and special interests, shouting and vying for influence, heightened his disdain for Austrian society and politics. Where some saw a human comedy in this polyglot society – the funniest expression of the empire's identity crisis was *The Good Soldier Švejk*, the classic novel by Czech writer Jaroslav Hašek, whose hero is utterly confused over which nation he is supposed to be fighting for in the First World War[3] – Adolf Hitler saw only a shambles of lesser races cavorting for power. Vienna's racial mélange affronted his dream of a greater Germany, a Pan-German hegemony over Austria and its vassal states. He felt contempt for Vienna's Parliament, for the inability of its barking politicians to get anything done in the name of democracy, for the very notion of democracy itself, primitive as it then was:

How soon was I to grow indignant when I saw the lamentable comedy that unfolded beneath my eyes! Present were a few hundred of these popular representatives who had to take a position on a question of the most vital economic importance . . . The intellectual content of what these men said was on a really depressing level, in so far as you could understand their babbling at all; for several of the gentlemen did not speak German, but their native Slav languages or rather dialects . . . A wild gesticulating mass screaming all at once in every different key, presided over by a good-natured old uncle who was striving in the sweat of his brow to revive the dignity of the House by violently ringing his bell and alternating gentle reproofs with grave admonitions. I couldn't help laughing.[4]

The experience utterly disabused him of any interest he might have had in 'parliamentary democracy'.[5] As he sat in the public gallery, aghast at the ugly rant that passed for public debate below, Hitler's mind slowly closed on a vision of Europe led by a strong, authoritarian ruler, a German ruler, who would tolerate none of the delays, duties and decencies of an elected Parliament.

In contrast with his absorption in Parliament, young Hitler showed little if any interest in the large number of Jews in pre-war Vienna. Many had been refugees from Russian persecution, many had fled Hungary or Galicia (in present-day Poland) and settled in the poorer districts of Vienna, relieved to find themselves living in a relatively tolerant city, free of terror. In 1910, there were 175,318 Jews living in Vienna, comprising 8.6 per cent of the city's population (up from 6,000, or 2 per cent, fifty years earlier[6]), a higher proportion than in any other Central European city. In some areas, Jews formed about a third of the population, and 17 per cent of the residents of the impoverished Brigittenau district, where Hitler would spend his last years in Vienna, were Jews.

The city's Jews were themselves divided, along ethnic and socio-economic grounds. The old Viennese Jewish families tended to be assimilated and respected. The orthodox eastern Jews, descendants of refugees from Russia's pogroms, were poor traders who lived on the fringes of society, 'accepted by none, hated by many', Kershaw writes,[7] as alien to the wealthy Viennese Jews as to the gentile rump. And, as in many European cities, the wealthier Jews were highly influential in the cultural life of the capital, thanks to their hard work, education and commercial connections, as Brigitte Hamann's superb study shows.[8] They tended to be university educated and held a disproportionate share of senior roles in medicine, law, art, commerce and the media, fomenting the usual envy and resentment among elements of the non-Jewish population.

Politically, too, they were high achievers. But they did not, and never would, correspond to a communist bloc, as Hitler would later hysterically claim. Jews had prominent roles in all political parties in pre-war Vienna, and while it is true to say they preponderated on the left, most of these were moderate socialists, not violent Marxists. And contrary to what he later claimed in *Mein Kampf*, Hitler was only passingly aware of the Jewish presence in Vienna and a long way from seeing them as a monolithic threat; nor had he yet developed any racial or 'Aryan' conception of his dream of a Greater Germany.

Hitler shunned the attractions that usually occupied young men in a big city: taking out girls, making money, drinking, attending dances and parties. He even failed to follow up an invitation – arranged through Magdalena Hanisch, his mother's former landlady in Linz – to meet the great set designer Alfred Roller, whose operas Adolf had seen a year earlier. Hanisch had generously written a reference to a friend who knew Roller, in which she described Hitler as 'a serious, ambitious young man, very mature for his age of 19, from a completely respectable family.'[9] Roller himself replied to the reference: 'Young Hitler should come see me and bring samples of his work so that I can see what they're like.' Poring over these words, from the master whom he revered, Hitler mysteriously failed to respond. He would later claim he had been too shy to meet the great Roller. The more likely explanation is that he knew his work fell short of the mark and so avoided the possibility of another rejection.

Hitler's acute disappointment at his failure to gain admission to the Academy of Fine Arts, which he had not mentioned to Gustl, deepened with every sign of Kubizek's progress as a music student. The pair argued, and one night Hitler exploded, admitting that the academy had 'rejected me', as Kubizek recalled:

'This academy!' Hitler yelled. 'Nothing but a pack of cramped, old, outmoded servants of the state, clueless bureaucrats, stupid creations of the civil service! The whole academy should be dynamited.' His face was pale, his lips were pressed so tightly together that they went white. His eyes were glowing. How uncanny his eyes were! As if all the hatred of which he was capable were burning in those eyes.[10]

Hitler's contempt for the academy spread to its graduates and the wider artistic movement. He detested the new masters of the Modernist movement. The work of artists such as Gustav Klimt, Oskar Kokoschka and Egon Schiele he would later dismiss as 'nothing more than crippled spattering'. He found similarly repulsive their counterparts in architecture and music. He simply failed to comprehend the artistic upheaval going on around him. He passed through Vienna indifferent to the music of Richard Strauss; the architecture of Josef Hoffman, Adolf Loos and Otto Wagner; and the poems of Rainer Maria Rilke. The Jewish-born experimental composer Arnold Schoenberg would be a source of particular revulsion, later condemned by the Nazis. Hitler perceived merely the sounds and scenes of a monstrous decadence.

In the visual arts, his heroes were nineteenth-century figurative and realist painters, such as Anselm Feuerbach, Carl Rottmann and Rudolf von Alt; and in architecture, the Neoclassicists Gottfried Semper and Karl Friedrich Schinkel. His artistic taste would always default to safe, middle-class respectability, the certain forms and solid outlines of a passing world. He closed his eyes and ears to the new revolution in aesthetics, which, despite the fact that few of its leading lights were Jews, was often construed as 'Jewish Modernism'. In Hitler's mind the seeds of a bizarre conflation were being sown.

Nor had he the patience or intellect to bother with Vienna's intelligentsia, whose rising stars were the Jewish psychologist Sigmund Freud and the Jewish philosopher Ludwig Wittgenstein (who had been in his school in Linz). Hitler moved in a very different city, a Sodom of soaring inflation and rising taxes, of prostitutes, vagrants and anarchic students; a Gomorrah of violent dissent, political oppression and crushing poverty.

Furious at society's indifference to what he saw as his obvious gifts, young Adolf threw himself into various pursuits, none of which yielded fruit: he churned out scores of sketches and watercolours; he immersed himself in plans to write dramas based on German legends; and he remodelled the grandest architecture of the Austrian capital, devoting days to the Ringstrasse alone. Opera consumed him: he later claimed he had heard *Tristan* between thirty and forty times in Vienna. His moods oscillated between fury and despair, lethargy and anxiety. 'Incessantly, he talked, planned, raved, possessed by the urge to justify himself, to prove that he had genius,' wrote the biographer and historian Joachim Fest.[11]

Returning home from his music studies in the evening, Kubizek would cautiously enquire of his friend how he had spent his day, dreading some explosive reaction. On one occasion, Adolf stunned Gustl by announcing that he was writing an opera, to be called 'Wieland the Blacksmith' – despite never having composed a line of music, or mastered the ability to read it, and regardless of his inexperience of the smithy trade. The project came to nothing, notwithstanding Gustl's encouragement. Another time, when Gustl asked about his daily activities, Hitler solemnly announced: 'I am working on a solution to the wretched housing conditions in Vienna and carrying on studies to that end.'[12]

Conscious of the poverty that surrounded him, Hitler directed his disgust at the politicians he deemed responsible. He felt little compassion for the victims, whose condition he found repellent or pathetic, something to be cleaned away; and yet he could write with eloquence of the misery around him:

Dazzling riches and loathsome poverty alternated sharply . . . The host of high officers, government officials, artists, and scholars was confronted by an even greater army of workers, and side by side with aristocratic and commercial wealth dwelt dire poverty. Outside the palaces on the Ring loitered thousands of unemployed, and beneath this Via Triumphalis of old Austria dwelt the homeless in the gloom and mud of the canals.[13]

If he were in charge, he wrote, he would bundle the poor off the streets and order them into uniforms, as servants of the state. There spoke the civil servant's son, assuming he could fix by diktat chronic economic problems of which he knew nothing. At the time, Hitler reputedly carried a photo of his father in parade uniform and proudly referred to him as a top official in 'His Imperial Majesty's Customs Service'. It was indicative of Hitler's true character in Vienna. Far from being a bohemian or a revolutionary, as he later portrayed himself, he was 'full of sentimental admiration for the bourgeois world. He craved a share in it . . . Social disdain he felt to be far more painful than social wretchedness.'[14]

His reaction to a huge rally for the unemployed outside the Viennese Parliament in February 1908 revealed a cast of mind without a scintilla of sympathy for the poor. At one point a man sat down on a tramway line and screamed, 'I'm hungry!' Hitler watched this with lofty detachment, as though taking mental notes on how not to behave if you wanted to start a revolution. 'He took everything in so dispassionately and thoroughly,' wrote Kubizek, 'as if all that was important to him – just like during his visits to Parliament – was to study the *mise-en-scène* of the whole event, the, as it were, technical execution of a rally.'[15] When a line of workers passed him on a Viennese street, Hitler stood 'watching with bated breath the gigantic human dragon slowly winding by'.[16]

Much as he claimed to feel solidarity with the 'little people', Hitler considered it beneath him to participate in demonstrations. Only later that night would he vent his fury – at the politicians, i.e. the new socialists, who 'organised rallies like that': 'Who is leading this suffering people?' he shouted at Kubizek. 'Not men who have experienced the hardships of the little man themselves, but ambitious, power-hungry politicians . . . who enrich themselves with the misery of the masses.'[17] His visits to Parliament exacted a similar, incendiary response: he would stand up and shake his fists from the visitors' gallery, 'his face burning with excitement'.[18]

Kubizek spent the summer of 1908 with his family in Linz. He returned to Vienna in November to find their flat deserted. Adolf had disappeared, leaving no contact address. During their months apart, he had corresponded with Gustl as usual, giving no sign of his impending flight. He spoke of his loneliness, bronchitis and the bed bugs, and claimed that he was 'writing a lot'. In October, the letters stopped coming.

Hitler's shame at rejection and looming penury probably explained his disappearance. In September he had again applied to and been rejected by the Academy of Fine Arts, deepening his sense of personal failure. At the same time, Kubizek was progressing in his musical studies, arousing his friend's bitter resentment. (After Hitler's flight, Kubizek would not see him again until 1938 when, to his amazement, Hitler visited Linz as chancellor. In the meantime, Kubizek had pursued a career as a musician and become conductor of the Marburg orchestra before the Great War. Wounded on the Eastern Front in 1915, he later worked as a council official in Eferding, Upper Austria.)

Adding to Hitler's woes were acute financial difficulties. He had almost exhausted his mother's funds. Poverty beckoned.

He now entered, as he later portrayed it, the nadir of his life, a Stygian realm of stinking hunger and despair. In November, when he left Frau Zakreys, he moved to a cheaper room at Felberstrasse 22, in the Fünfhaus district of Vienna, an impoverished inner-city area, where he stayed until 20 August 1909, followed by a month in another, cheaper room at Sechshauserstrasse 58 (in the same district). He then disappeared from view and probably spent two months – mid-September until November – living on the streets, sleeping rough and scrounging among the city's poor and most desperate. He 'sank into the bitterest misery,' writes his first biographer, Konrad Heiden.[19] He slept on park benches and in cafés, until the onset of winter forced him to find shelter.

Hitler failed or refused to find work as an ordinary labourer. The man who would seduce Germany with the idea of 'national socialism' felt no affinity for the unions. In *Mein Kampf* he would claim a brush with the city's working class during a short-lived job as a construction worker (the facts of which are unconfirmed), which he presents as an experience that reinforced his disgust for unionized labour. He sat by them, not with them, on the building site and 'drank my bottle of milk and ate my piece of bread somewhere off to one side, and cautiously studied my new associates.' His fellow workers, Hitler wrote, 'rejected everything' and 'infuriated me to the extreme'. They dismissed the state as an invention of the 'capitalistic' classes, and the Fatherland as 'an instrument of the bourgeoisie for the exploitation of the working class'. To them, the authority of the law was merely 'a means for oppressing the proletariat'; school, 'an institution for breeding slaves and slaveholders'; religion, 'a means for stultifying the people and making them easier to exploit'; and morality, 'a symptom of stupid, sheeplike patience . . .' As they familiarized themselves with the views of this strange new labourer, Hitler's fellow workers grew so angry they threatened to throw him off the scaffolding – or so he later claimed in *Mein Kampf*, a story of dubious merit made up or exaggerated to enhance his anti-Marxist credentials.[20]

Indeed, it would be wrong to conclude that his loathing for Marxism originated on building sites or in other menial jobs around Vienna. Like so much else in his autobiography, as we shall see, Hitler was, at worst, indulging in pure fabrication or, at best, projecting backwards emotions that emerged several years later in Bavaria in the aftermath of the war.[21]

Hitler's circumstances struck rock-bottom in late 1909. In November we find him, aged twenty, queuing up at a shelter for homeless men in the poor district of Meidling. Witnesses recount a dirty, dishevelled tramp, unrecognizable from the debonair dandy of Linz. He wore an unruly beard and long hair to his shoulders, and the soles of his shoes had been worn through and replaced by paper. His shirt was 'notoriously dirty' even among the destitute: 'he was once in danger of expulsion from the Hostel as too unkempt,' observed witnesses, who remembered him as 'shy, never looking a person in the eye. The sole exception was during ecstasies when he talked politics.'[22] His volatile character and fierce argumentativeness drew mockery, not respect. The hostel director described him as 'the oddest resident' and his fellows in the shelter laughed at and impersonated their strange, combustible companion. Some residents respected him, most laughed at him and 'many considered him a fanatic': 'He brooked no contradiction but lost control and showered abuse on any who attempted discussion. He was incapable of reasonable debate, as he was of ordinary companionship. If he could not dominate an argument, his wrath would be followed by sullen silence. His irritability and hatreds caused the atmosphere around him to be uncomfortable, even hostile.'[23]

A vagrant called Reinhold Hanisch, who slept in the adjoining bed to Hitler, recalled how he first set eyes on a gaunt young man, dead tired, whose feet were bleeding and sore from tramping the streets:

For several days he had been living on benches in the park where his sleep was often disturbed by policemen . . . His blue-checked suit had turned lilac, from the rain . . . We gave him our bread because he had nothing to eat. An old beggar standing nearby advised him to go to the convent in the Gumpendorferstrasse; there every morning between nine and ten soup was given to the poor. We said this was 'calling on Kathie' probably because the name of the Mother Superior was Katherine. My neighbour's name was Adolf Hitler.

He was awkward. The Asylum [shelter] meant to him an entirely new world where he could not find his way, but we all advised him as best we could and our good humour raised his spirits a little . . . He told us that he was a painter, an artist, and had read quite a lot . . .

he had come to Vienna in the hope of earning a living here, since he had already devoted much time to painting in Linz, but had been bitterly disappointed in his hopes. His landlady had dispossessed him and he had found himself on the street without shelter.[24]

Hitler was now broke, Hanisch recalled. 'One night in his great distress he begged a drunk gentleman for a few pennies but the drunk man raised his cane and insulted him. Hitler was very bitter about this, but I made fun of him saying, "Look here, don't you know you should never approach a drunk".'[25]

Hitler had been reduced to a beggar, preying on misfits and drunks, the furthest one could imagine from a future leader of Germany. One witness, who called himself 'Anonymous' and who met Hitler that spring, described him:

The upper half of his body was covered almost down to his knees by a bicycle coat of indeterminate colour, perhaps grey or yellow. He had an old, grey, soft hat whose ribbon was missing . . . In response to my question of why he never took off his coat, even though he was sitting in a well-heated room, he confessed with embarrassment that unfortunately he didn't have a shirt either. The elbows in his coat and the bottom of his pants were one single hole as well.[26]

Some of these testimonials were biased or exaggerated, or told many years later, when Hitler's early associates had a political or financial incentive to twist or embellish their stories (Kubizek was an exception). None the less, Hanisch conveyed a fair impression of Hitler's incendiary, somewhat pathetic, character in Vienna, one that conforms with others' recollections – so much so that, as Führer, Hitler would go to murderous lengths to suppress any account of his 'lost' years, and in 1936 ordered Hanisch hunted down and killed (he would die in captivity in Vienna in February 1937, allegedly of a heart attack).

In 1909, however, they struck up a working relationship. As a veteran conman, Hanisch easily insinuated himself into Hitler's miserable life. On learning that his new friend was a visual artist – not a house-painter, as he had first supposed – he persuaded him to paint a series of postcards that he, Hanisch, would sell to tourists. They'd split the profits. Having little else to do, Hitler agreed and borrowed money from his aunt to buy paints and brushes.

He spent his days roaming the city, painting postcards of buildings and monuments and street scenes, which his new agent hawked to visitors. If technically accomplished, his pictures struck later observers as curiously soulless, though perhaps this was a case of reading the artist's murderous future into a collection of innocuous images. The partnership prospered and in time Adolf won commissions from local advertisers, sketching posters for consumer products such as hair tonic, mattress stuffing, soap and an antiperspirant powder called 'Teddy'.[27]

CHAPTER FIVE

'Is this a German?'

In February 1910 Hitler and Hanisch moved into a new home for men at Meldemannstrasse 27, in Vienna's working-class district of Brigittenau. The shelter was something of a model of social welfare, partly financed by Jewish charities: newly built, clean, with proper beds, and serving three meals a day for 1,000 men. It even had a reading room, with a small library, the scene of vigorous discussion. Here, Adolf would live for more than two years. He had survived the darkest period of his young life with remarkable resilience and, though his lungs were weak and his teeth in bad shape, his health was improving.

When he wasn't running around the city sketching postcards for Hanisch, Hitler would withdraw to 'his' corner of the reading room and quietly read or sketch. When he disagreed with the ambient discussion, he would fly into a rage, leap up and burst into one of his long tirades, about the greatness of Germany, the decadence of Vienna, or whatever subject seized his imagination, chopping his hands in the air and shouting, to the bemusement of his homeless comrades, before he quietened down and returned to his corner.

'Propaganda, propaganda!' he yelled on one occasion, in response to his mates' disapproval of a story about a woman who'd sold hair tonic using false testimonials. 'You must keep it up until it creates a faith and people no longer know what is imagination and what is reality . . .

Propaganda,' he cried, is the 'essence of every religion . . . whether of heaven or hair tonic.'[1]

Of unconfirmed provenance, this outburst none the less chimes with Hitler's early ideas about the uses of propaganda for mass manipulation and how to exercise it, as he would describe in *Mein Kampf*: banish the truth through threats or violence, fill the empty space with falsehoods that serve the purpose, and reinforce those falsehoods over and over until the people not only believe them, they want to believe them.

His new companions soon tired of Hitler's furious interjections and bombastic speeches, and simply ignored him. Understandably, given their meagre circumstances, they failed to see the hard-edged nature of this man, to fathom the formidable will that would propel him from the troughs of Vienna to the highest office in the German Reich. Hitler's resilience, autodidactic arrogance and the very nature of his *thought* went largely unnoticed. Unable to keep pace with their strange young companion's stormy discourse and agile mind, many of them resorted to laughter and mockery.

In 1910, Hanisch, who had successfully sold many of Hitler's paintings, turned against his younger charge. It infuriated him that Hitler also sold his postcards through Josef Neumann, a Hungarian Jewish copper-polisher who also lived in the men's home. On one occasion Hitler and Neumann disappeared together for five days. When Hitler accused Hanisch of short-changing him on the sale of a picture of the Viennese Parliament, which the artist claimed was worth 50 crowns, their relationship collapsed. Hitler even testified against Hanisch at the local police station, accusing him of theft, for which his former friend received a week in jail.

As such, it was a fellow German, and not his Jewish colleagues, who defrauded and preyed on Hitler in Vienna. In fact, Neumann shared Hitler's love of 'Germany' and gave his friend an old black overcoat, which became something of a trademark item of clothing around the doss house and preserved his health during the winter of 1910/11.

*

Young Adolf, it seems, had no recorded sexual adventures or relationships in Vienna. Female guests were strictly forbidden in the men's home, but that didn't matter to Hitler. According to his comrades, he shunned female company. While susceptible to feminine beauty, commenting on attractive women from a distance, he displayed, or affected, a marked *froideur* towards the opposite sex on the few occasions he actually came into contact with them. Yet women seemed to notice him, especially at the opera, where he would loiter with pointed indifference, according to Kubizek, who theorized that women wanted 'to test this male source of resistance'.[2]

Many years later, in his 1942 'Table Talk' monologue, Hitler claimed he had encountered 'many beautiful women in Vienna' and had taken a special shine to 'big blonde' girls.[3] Yet he never seemed to get to know any, as Ullrich concludes. He certainly seems to have been afraid of women; and he later described his ideal woman as 'a cute, cuddly, naïve little thing – tender, sweet and stupid.'[4] He had a horror of syphilis, and the idea of sexual intercourse affronted his standards of personal hygiene. Now that he could wash and stay clean, he felt only disgust at the memory of the dirty tramp he had become during the worst days in Vienna.

It was not out of any religious duty or pangs of conscience that Hitler shunned pre-marital sexual relationships. Rather, it seems he subscribed to conservative notions about masculinity prevalent at the time, which lauded celibacy as a test of male self-control, of stoic self-abnegation. It was a kind of self-love, underscoring his strength of will.

In choosing to abstain from sex, he took a leaf out of the 'moral code' of the radical leader Georg Ritter von Schönerer – to remain celibate until the age of twenty-five, to have no sex with 'lesser' or 'impure' races, and to consume no meat or alcohol. 'Extended celibacy' greatly benefited young people, Schönerer claimed. Celibacy 'quickens the wits, refreshes the memory, inspires the imagination and fortifies the will,' he wrote – all nonsense of course, peddled by a man with no medical expertise, but widely believed. It enabled Hitler to fashion a virtue out of his abstemiousness and hatred of 'decadence': prostitution and homosexuality disgusted him; he even refrained from masturbating, according to Kubizek.[5]

In sum, Schönerer's masculine code served as a convenient cover for Hitler's fear of sexual inadequacy, which was hardly unusual in young men of the time. In later years he pursued a few female relationships with gusto, but would not marry his long-standing companion, Eva Braun, until forty hours before they consummated their suicide pact, on 30 April 1945, in the Führer's Berlin bunker.

If Hitler stayed celibate in Vienna, as seems likely, he would have entered his twenty-fourth year a virgin.[6] In 1912 he threw his time and surplus energy instead into his political 'education', an exercise in defining himself by what he most despised – chiefly Marxism, the Slavs, modern art and the Habsburgs – and dreaming of what he most desired: a world ruled by Germany.

Hitler's faith in 'Germany' and the 'Germans' had been unassailable since his boyhood. As a member of Austria's German minority, he had always felt an acute sense of historic displacement, instilled in him by his Pan-German teachers and family, and manifested by a longing to return to the homeland. The ideas of Germany as the saviour of Europe and the German people destined to rule it were well formed in his youth. Prussian military prowess impressed him: the only book he possessed at this time was a history of Prussia's victory over France in 1870–71.

The greatest champion in his pantheon of German heroes was Count Otto von Bismarck, whose towering achievement was the unification of Germany in 1871. Bismarck was one of the few men Hitler unreservedly admired throughout his life, chiefly for the Iron Chancellor's 'blood and iron' leadership, hatred of social democracy and non-Germans, and policies of *Kulturkampf*, the supremacy of secular rule over the Catholic Church. All these would find new expression in the most brutal form during Nazi rule.

In the 1900s, the new Germany was making huge strides, announcing to the world the arrival of an economic and cultural force. Yet there was a sinister side to German economic and political success. Pride in the new empire's achievement bred a fervent, even fanatical patriotism, utterly loyal to the Fatherland. By extension, and with varying intensity in the coming years, this new sensibility excluded non-Germans, or non-Teutonic breeds, to use the racially charged language of the era of Social Darwinism.

According to this thesis, Slavs and Jews were explicitly lesser breeds and had no right to exist in the front rank of nations, of which 'Deutschland' was the gleaming showcase. In this sense, the creation of Germany expressed a new *racial* consciousness, a full-blown 'German' consciousness. The drawing together of the reins of Deutschland was the single most arresting political and economic fact in Europe in the first decade of the twentieth century. Hitler absorbed all this in a most virulent form. The disturbed orphan cleaved to Germany as his saviour, his only hope. It is not fanciful to suggest that he projected his longing for his lost mother on to Deutschland, his Teutonic mother country.

In Vienna, Hitler's love of Germany rose as his disgust for the Austrian Parliament and the charade of democracy intensified. He was more receptive to the authoritarian uses of political power, as exemplified by Bismarck, at a time when the Austrian Parliament was struggling to provide adequate living standards, jobs or hope. Local politicians had failed to find a solution to this wretchedness, and periodically tried to divert attention from their failure to popular scapegoats: minorities such as Jews, gypsies, Serbs, Czechs, Italians, Hungarians or Romanians.

All this tended to dismay the German Austrians, most of whom were fiercely opposed to the lacklustre old methods of the Habsburgs. Like Hitler, they wanted rapier blows against external threats and decisive action in the Balkans. In the late nineteenth century the Habsburgs had tried to expand their empire into the Balkan peninsula (chiefly because the landlocked country needed access to the sea), with first the occupation of Bosnia and Herzegovina in 1878 and then their annexation in 1908. Yet strong-arm tactics and decisive action ran against the grain of the regime, whose guiding animus was muddling along, not crashing through. The Habsburgs were essentially landlords, after all, not rulers, and played off the empire's constituent parts in a constant game of divide and conquer. 'The Habsburg lands were not bound together either by geography or by nationality,' observed A. J. P. Taylor.[7]

For centuries, the Ottoman Turks had traditionally been the biggest threat to Habsburg rule. That ended in 1912, with the eviction of Turkey from the Balkans in the First Balkan War. The Slavic people then replaced the Muslims as Austria–Hungary's 'necessary' enemy. Vienna cast a covetous eye over the recrudescent Slavs in the peninsula, chiefly the strongest and most threatening, the Russian-backed Serbs. Franz Joseph and his fiercely anti-Slav court – which did not include his nephew and heir, Archduke Franz Ferdinand, who, in one of history's more bitter ironies, advocated a moderate policy towards the Slavs – were determined to control the Balkan territory vacated by the Turks and, with German support, freeze Russia out of the peninsula.

Young Hitler shared this goal in a most aggressive form. He was violently opposed to the Slavic dominance of the Balkans. He reckoned the Austrian policy of encroaching on the peninsula fell well short of what was required: the annexation of Bosnia–Herzegovina should have initiated a process of complete conquest of Serbia and other Russian-backed strongholds. He despised the bumbling nobility in Austria, and in Germany too. He loathed Franz Ferdinand and his moderate followers. He scorned the dithering Kaiser Wilhelm II. The only aristocratic courtier he admired was the bellicose Count Conrad von Hötzendorf, chief of staff of the Austrian armed forces, who had constantly pressed the Viennese government to crush Serbia.

For Hitler, whose political sensibility was gradually unfolding, only the binding power of a united 'Germany', a Pan-Germany, could deliver a coherent solution to the racial shambles of Central Europe and control the Slavs to the south. Hence his strong attachment to the Pan-German demagogues and racial theorists who proliferated in Vienna at the time, some of whose ideas he shared – but did not swallow. Their theories of racial preservation and methods of political manipulation struck him more powerfully than their overt anti-Semitism, which he simply took for granted, it was so widespread.

Hitler's reading habits at this stage of his life in Vienna were unsystematic, arbitrary and impulsive. He rarely read literature for enjoyment, as Kubizek observed, with the exception of his lifelong love of Germanic myths and sagas of Teutonic heroism. It is highly unlikely that he had actually read a full-length work of philosophy by Arthur Schopenhauer or Friedrich Nietzsche, despite Kubizek's claim that their books surrounded him in their flat.[8] The twenty-one-year-old preferred the popular press and short political pamphlets. In this time before public radio and television, newspapers were immensely powerful. Viennese papers were split between the 'Jewish press' and the 'anti-Jewish press'; the latter peddled Pan-German ideas and racial 'purity'. Hitler chose the tabloids for his news, chiefly the anti-Semitic rag *Deutsches Volksblatt*.

He squirrelled away snippets of political, religious and racial theory that reinforced his own views, collecting knowledge rather like a jackdaw collects shiny objects. His mental 'nest' was a combobulation of facts, opinions and plain lies that buttressed his emerging personal 'philosophy' and its attendant prejudices. He gathered up whatever accorded with this mental excrescence and dismissed the rest, as though he were following a pre-ordained plan.

Hitler considered this approach an intellectual strength, as he later told the readers of *Mein Kampf*: The 'art' of proper reading, he explained, lay in 'sifting what is valuable for them in a book from that which is without value, of retaining the one forever, and, if possible, not even seeing the rest, but in any case not dragging it around with them as useless ballast.'[9] Or, in another translation, 'The art of reading and studying consists in remembering the essential and forgetting what is not essential.'[10]

'Essential facts' and 'useless ballast' meant whatever Hitler chose them to mean. Reading, for him, meant seizing on information that reinforced his prejudices and facilitated his 'life's work'. Hard evidence that contradicted his ideas he simply rejected or ignored as useless. He had no use for proper context, for weighing pros and cons, far less a dialectical or hypothetical approach to the pursuit of truth. He had no truck with 'experts' and 'intellectuals', of course. He drew on tabloid rants, rabid political rhetoric and smatterings of philosophy to feed his *Weltanschauung*, his 'philosophy of life'. His excellent memory harvested quotes and fragments that made his unschooled companions think of him as a philosopher tramp, a wayward intellectual.[11]

At this time, his mind was greatly exercised by themes of German greatness, the rise of the Fatherland and the German people's right to rule, which fed his ever-strengthening Pan-German world view. His sympathies at the time were 'fully and exclusively with the Pan-Germanic movement,' he later plausibly claimed. It was now that the concept of an 'Aryan' race started to impinge on Hitler's mind: it seemed an ancient people of Indo-Iranian origin and mythical powers of mind and physique were the forebears of the tall, blonde Nordic champion who animated far-right literature. We should not make too much of the influence of these mythical *Übermenschen* on his mind at the time, however: in Vienna, Hitler was nowhere near formulating the 'theory of race' that would drive the Nazi Party to genocide. Yet he was undoubtedly receptive to any ideas that cemented notions of German supremacy.

In pre-war Vienna, such ideas proliferated. Hitler attended talks and read pamphlets on German racial supremacy by an array of soap-box speakers, incendiary Pan-Germans, racial theorists and pseudo-scientists. They included Guido von List, the charlatan 'visionary' and mystical Pan-German who urged the 'demixing' (i.e. cleansing) of the population and who described the swastika as the sign of the 'invincible' and 'strong one from above'; Josef Adolf Lanz von Liebenfels, a former monk and publisher of *Ostara*, a journal devoted to cultivating the 'Master Race', who adopted the swastika as the symbol of his 'racially pure' society of New Templars and proposed 'pure-breeding' colonies to protect pristine Aryan blood from inferior races (ironically, Liebenfels himself was partly Jewish); Hans Goldzier, a self-taught 'scientist' who branded Newton's theory of gravity 'false' and who peddled an especially crude form of Social Darwinism; the

Pan-German Franz Stein, whose contempt for Parliament would teach Hitler a lesson in how to undermine democracy; Karl Hermann Wolf, leader of the 'Free German', the most radical of the Pan-German parties; and Houston Stewart Chamberlain, the English author turned German citizen, whose massive work of pseudo-scientific history, *The Foundations of the Nineteenth Century*, conceived of all human history as a racial struggle between the Nordic, Teutonic and Anglo-Saxon peoples and the rest, singling out the Jews as a parasitic growth on the Aryan achievement – he likened the Gothic tribes who pounded Rome to dust to modern Prussians.

Two intriguing influences on Hitler's young mind were Jewish-born 'intellectuals' who had rejected their religion, and whom he most likely read about in newspapers: Arthur Trebitsch, an Austrian author and paranoid 'racial theorist', who, despite being the son of a wealthy Jewish industrialist, turned against Judaism and persuaded himself of an 'international Jewish world conspiracy' against the German people, fearing that the Jews were trying 'to poison him with electric rays';[12] and Otto Weininger, a precociously gifted academic and Christian convert who, perhaps overcompensating for his failure to eradicate his 'inner Jew', damned the Chosen People as a 'race' of 'Mongrels' and 'Negroes', thus rendering his conversion pointless: if the Jews were a race, as he implied, then he would always be a Jew. Unable to find a way out of this self-eliminating logic, Weininger dutifully killed himself. He was twenty-three. (The Nazis would later use his case against the pleas of Jews who had converted to Christianity: your 'race', not your religion, would ultimately determine whether you lived or died.)

In Vienna, he was also exposed to the bastardized theory of Social Darwinism, widely believed in Europe, which argued that 'natural selection' could be fast-tracked and applied to a living society, in which the 'fittest' race ruled. Stripped of its pseudo-scientific jargon, the idea merely unloosed the law of the jungle on civilized Europe. To Hitler, it made perfect sense, because it buttressed his belief in the Aryans as the 'fittest' race.

Such notions of racial purity and German power were all part of a common discourse in pre-war Vienna – and, indeed, throughout Europe – in which racist feelings were always on the conversational menu. In this milieu, to feel disdainful towards the Jews or 'lesser breeds' – Slavs, Poles and so on – was 'normal', a default mode of thought. And none of the Pan-German, racial supremacists Hitler associated with, read or listened to during his time in Vienna dismissed these ideas as stupid, bigoted or uncivilized, because they all shared them.

In *Mein Kampf* Hitler claims that he left Vienna feeling a violent hatred of the Jewish people and that his racial programme was already fully formed.[13] In Vienna, he insists, 'I underwent the greatest internal upheaval I have ever experienced. I went from cosmopolitan weakling to fanatic anti-Semite.'[14] That was sheer confabulation. In Vienna, and later in Munich, Hitler in fact displayed no systemic hatred of Jews or other minorities, despite his exposure to a gallery of racist influences and thinkers. Their ideas merely reinforced his belief in Germans as the Master Race, but did not at this stage lead him to a specific and acute hatred of singular 'races'.

His 'anti-Semitism' during this period amounted to little more than the general hostility of the city, where such views were mainstream: like most people, he simply bundled up the Jews with what were popularly dismissed as the ethnic detritus in Vienna's melting pot. 'Hitler did not experience an anti-Semitic epiphany in Vienna,' concludes Volker Ullrich. The truth, as he and others remind us, was far murkier.[15] It is none the less true that the seeds had been sown and lay dormant in his mind, to emerge years later, fertilized by his intense experience of the Great War and its aftermath.

Indeed, Hitler's experiences of Vienna's Jews tell a different, far messier story. His first encounter with orthodox Jews, in their traditional black kaftans, broad hats, beards and tzitzit tassels, provoked a morbid curiosity, not a murderous hatred, as he recounted in *Mein Kampf*:

> Once, as I was strolling through the inner City, I suddenly encountered
> an apparition in a black caftan [*sic*] and black hair locks. Is this a Jew?

was my first thought. For, to be sure, they had not looked like that in Linz. I observed the man furtively and cautiously, but the longer I stared at this foreign face, scrutinizing feature for feature, the more my first question assumed a new form: Is this a German?[16]

He claimed this experience drove him to 'study' the Jewish people and the Zionist political movement: 'For a few hellers [half a pfennig] I bought the first anti-Semitic pamphlets of my life.' And soon, it seemed, there was nowhere he could turn without bumping into another man in a black kaftan. 'I suddenly encountered him in a place where I would least have expected to find him. When I recognized the Jew as the leader of Social Democracy, the scales dropped from my eyes. A long soul struggle had reached its conclusion.'[17] The face of his true enemy had been revealed, he later claimed: the Jews were a 'spiritual pestilence, worse than the Black Death'.[18]

This is another *ex post facto* fabrication. Hitler did not experience a sudden 'conversion' to violent anti-Semitism, either in Vienna or elsewhere. As we shall see, it would be a gradual process, combining political opportunism and genuine hatred. He contrived this apparent psychological upheaval many years later, to enhance his political ambitions and to establish the 'continuum' of a man of destiny. In fact, his actual first encounter with Jews in Vienna had little purchase on his thoughts. He simply let the matter slide. To him, 'the Jews' were another passing curiosity, a social carbuncle like the abundance of 'aliens', poverty and prostitution.

In fact, two of his close friends at the time were Jews, according to Brigitte Hamann's forensic research for her book *Hitler's Vienna*: Josef Neumann, the Hungarian Jewish copper-polisher with whom he went into business, and Simon Robinson, a one-eyed locksmith. And Jews were among the biggest buyers of Hitler's postcards, which Siegfried Loffner, a Jewish friend of Neumann's, and two Jewish picture framers, Jakob Altenberg and Samuel Morgenstern, promoted and sold to their communities. Hitler avoided falling back into absolute poverty thanks to their help.

In the hostel's reading room, Hitler was sometimes heard defending the Jewish people, praising their charity and citing examples of great Jewish musicians and artists, according to Hanisch.[19] Of course, Hanisch was writing in the early 1930s after he had fallen out with Hitler and was trying to discredit his old business pal.[20] His statements cannot be completely dismissed, when set against other witnesses whose observations were also sometimes biased, self-serving or politically motivated; yet taken together they build a coherent, if limited, portrait of their disturbed and embittered young comrade. 'In those days Hitler was by no means a Jew hater,' Hanisch wrote in an article posthumously published in the *New Republic* in 1939. 'He became one afterward. He used to say even then that the end sanctions the means, and so he incorporated anti-Semitism into his program as a powerful slogan.'[21]

In fact, Hitler often spoke admiringly of the Jewish people, claimed Hanisch, with whom he discussed the subject on their evening walks:

[H]e admired the Jews most for their resistance to all persecutions. He remarked of Rothschild that he might have had the right of admission to court but refused it because it would have meant changing his religion. Hitler thought that was decent, and that all Jews should behave likewise. During our evening walk we discussed Moses and the Ten Commandments. Hitler thought it possible that Moses had taken over the commandments from other nations, but if they were the Jews' own they had produced as a nation one of the most marvelous things in history, since our whole civilization was based on the Ten Commandments.[22]

Other accounts bear witness to Hitler's admiration for Jewish resilience, and their ability to survive and retain their faith despite centuries of oppression. According to 'Anonymous', the doss-house comrade whose identity is unknown but whose remarks have been treated as credible, Hitler 'got along well with Jews. Once he said they were a clever people who stuck together better than the Germans.'[23]

Indeed, Hitler's later murderous hatred of the Jewish people arose in part from his fear that this 'pure' and successful 'race' posed a serious threat to his Aryan fantasy.

In summary, Hitler displayed no signs of vicious anti-Semitism or 'racial' hatred towards the Jews in Vienna. He himself stated in *Mein Kampf* that he barely registered the city's Jews at first, and when he did, he studied them as if they were a passing oddity: 'Notwithstanding that Vienna in those days counted nearly two hundred thousand Jews among its two million inhabitants, I did not see them . . . For the Jew was still characterized for me by nothing but his religion, and therefore, on grounds of human tolerance, I maintained my rejection of religious attacks in this case as in others.' He considered the vicious tone of the city's anti-Semitic press 'unworthy of the cultural tradition of a great nation'.[24]

Years later, his youthful companions, the homeless, the unemployed, street hawkers, 'agents' and students – including Hanisch, the source known as 'Anonymous', fellow hostel-dwellers Karl Honisch and Rudolf Häusler, and of course Kubizek – verified this. Hitler's associates in the men's shelter were thus astonished to learn that their earnest, prudish companion, who never drank, took no interest in girls and never seemed to enjoy himself, was the same violent Jew-hater who was elected Reich Chancellor. They had seen nothing in what Hitler did or said between 1908 and 1914 that marked him out as a future leader of Germany, conqueror of Europe and exterminator of the Jews.

Two Viennese politicians made a deeper impact on Hitler than the hell-raisers and soap-box theorists, and powerfully influenced his later political career: the ferocious anti-Semite Georg Ritter von Schönerer and the city's mayor, Dr Karl Lueger. Schönerer and Lueger were his touchstones, both of whom he would portray in *Mein Kampf* as admirable failures.

By the time Hitler arrived in Vienna, Schönerer, the once-popular leader of the Pan-German movement, was a near-spent force, a fuming anti-Catholic, anti-Habsburg, anti-Liberal and fierce anti-Semite, defined merely by what he despised. Though Schönerer's political career was over, his ideas proliferated and any number of upstart demagogues waved the baton of Schönererism, or aspects of it. Schönerer had routinely called for the elimination of the Jewish influence in all areas of public life. His extremism and eccentricity – he anointed himself 'Führer' and insisted on the '*Heil*' greeting – failed to appeal to anyone beyond his immediate, dwindling circle, and he received a humiliating 20 votes in the 1911 elections. Schönerer's chief mistakes, Hitler later decided, were to ignore the importance of mass appeal and to confuse and divide his followers by offering no fixed group on whom to focus their hatred. And plainly Schönerer's 'Away from Rome' programme alienated Vienna's large Catholic community.

Years later, as Führer, Hitler would act on these 'lessons' by mobilizing a powerful propaganda machine, softening his anti-Catholicism when expedient, and turning the full wrath of the Nazis on a single target. At this point, however, he possessed a ragbag of incoherent ideas about race and politics, which were gradually turning into something sharp and unyielding.

Dr Lueger, Vienna's mayor from 1897 until 1910, leader of the Christian Social Party and so-called 'Lord of Vienna', had a profound, practical influence on the young Hitler. No doubt Lueger was a fine lawyer and a good mayor, in the traditional sense: he built hospitals, schools and churches; he overhauled the transport network and water supply (all of which impressed Hitler's sense of civic pride and municipal duty). The mayor was also a fully fledged Pan-German, who sought to preserve the city's German-ness in a sea of racial chaos.

Lueger's extraordinary oratory, coupled with his simple slogans, moved and impressed Hitler. 'Vienna is German and must remain German!' Lueger was fond of declaring, in the face of a huge influx to the city of Slavs, arriving to look for work and to escape the troubles in the Balkans. Or: 'Greater Vienna must not turn into Greater Jerusalem!' When attacked in the media for refusing to extend full suffrage to Vienna's Jews, which would have empowered the Jewish-led Social Democrats, Lueger simply condemned the 'Jewish Press', which delighted his followers and cemented his ascendancy.[25]

The mayor used the Jewish scapegoat to devastating effect. 'Lueger knew how to focus all his voters' negative images in one powerful movement: anti-Semitism,' writes Brigitte Hamann. 'He reduced everything that was contrary to the simple formula: the Jew is to blame.'[26] He declared that he was fighting to defend Christianity against 'a new Palestine' and regularly invoked the old Catholic hatred of these 'Christ killers'. His racist harangues dredged the swamp of anti-Semitic cliché. He rallied his constituents against the 'press Jews' and 'ink Jews' (intellectuals), 'stock exchange Jews' and 'beggar Jews' (Eastern immigrants).[27] He turned Jew-hating into a show, a game of outrage, to score political points. 'Beheaded! is what I said,' he shouted, when accused of saying that it was a matter of indifference to him whether the Jews were hung or shot.[28]

Lueger's outbursts were archly timed (around elections) and pointedly applied, suggesting his anti-Jewish stance was little more than political posturing. Certainly he knew how to exploit the bigotry of this viciously prejudiced city. He chose the Jews 'as a kind of political glue to unite prince and peasant, scholar and servant, in a classless social movement,' concluded the scholar Ewart Turner.[29]

For Lueger, this was all a political game. He never went 'too far': he had powerful Jewish friends and never threatened Jewish businesses. His anti-Semitism was clearly designed to shore up his support among Catholics and workers. From Lueger, Hitler received an absorbing tutorial in the art of political persuasion and the power of oratory and propaganda. Later, he would ominously dismiss the mayor's anti-Semitism as a half-hearted sham.

While these politicians and radicals informed Hitler's early thinking, they did not dominate it (none of them had met the strange young man who lingered at their meetings and devoured their pamphlets). Hitler decided early on that he would be nobody's disciple. He neither joined their parties nor agreed with everything they said. He studied their policies. He read their work, heard them speak, and extracted the elements that appealed to him or conditioned his inchoate prejudices. Though he openly admired them, none was a 'role model' or mentor.

Rather, they offered Hitler morsels that he would absorb now and use later. He scavenged at the entrails of others' political ideas.

A vital ingredient distinguished Hitler's emerging Pan-German vision from the rest: the control of the masses. Only a mass movement would catapult Germany to power. So long as bourgeois moderation infected the German Austrian population in Vienna, little could be achieved, he later argued. Intellectual dilettantes and meek parliamentarians would be useless in the coming 'revolutionary struggle':

> [T]he broad masses of the people can be moved only by the power of speech. And all great movements are popular movements, volcanic eruptions of human passions and emotional sentiments, stirred either by the cruel Goddess of Distress or by the firebrand of the word hurled among the masses; they are not the lemonade-like outpourings of literary aesthetes and drawing room heroes. Only a storm of hot passion can turn the destinies of peoples, and he alone can arouse passion who bears it within himself.'[30]

On the contrary, rousing words that fell on the sawdust of a beer hall were not enough to sustain a lasting revolution. A mass uprising and revolution needed *morally* powerful ideas to sustain it, not just an inspiring speaker – ideas such as those of the brilliant, lawyerly, 'intellectual revolutionaries' Danton, Robespierre or Marx (whom Hitler could admire for the strength of his beliefs, even though he deplored his politics). Such ideas were lacking in what was, at this stage, Hitler's mass-driven fantasy.

Hitler later claimed his Vienna years formed the 'granite foundation' of his political struggle against Marxism and world Jewry. Clearly, this statement in *Mein Kampf* was a deliberate lie, an attempt to validate retrospectively his life as a heroic continuum from impoverished artist to political thinker to revolutionary leader. Like so much of his memoir, it served his personal mythology: to re-create his past as the self-realization of a born leader.

The reality was far from it. Hitler left Vienna in 1913 with no political ambitions, no plans, no job and little hope. He had some money, having now come into his father's inheritance. And he had picked up a rag-tag collection of ideas and theories about race and Social Darwinism. What Hitler learned in Vienna, observed historian and biographer Werner Maser, was 'that life is but a continuous, bitter struggle between the weak and the strong, that in that struggle the stronger and abler will always win, and that life is not ruled by principles of humanity but by victory and defeat'.[31]

There was nothing new or unusual in this. Before the First World War, millions of Europeans shared Hitler's notion of the survival of the fittest. Racial cleansing through Francis Galton's concept of 'eugenics' – inter-breeding to produce a 'superior' race in tandem with the forced sterilization of the 'inferior' – was popular right across the political spectrum. Nice liberals and cosy clergymen were among the strongest supporters of eugenics. There was something ominous, however, in Hitler's notion of racial 'purity' that distinguished it from the main-stream: in his world view, only German power had the strength and vision to procreate an Aryan Master Race: 'German' and 'Aryan' were mutually reinforcing, indivisible. The seeds of these ideas were planted in Hitler in Vienna; the full-grown beast would not emerge until much later, after a world war had poisoned the political soil.

What Hitler's personality was yet to project, though a form of it smouldered within him, was that defining feature of his mature character: hatred, pure, unalloyed hatred, of an intensity that only some cataclysmic intervention in the course of his life could have forged and nurtured, such that he would shout at a crowd in 1921: 'There is only defiance and hate, hate and again hate!' Life taught only one lesson, he yelled: 'to hate and to be hard . . . a lesson devoid of love'.[32] This, though, was not a lesson he learned in Vienna.

His journey now took him to Munich, to where he dragged this bag-gage of ideas about German greatness, Habsburg weakness and Aryan supremacy, as well as his fear and loathing of the 'giant human dragon' of socialism. Bavaria would deepen and entrench these feelings into something more dangerous, more monolithic. Yet it would take a war of unprecedented scale and horror for Hitler's full-blown *Weltanschauung* (philosophy of life) to step forth. And before that, he would find, for the first time in his life, an anchorage, a sense of belonging and the closest thing to a home, in his beloved regiment.

CHAPTER SIX

'I fell down on my knees and thanked Heaven'

The reasons Hitler gave for his sudden move to Munich, on 25 May 1913, bore little relation to the truth. He later blamed Vienna's racial diversity and degradation for his flight. 'I was repelled,' he wrote in *Mein Kampf*, '. . . by this whole mixture of Czechs, Poles, Hungarians, Ruthenians, Serbs, and Croats, and everywhere, the eternal mushroom of humanity – Jews and more Jews. To me the giant city seemed the embodiment of racial desecration . . . For all these reasons a longing rose stronger and stronger in me, to go at last whither since my child-hood secret desires and secret love had drawn me.'[1]

In truth, none of this drove Hitler from Vienna. He was in fact fleeing an order to fulfil his military service to Austria, an obligation under Austrian law. He was a 'draft dodger' on the run. But this was no ordinary conscientious objector, motivated by fear or religious constraints: Hitler had decided he would not join the Austrian Army, which in the event of a war would have sent him to Galicia or some-where on the Eastern Front with Russia. He was determined to fight, if war came, in a German uniform.

There were also 'pull' factors. The Bavarian capital appealed to the young artist, partly because he still harboured dreams of becoming one, of using his skill as a draughtsman in a useful job: 'I hoped some day to make a name for myself as an architect and thus . . . to dedicate my sincere services to the nation.'[2] Elsewhere he wrote: 'I went to Munich with joy in my heart. I intended to keep learning for three more years and then, when I turned 28, to become a draughtsman at [a local construction firm].'[3]

He would do nothing to fulfil these ambitions. In truth, he went to Munich to submerge himself in his childhood dream: '. . . I want[ed] to enjoy the happiness of living and working in the place which some day would inevitably bring about the fulfillment of my most ardent and heartfelt wish: the union of my beloved homeland with the common fatherland, the German Reich.'[4]

Hitler would remember his first year or so in Munich, May 1913–August 1914, as 'by far the happiest and most contented time of my life'. The city was the throbbing heart of his beloved Fatherland:

> [T]here was this heartfelt love which seized me for this city more than for any other place that I knew, almost from the first hour of my sojourn there. A German city! What a difference from Vienna! I grew sick to my stomach when I even thought back on this Babylon of races. In addition, the dialect, much closer to me, which particularly in my contacts with Lower Bavarians, reminded me of my former childhood.[5]

To young Hitler, Bavaria felt like a home away from home. 'But most of all,' he would say, 'I was attracted by this wonderful marriage of primordial power and fine artistic mood, this single line from the Hofbräuhaus to the Odeon, from the October Festival to the Pinakothek . . .'[6]

He arrived in Munich, aged twenty-four, in the company of Rudolf Häusler, a twenty-year-old comrade from the Vienna doss house, who had been ejected from his wealthy family's home for a misdemeanour and was also now heading to Munich to start a new life. They shared a small flat in an apartment block at Schleissheimerstrasse 34, owned by Joseph Popp, a master tailor.

Hitler admired the city's neat beauty, with its broad, crowded squares and tree-lined streets, its cathedrals and palaces. At night he joined the flow of lederhosen and feathered caps going into the beer halls, whose raucous atmosphere offered a sweaty, shouting contrast to the restrained and upright society outside.

Munich was, before the war, one of the more culturally confident and innovative cities in Europe, belying the conservatism of the Bavarian state of which it was the capital. It was a transit point between the ancient and modern, radical and traditional, safe and experimental. So Hitler encountered a city that was indeed pulsing with artistic spirit, but not quite in the direction he approved of: at the time, Munich was the centre of various strands of Modernism and Expressionism, radical artistic movements that Hitler swiftly dismissed as degenerate. Wassily Kandinsky, Paul Klee, Alexej von Jawlensky and August Macke were among the artistic luminaries who lived in or were associated with the city. Richard Strauss and Thomas Mann also lived there around this time, though Vladimir Ilych Lenin had recently departed. None of them left much trace on Hitler's mind, except to repel it.

In this line-up, his pastel postcards were but the faintest ephemera. Not that he intended to exhibit his work; his passing exposure to Munich's artistic efflorescence simply reinforced his general loathing of 'degenerate art', which he would later ban. His own taste remained resolutely 'locked in the 19th century'.[7] He loved the Old Masters at the Alte Pinakothek. He was a great admirer of Anselm Feuerbach, Arnold Böcklin and the German realist painter Adolph von Menzel, whose work the Nazis would later use in their propaganda.

And so this searching, angry young man once again fell among the idlers, wastrels and revolutionaries who inhabited the beer halls, cabarets and cafés, chiefly in the fashionable bohemian district of Schwabing, where he would sit sipping coffee and eating sugary desserts, poring over his newspapers and loudly disburdening himself of his opinions to anyone who'd listen – an activity he later digni-fied as a 'political awakening'. His favourite tavern was Café Stefanie, reminding him of his childhood sweetheart; it was also nicknamed the Café Megalomania, on account of its radical student clientele. At other times, he spent his days turning out pictures of tourist landmarks, copied from postcards – the Theatinerkirche, the Hofbräuhaus, the Altes Rathaus, the Sendlinger Tor and many others – which he peddled in the cafés and beer gardens. They sold well, and he later estimated his annual income was around 1,200 marks a year (about £4,500 or US$6,100 in absolute terms today).

He painted, and 'studied' – his chief interest, he later claimed, being 'the relations between Marxism and Jewry', although there is no evidence he spent much time reading Marx's works. He made few friends and, according to his landlady, Frau Anna Popp, received not a single visitor to his apartment in his two-year tenancy.[8]

On 18 January 1914, the Linz police finally tracked Hitler down to Schleissheimerstrasse 34. The receipt of a summons to appear in Linz two days later alarmed him: evading military service carried a possible jail term and heavy fine. On the 19th the police escorted him to the Austro-Hungarian consulate in Munich, where he realized the seriousness of the situation.

The fear of disgrace energized Hitler to try to explain himself to the Linz magistracy and so justify his absence. He hired a lawyer, Ernst Hepp, who advised him to apologize to the magistracy for neglecting to register for military service, and to explain that he had been living in Vienna and his papers had not arrived. Hepp further urged his young client to plead for the court's sympathy: he was an orphan in a dire financial situation and 'worthy of special consideration'.[9] His letter to the military authorities, which he sent on 21 January, is an astonishing record of his early years, awash with ingratiating self-importance, traces of self-pity and the cunning turn of phrase of an emerging master manipulator:

> In the summons I am called an artist. Although I am rightly accorded this title, it is nevertheless only conditionally correct. It is true that I earn my living as a free-lance painter, but only, since I am entirely without property (my father was a government official), in order to

further my education. I am able to devote only a fraction of my time to earning a living, since I am still training myself as an architectural painter. Therefore my income is a very modest one, just large enough for me to get along.

I submit as evidence of this my tax statement and request you kindly to return this document to me. My income is estimated as 1200 marks, rather too much than too little, and does not mean that I make exactly 100 marks a month. Oh no. My monthly income is extremely variable, but certainly very bad right now, since the art trade sort of goes into its winter sleep around this time in Munich . . .

As far as my sin of omission in the autumn of 1909 [i.e. his failure to register for military service in Austria] is concerned, this was a terribly bitter time for me. I was an inexperienced young man, without any financial aid and also too proud to accept any from anyone, let alone to ask for it. Without any support, dependent on myself alone, the few crowns or often coppers I earned from my works were scarcely sufficient to provide me with a bed. For two years I had no other friend but care and need, no other companion but eternally gnawing hunger. I never knew the beautiful word youth. Today, even after five years, I have the mementos in the form of chilblain sores on my fingers, hands and feet. And yet I cannot recall this period without a certain rejoicing, now that I am after all over the worst. In spite of the greatest misery, in the midst of often more than dubious surroundings, I have always preserved my name unsullied, am altogether blameless before the law, and pure before my own conscience . . .[10]

After a fortnight of delays and mistimed telegrams, on 5 February 1914 Hitler appeared before the Salzburg draft board and pleaded various excuses – poverty, absence and the fact that he had belatedly registered. The court lent a sympathetic ear. The army examined him on 23 February and declared him medically 'unfit for military service' – the result of five years of privation – 'unsuitable for combat and support duty, too weak, incapable of firing weapons'.[11] The case was closed.

Hitler would later seek to hide the truth, for obvious reasons: a record of avoiding military service, whatever the cause, hardly chimed with the martial note of the Nazi regime and would be a career-stunting gift to his enemies. Not until 1950 would the evidence emerge that he had lied about the reasons for and timing of his move to Munich.

No example better illustrates Hitler's re-creation of himself as Führer and prophet than what he wrote about the outbreak of the First World War. In *Mein Kampf,* written a decade after the war began, he would retrospectively endow himself with the prescience of a political seer. In Munich in 1913, he would claim, he had sniffed war in the air 'better than the so-called official "diplomats", who blindly, as almost always, rushed headlong toward catastrophe'.[12]

The young prophet had seen the future more clearly than any politician or 'expert'. In describing the coming struggle, he would deploy the usual meteorological imagery indulged in by self-aggrandizing politicians and secular seers:

> As early as my Vienna period, the Balkans were immersed in that livid sultriness which customarily announces the hurricane, and from time to time a beam of brighter light flared up, only to vanish again in the spectral darkness. But then came the Balkan War and with it the first gust of wind swept across a Europe grown nervous. The time which now followed lay on the chests of men like a heavy nightmare, sultry as feverish tropic heat, so that due to constant anxiety the sense of an approaching catastrophe turned at last to longing: let Heaven at last give free rein to the Fate which could no longer be thwarted. And then the first mighty lightning flash struck the earth; the storm was unleashed and with the thunder of Heaven there mingled the roar of the World War batteries.[13]

That lightning flash was the assassination of Archduke Franz Ferdinand, heir to the Austrian throne, by Gavrilo Princip, a Bosnian Serb, in Sarajevo, capital of Bosnia–Herzegovina, on 28 June 1914. Austria–Hungary sought to pin the assassination on Serbia, whom they held responsible for orchestrating the murder. The Austrian government, with Germany's open-ended support, used the murder to contrive a case for swift retribution, turning a crisis that could have been contained into a *casus belli*. In other words, the decision to go to war in 1914 was another human – all too human – case of paranoia, incompetence and the disastrous misuse of power; it was not, as Hitler's mind conceived it, Heaven-sent or willed by the masses, most of whom, with the exception of a shrieking minority, did not want war.

There was nothing inevitable or accidental about it: by this point, Germany and Austria had *decided* to go to war, at least in the Balkans. They seized upon the death of poor old Franz Ferdinand, whom nobody in the Austrian court much cared for, as the perfect catalyst. Any other trigger might have set the process rolling – Russian mobilization, French colonial provocation – given the political enthusiasm for war. In those delirious July days, the one wildcard, the face of which nobody knew, was Britain: would she remain neutral or join France and Russia, her Triple Entente partners, in a war against Germany?

Despite his later claim that he saw it coming, in truth when Austria–Hungary declared war on Serbia on 28 July, young Adolf was as stunned and enthralled as thousands of other young men. He knew little of the deeper causes. Having read about it in the press in a café, he later projected back on to his youthful ignorance his insights into the national mood: 'People wanted at length to put an end to the general uncertainty. Only thus can it be understood that more than two million German men and boys thronged to the colours, prepared to defend the flag with the last drop of their blood.'[14]

All his dreams of a greater Germany coalesced around that moment, all his youthful fantasies seemed to be realized at last:

To me those hours seemed like a release from the painful feelings of my youth. Even today I am not ashamed to say that, overpowered by stormy enthusiasm, I fell down on my knees and thanked Heaven from an overflowing heart for granting me the good fortune of being permitted to live at this time.

A fight for freedom had begun, mightier than the earth had ever seen; for once Destiny had begun its course, the conviction dawned on even the broad masses that this time not the Fate of Serbia or Austria was involved, but whether the German nation was to be or not to be.[15]

The 'stormy enthusiasm' for war was not a fleeting phenomenon, he later insisted. It contained a 'necessary grave undertone', which made the 'national uprising more than a mere blaze of straw'. He rejoiced in the certainty of a 'gigantic struggle': 'at last war would be inevitable'.[16] A talent for boiling down profound historical upheavals into the simplest message – e.g. that 'popular spirit' drove the world to war – would define Hitler's thought and political style throughout his career.

Were European leaders so impressionable? Had the 'popular spirit' compelled the German, French, Russian and British governments to declare war, as Hitler claimed? In fact, a few thousand extreme nationalists and a complicit media made a big noise but were hardly representative of the general mood in Europe. Most German, French, British and Russian people did not want war, but they were powerless to stop it. 'Militarism was far from being the dominant force in European politics on the eve of the Great War,' observed historian Niall Ferguson. 'On the contrary, it was in political decline . . . The evidence is unequivocal: Europeans were not marching to war, but turning their backs on militarism.'[17] The warmongering on display that July in Munich, Berlin, Vienna and Paris did not reflect the feelings of millions of quiet, unasked families, who dreaded the loss of their sons, brothers and husbands in the coming conflagration.

War fever certainly gripped the jingoistic minority in Bavaria in July 1914. Distempered, marginalized characters like Hitler were in thrall to the greatest excitement of their time. War put meaning into their meaningless lives. And few were bathed so completely in the exuberance of those warm July days as this solitary young man, just twenty-four years old, friendless, orphaned and unemployed, for whom the declaration of war gave his life a sacred new direction. War would rescue Hitler from the pattern of serial failure, rejection and loneliness.

In the days before and after Germany declared war on Russia – which had mobilized in support of Serbia – on 1 August (it would declare war on France two days later), crowds formed in Munich's main square, the Odeonsplatz. Hitler appears in the famous Heinrich Hoffmann photo of the Odeonsplatz, wedged in among the people, delighted, open-mouthed, wild with anticipation. He sang the German nationalist hymn *'Die Wacht am Rhein'* ('The Watch on the Rhine', the unofficial patriotic anthem) until he was hoarse. The jubilant scene belied the fact that only a fraction of Munich's 600,000 people had turned out, and they tended to cheer on cue when they knew the camera was on them.[18] Otherwise, the mood was sombre, anxious, contrary to the popular notion that most ordinary Germans rushed to support the war.

Hitler's case for war was 'simple and clear', he later wrote. Germany faced an existential threat:

[F]or me, it was not that Austria was fighting for some Serbian satisfaction, but that Germany was fighting for her existence, the German nation for life or death, freedom and future. The time had come for Bismarck's work to fight; what the fathers had once won in the battles from Weissenburg to Sedan and Paris [all battles in the Franco-Prussian War], young Germany now had to earn once more. If the struggle were carried through to victory, our nation would enter the circle of great nations . . .[19]

CHAPTER SEVEN

'I passionately loved soldiering'

On 3 August, the British foreign secretary, Edward Grey, laid down an ultimatum to Germany to withdraw from Belgium or face war. Nobody in power in Berlin paid the slightest attention. The first stage of the Schlieffen Plan, the huge wheeling movement that was supposed to surround and conquer Paris from the north and north-west within six weeks, was already in motion: the first columns of 750,000 German soldiers had started the invasion of Belgium.

Britain's civilian leaders, several of whom, including the future prime minister David Lloyd George, had opposed the war until that point, were shocked by the magnitude of what was happening. Tears breached the dam of English reserve. The resolute calm of the Foreign Office and the prim punctiliousness of Whitehall yielded to the open sobbing of old men conscious of their role in the tragedy of the world. The German invasion of Belgium had swung the 'neutrals' in government behind the war.

Margot Asquith joined her husband, Herbert 'H.H.' Asquith, the prime minister, in his office in the House of Commons. 'So it's all up?' she asked. 'Yes it's all up,' he answered, without looking at her. He sat at his desk, pen in hand, and she leant her head against his. She later wrote, 'we could not speak for the tears'.[1]

That evening, as Edward Grey stood at a window in Whitehall, watching the sun set over St James's Park and the street lamps being

74

lit on the Mall, he said to a friend, 'The lamps are going out all over Europe; we shall not see them lit again in our lifetime.'[2]

At dawn on 4 August 1914, Chancellor Theobald von Bethmann-Hollweg rose to address Germany's Parliament, the Reichstag:

> A stupendous fate is breaking over Europe . . . [W]e wished to continue our work of peace [but], like a silent vow, the feeling that animated everyone from the Emperor down to the youngest soldier was this: Only in defence of a just cause shall our sword fly from its scabbard. That day has now come when we must draw it, against our wish, and in spite of our sincere endeavours. Russia has set fire to the building. We are at war with Russia and France – a war that has been forced upon us . . .[3]

Bethmann-Hollweg then gave a heavily truncated version of the July crisis that had precipitated the outbreak of war, distorted by untruths and omissions, and redounding always to Germany's honourable intent amid the perfidy of its neighbours. He unwittingly laid bare the siege mentality of a people perennially wronged, never the wrongdoers.

He dismissed the warnings Tsar Nicholas had given that Russia would not stand by if Austria–Hungary crushed Serbia, ignoring the fact that everyone in power knew this 'Third Balkan War', which Germany had provoked, could not be confined to the peninsula. He said nothing of Germany's role in engineering this outcome, of handing Vienna a blank cheque to do as it pleased against Serbia, confident of German support. He excised from the script Berlin's refusal to engage constructively in mediation attempts. He made much of Russia's reckless decision to order partial mobilization, which was admittedly the greatest error made by the Triple Entente.

Towards the end of his speech, Bethmann-Hollweg declared: 'Gentlemen, we are now in a state of necessity, and necessity knows no law.'[4] The remark horrified the embassies of Europe: was the civilized world, then, to revert to barbarian lawlessness? The chancellor later sourced his words to Helmuth von Moltke, chief of the German General Staff, who believed that fighting a war on two fronts made the invasion of Belgium a case of 'absolute military necessity': 'I had to accommodate my view to his,' were the chancellor's weasel words.[5]

From that point, the German government tossed aside all the customary rules that exist between nation states, in war and peace. Henceforth, Germany would behave as if centuries of evolving diplomacy and international law traceable to the Treaty of Westphalia in 1648, which ended the European wars of religion, were as nothing and revert to the blood pact of a gang of Visigoths. In waging war on Europe, the Reich would act outside all the accepted rules drawn up by the Hague Conventions. And the Entente powers would soon respond in kind.

In phrases that heaped shame upon ignominy, Bethmann-Hollweg then admitted that Germany had already committed two 'necessary' lawless acts – the invasions of Luxembourg and Belgium:

> Our troops have occupied Luxembourg and perhaps have already entered Belgian territory. Gentlemen, that is a breach of international law . . . [But] we were forced to ignore the rightful protests of the Governments of Luxembourg and Belgium. The wrong – I speak openly – the wrong we thereby commit we will try to make good as soon as our military aims have been attained. He who is menaced as we are and is fighting for his highest possession can only consider how he is to hack his way through [*durchhauen*].

His words drew 'great and repeated applause'.[6]

Belgium quaked at the realization of what she was about to endure: the full force of the German Army, unconstrained by the treaty obligations of Belgium's neighbours. Astonishingly, Bethmann-Hollweg still seemed to think British neutrality negotiable, despite his defence of German lawlessness:

> We have informed the British Government that, as long as Great Britain remains neutral, our fleet will not attack the northern coast of France,

and that we will not violate the territorial integrity and independence of Belgium [a bizarre statement, having admitted that Germany had already done just that]. These assurances I now repeat before the world, and I may add that, as long as Great Britain remains neutral, we would also be willing, upon reciprocity being assured, to take no warlike measures against French commercial shipping . . .

Gentlemen, so much for the facts. I repeat the words of the Emperor: 'With a clear conscience we enter the lists.' . . . Now the great hour of trial has struck for our people. But with clear confidence we go forward to meet it. Our army is in the field, our navy is ready for battle – behind them stands the entire German nation – the entire German nation united to the last man . . .[7]

If the chancellor's remarks shocked millions of Germany's neighbours, they exhilarated young Hitler, who approved of stamping all over small, neutral countries. To him, nothing should be allowed to stand in the path of German power, least of all international laws and old treaties. His hatred of meddling lawyers and prying bureaucrats had been well honed in Vienna, and was rooted in his contempt for the patient civil service of his father.

On the brink of war, the chancellor and Kaiser made rousing public noises, but behind the scenes were weighed down by the sheer enormity of what they had committed their country to do. In the eyes of Admiral Alfred von Tirpitz, secretary of state of the Imperial Navy, Bethmann-Hollweg resembled a 'drowning man'; and the Kaiser, according to a friend, wore 'a tragic and disturbed face'.[8] In rushing to mobilize, Germany's civilian leaders knew they had exhausted any hope of a diplomatic solution and had ceded power to the Prussian generals. Bethmann-Hollweg's rudderless diplomacy had dismally failed to avoid the descent into conflict and done much to start it. The destiny of the country, and Europe, now lay in the sights of the Prussian military class.

The final blow fell that same day, 4 August, when Britain revealed its true position. Having heard no response to its ultimatum, Britain declared war on Germany that day, killing Bethmann-Hollweg's last hope that the world's greatest sea power would stay neutral. Young Hitler could scarcely contain his excitement.

The next day Hitler eagerly volunteered for the German Army. He was rejected. He tried again on 16 August and this time was accepted, as a trainee infantryman in a Bavarian battalion. He would absurdly claim, in *Mein Kampf*, that as an Austrian he had had to petition Bavaria's King Ludwig III for a special dispensation to join the German Army. This was preposterous grandstanding. In the rush to enlist, a bureaucratic oversight had failed to pick up his nationality and landed him in a Bavarian unit by mistake. On 16 September he was assigned to the 16th Bavarian Reserve Infantry Regiment, of the 6th Bavarian Reserve Division; it was known as the 'List Regiment' after its first commander, Colonel Julius List.

Hitler had found a home, at last. For the first time in his life he had discovered a cause, regular employment and comradeship. 'I passionately loved soldiering,' he would later say.[9] The war would be 'the greatest and most unforgettable time of my earthly existence'.[10] His regiment quickly became his family, which he would refuse to abandon even when wounded or offered the prospect of promotion to a more effective unit.

Far from being members of a well-oiled fighting machine, the List Regiment's 3,500 soldiers formed a 'motley assortment of callow youths and not always young, or fit, men, from a range of backgrounds'.[11] It contained homeless misfits, romantic students, unemployed workers and, of course, idealists and Pan-Germans like Hitler (there were also fifty-nine Jews, who served mostly as privates or non-commissioned officers[12]). The List Regiment ranked well down the food chain in the German Army, receiving outmoded rifles with which to practise, not the weapons they would use in combat.[13]

Poorly trained and ill-equipped, these bumbling conscripts (volunteers like Hitler made up only 15 per cent of his regiment[14]) were thrown together into new formations and, on 10 October, dispatched to the training grounds at Lechfeld, near Augsburg. Hitler described the first five days of combat training as 'the hardest of my life'. 'Every day,' he wrote to his Munich landlady, Anna Popp, on 20 October, 'we have a long march, major exercises, and a night-time march of up to forty-two kilometres, followed by major brigade manoeuvres.'[15]

They trained for ten days before their departure for France and the Western Front. 'The volunteers of the List Regiment may not have learned how to fight properly,' Hitler would later say of his comrades, 'but they knew how to die like old soldiers.'[16]

Brave they certainly were. The Listers would fight with blind courage, obedient cannon fodder in the coming slaughter. Some 16,000 men would pass through the regiment between 1914 and 1918, a horrific turnover rate, but not so extreme on Germany's scale of losses. The German front desperately needed these young recruits during the first, devastating confrontations. By the time Hitler's regiment arrived on the Western Front, in late October, French and British forces had confounded the German Schlieffen Plan at the great Battle of the Marne on 5–12 September, driving the invaders back from the gates of Paris and crushing Prussian hopes of a swift victory.

In October, the focus of the German attack turned to Flanders, deemed an important link in the Allied defences: strategically close to the Channel ports of Dunkirk and Calais, vital to the maintenance of the British supply line to France. Their goal was to burst through the British and French defences and seize the town of Ypres, shutting off the British lifeline. Hitler and his comrades were to be thrown into the attack. But first, he would have to travel to Lille, Germany's new headquarters in northern France, through the aftermath of the invasion of Belgium.

Chapter Eight

'Louvain was a heap of rubble'

Nobody expected little Belgium to put up any resistance, least of all the Germans. The 'rage of dreaming sheep' was how a Prussian statesman had described the Belgians' willingness to defend their neutrality. 'I will go through Belgium like *that!*' the Kaiser, with a chop of his hand, had indiscreetly confided in a British officer before the war.[1]

At 8.02 on the morning of 4 August, the first grey lines of German infantry crossed the Belgian border at Gemmenich. Belgian sentries promptly opened fire, not realizing they had shot the spearhead of three German armies – nearly 800,000 troops – the vanguard of whom were now bristling to invade French territory. The reconnaissance patrol briefly dispersed, but the Germans soon returned, in force. They didn't expect any delays. The occupation of Belgium was meant to be just the rapid first stage in the Schlieffen Plan.

Within an hour, the brunt of the German invasion – the cavalry – had made short work of the border resistance and entered Belgian territory proper, hoisting the black eagle standard in every village and issuing proclamations that the destruction of roads and bridges by the locals would be considered hostile acts. As they barged into each community, the Germans were, at first, almost apologetic: they had violated Belgian territory 'with regret' and meant no harm, so long as the Belgians stood aside.

Advancing across Belgium that morning were General Alexander von Kluck's First Army on the right wing; General Karl von Bülow's Second Army in the centre; and General Max von Hausen's Third Army on the left wing. Line after line of grey-uniformed soldiers crammed every road and lane, in columns 30–40 miles (50–60 km) long, accompanied by reconnaissance motorcyclists, officers in automobiles, field kitchens, medical units, engineers, horses with carts of supplies, ammunition trucks and piece after piece of horse-drawn artillery. Not yet visible were the huge Krupp and Skoda guns – including the 16.5-inch Big Bertha super-heavyweight howitzers, the largest of their kind, specially designed to demolish modern fortresses with their concrete-smashing shells. They would soon destroy the city of Liège in an agony of pounding.

One after one, the Belgian villages stirred, murmuring 'Uhlan' and 'Hun' at the German approach. The people stood silently aside as thousands of grey-uniformed troops passed through bearing a forest of flags. The great crump of boots on the cobblestones and the rising chorus of the German anthem and patriotic songs were all that could be heard. A verse from a favourite ran:

> So a whole world is threatening us – so what?
> We are of good cheer
> And if someone should try to get in our way
> Give us our rifles! We are good shots.
> Brothers, move on! To the Vistula, to the Rhine!
> Dear Fatherland, no need to fear!
> Just and good, that is our war!
> Now lead us, Emperor, into battle and to victory![2]

Private Hitler sang the same song as his regiment approached the front, though the Listers would not pass through Belgian territory until October, when Hitler would witness the aftermath of one of the lesser-known atrocities of the First World War. How Germany dealt with Belgium would have a profound impact on the mind of the future dictator. To understand why, we must enter the maelstrom of those first few weeks of conflict.

The 'Martyrdom of Belgium'[3] began in the villages and farms, up against church walls and in the flames of people's homes. For General von Kluck, the 'shooting of individuals and the burning of houses' were 'punishments under martial law', which, he later wrote, were 'slow in remedying the evil'.[4] Other generals shared his view that whole villages of innocent people should be massacred as punishment for the actions of a few *francs-tireurs*, the civilian resistance.

German retribution was merciless and bloody. It expressed a policy that blamed Belgium for any disruption to the German Army, part of a 'general system of terror' directed at innocent communities. Revelations of the slaughter of Belgian civilians – old men, women and children – and the mass rape of women would soon astonish the world. Whole towns were selected for destruction without any evidence that the inhabitants had resisted the occupying force. A stray explosion, a broken bridge, a destroyed road, the shout *'Vive la France!'* – as some Belgian French, aware of the ultimate goal of the invasion, would call out – was enough to bring down the wrath of the Uhlan, the feared Prussian cavalrymen.

The people of Namur in southern Belgium dared not resist the German lines, yet they would be severely punished, *pour encourager les autres*. The murder of residents and the burning of their homes began at 9 p.m. on 24 August. 'Six dwellers in the Rue Rogier, who were [fleeing] their burning houses, were shot on their own doorsteps,' noted the Official Belgian Commission of Inquiry, based on the evidence of hundreds of witnesses (and the source for the testimonials that follow, unless otherwise stated).[5] The town panicked. People streamed from their homes, many in their nightgowns. Seventy-five were shot or burned to death.

At Andenne, on 20 August, a single shot and an explosion were heard as the German troops marched through town on their way to Charleroi near the French border. Nobody was hit. The Germans halted and fired back in disorder. They brought up a machine gun. The people fled, hiding in their cellars, bolting their doors and shutters. The destruction of the bridge and a nearby tunnel also provoked German fury. The pillaging began: windows and shutters were smashed, houses burned. The next day, the citizens were herded through the streets at gunpoint, their hands in the air. A man who tried to help his eighty-year-old father, who couldn't put up his arms, was struck in the neck with an axe. Anyone who resisted was shot; between forty and fifty people were selected at random and shot. Some were axed to death. More than 300 civilians were murdered at Andenne: 'no other Belgian town was the theatre of so many scenes of ferocity and cruelty'. The survivors later said that 'Andenne was sacrificed merely to establish a reign of terror'.[6]

The horror continued at Tamines, on the River Sambre. On 22 August, the Germans herded 400–450 men in front of the local church and opened fire – punishment for defying the occupation and shouting '*Vive la France!*' The Official Inquiry stated, 'as the shooting was a slow business the officers ordered up a machine gun, which swept off all the unhappy peasants still standing'.[7] The wounded hobbled to their feet and were shot down again. The next day, a Sunday, the people were ordered to bury a pile of corpses in the town square: 'fathers buried the bodies of their sons and sons the bodies of their fathers', while the German officers watched, 'drinking champagne'.[8] A gravedigger testified to burying 350–400 corpses. On leaving Tamines, the Germans burned 264 houses. The Official Inquiry estimates 650 dead; later research put the figure at 385.

The same atrocities were inflicted on many Belgian communities – at terrible cost, for example, to Dinant, in the district of Philippeville, and the villages of Hastière and Surice, according to the Official Inquiry. In these and other places, the populations were terrorized or killed, and the towns utterly destroyed. At Dinant, hundreds of bodies, including that of a three-week-old baby, were identified as the victims of two firing squads. The Inquiry listed 700 dead. Later research found evidence of duplication and placed the figure at 410.

In these communities, parish priests were routinely shot, and massacres of the menfolk usually followed. Women were hunted down and raped, by crazed, drunken soldiers whose officers were unwilling to restrain them. Nothing was sacred: in one village, a German infantry regiment broke up a church service, drove the parishioners on to the street and shot fifty of the men. During another massacre, women and children were forced to watch the execution of their husbands and fathers. At the village of Surice, a crowd of tearful women shouted, 'Shoot me too; shoot me with my husband!' German soldiers obliged, then plundered the corpses, taking 'watches, rings, purses and pocketbooks'.[9]

An act of barbarity that would for ever redound to German disgrace was visited upon the Belgian town of Louvain between 25 and 31 August. Over six days, the German Army burned Louvain's cathedral and university to the ground, murdered many of its residents and destroyed one of the world's finest cultural centrepieces: Louvain's peerless library, the cherished depository of 230,000 ancient volumes, including 750 medieval manuscripts. All were reduced to ashes. The sack of Louvain, reported in the world's press, provoked universal disgust. 'Are you descendants of Goethe or Attila the Hun?' wondered the writer Romain Rolland in a letter of protest.[10]

By the end of August, Belgium had been subjected to the horror of 'a medieval war'. The crucial point was this: the massacres, the rapes and the sacking of whole towns were not arbitrary acts of vengeance. They were organized. They were part of a strategy of civilian coercion laid down in the 1902 German Military Code, the *Kriegsbrauch im Landkriege*, or 'custom of war'. This explicitly stated that 'an energetically conducted war' should extend to 'the destruction of material and moral resources' (i.e. property, civilian lives, including women and children). 'Humanitarian' acts were in conflict with *Kriegsbrauch*.[11] In other words, German atrocities in Belgium were planned and *prescribed*, the corollary being the dismissal of the rules of law under the Hague Convention and the wilful suspension of conscience and compassion in the troops.

The man responsible for enforcing *Kriegsbrauch* was Field Marshal

Colmar Freiherr von der Goltz, appointed military governor of Belgium at the start of the occupation (he would later die of typhus or, some believe, poisoning by Turkish assassins). A dour, pitiless individual, von der Goltz grimly adhered to his rule book. 'It is the stern necessity of war,' he ordered in early September, 'that the punishment for hostile acts falls not only on the guilty, but on the innocent as well.' He clarified this on 5 October, shortly before Hitler's regiment passed through, in an order bearing his name:

In the future, villages in the vicinity of places where railway and telegraph lines are destroyed will be punished without pity (whether they are guilty or not of the acts in question). With this in view hostages have been taken in all villages near the railway lines, which are threatened by such attacks. Upon the first attempt to destroy lines of railway, telegraph or telephone, they will immediately be shot.[12]

The result was utter lawlessness, as German officers lost control of their men. By the end of August 1914, the Belgian civilian dead outnumbered their military casualties. In these acts, Germany revealed to the world 'a monstrous and disconcerting moral phenomenon', concluded the report on the Martyrdom of Belgium.[13]

In the early hours of 21 October, Hitler's regiment entrained for the front line – they knew not where, only that they were heading for the Western Front. 'I'm immensely looking forward to it,' Hitler wrote to Joseph Popp, his landlord, as the train shunted towards Belgium, via Cologne and Aachen.[14] The soldiers hoped they would be fighting the English.

At every German station crowds of supporters greeted Hitler's regiment with gifts of food and tobacco. The Rhinelanders left a deep impression on him: '. . . they received and feted us in a most touching manner'[15] – with stirring choruses of *Die Wacht am Rhein*. 'I will never forget the feelings that welled up in me when I first caught sight of this historic river,' he later said.[16]

Amid German jubilation at the fall of Brussels in late August, Hitler's chief fear had been that he would arrive too late for the fighting at the front. Scenes of the German path through Belgium soon relieved his impatience. He and his comrades witnessed a trail of destruction and heard stories of the rape and slaughter of Belgian civilians such as would horrify any morally sentient witness. Yet German propaganda muted their reaction: the Bavarian press retaliated with accounts of the *francs-tireurs* mutilating and blinding German officers. Hitler had surely read, as did most soldiers entering Belgium, the story of a Württemberger dragoon who had had his 'eyes plucked out, his hands hacked off and his tongue ripped out'.[17]

In a letter dated 5 February 1915, he wrote to Ernst Hepp, the lawyer who had helped him in Munich:

After a really lovely journey down the Rhine, we reached Lille on 23rd October. We could already see the effects of the war as we travelled through Belgium. We saw the conflagrations of war and heard its ferocious winds. As far as Douai our journey was reasonably safe and quiet. Then came shock after shock . . . We were now frequently coming upon blown up bridges and wrecked locomotives. Although the train kept going at a snail's pace, we encountered more and more horrors: graves. Then in the distance we heard our heavy guns.[18]

During the journey Hitler witnessed, unmoved, the ruins of Liège, pounded under shellfire. In a letter to Joseph Popp, dated 3rd December 1914, he dismissed the burned-out city of Louvain and its beautiful library as a 'heap of rubble'.[19] The slaughter of 248 of Louvain's citizens and the loss of 230,000 books, including many priceless, irreplaceable works, elicited no further comment in his letters or memoir.

Hitler took a lesson from the rape of Belgium that he would later apply as Führer: terrifying civilians was a tactic of war, vital to the effective occupation of an enemy country. As the German military governor of occupied Belgium, von der Goltz personally authorized the atrocities and terrorized Belgium for the duration of the war. His 'methods' impressed young Hitler, who would later deploy them on a far larger scale during the invasions of Poland, France, Russia, Ukraine and many other countries in the Second World War. The Nazis would think nothing of wiping out whole villages and towns and murdering their people as punishments for resistance elsewhere. In the First World War, this policy was applied to speed the flow of the German Army into France; in the Second, to destroy civilian resistance and unearth the racial enemies of the Third Reich (and infamously applied at the Czech village of Lidice, which was completely destroyed and 184 men massacred on Hitler's orders as punishment for the assassination of Reich Protector Reinhard Heydrich in the spring of 1942).

On the evening of 23 October, the List Regiment detrained at Lille station, a bombed-out shambles. The war had severely marked the city's civilian population: bombs had destroyed 1,200 homes and 'crying and begging women and children' crept among the rubble.[20] The German forces received three days' leave during which most of the men drank and caroused with French girls. Hitler spent his time reading.

Three days later the Sixth Army Reserve paraded before the Bavarian King Ludwig III and Crown Prince Rupprecht, before hastily preparing to attack the British lines east of Ypres. The alarm sounded in the German camp in Lille at 1 a.m. on 27 October. Hitler's regiment assembled in the Place de Concert, where the Crown Prince issued a rousing call to arms against 'the Englishman [who] has been at work for so many years in order to surround us with a ring of enemies and strangle us'.[21] They then departed on the 25-mile march towards the sound and flash of the heavy guns on the western horizon, in Flanders fields.

They marched through the night and all the next day, camping on the evening of the 28th. 'Four steps from my bundle of straw,' Hitler wrote, in the same letter to Hepp, 'lay a dead horse. The beast was already half decayed.' They got little sleep, as German guns fired round after round all night: 'They howled and hissed through the air, and then far in the distance you heard two dull thuds. Every man of us listened. We had never heard that sound before . . .'[22]

Late that night the regiment received their marching orders. 'Tomorrow we're attacking the English!' an officer announced. 'At last!' Hitler wrote. 'Every man of us was overjoyed.'[23] They rose at dawn on 29 October and, in dense fog, prepared to charge the British lines near the villages of Becelaere and Gheluvelt. 'Out there the first shrapnel was flying over us,' Hitler recorded, 'bursting at the edge of the woods, and tearing apart the trees like so much brushwood. We looked on curiously. We had no real idea of the danger. None of us was afraid. Each man was waiting impatiently for the command: "Forward!"'[24]

CHAPTER NINE

'I was right out in front, ahead of everyone'

Before the war arrived, Flanders looked much as it had for centuries: a bleak, rain-drenched land of gentle hills and ridges, pocked with woods of ash, chestnut and oak, set in heavy, blue 'Ypres clay'. It was a land of monotony and mist, 'with an air of melancholic sadness melting almost imperceptibly into the grey waters of the North Sea'.[1] General Ferdinand Foch, the future Supreme Allied Commander, gazed down from the tower of Ypres Cloth Hall on 'a sea of green, with little white islands marking the location of the rich villages with their fine churches and graceful steeples. To see open country in any direction was impossible.'[2]

The pastures were strewn with poppies that flowered in soil churned by plough and, soon, shellfire. Within days, this dreary farmland would be pounded beneath the guns and boots of four national armies. Within weeks, Flanders fields would be flattened to a lifeless moonscape. Within four years, the German and Allied armies would repeat the carnage, several times, culminating in the unspeakable horror of the Third Battle of Ypres, at Passchendaele, 1917, in which more than 500,000 would be killed or wounded in one of the bloodiest struggles of the war. Hitler would participate in several of these battles.

The town of Ypres had a long history of warfare and besiegement. The Romans had attacked it. So had successive forces of French, Dutch and English in the bloody parade of power through time. In

1383, Henry le Despenser, the Bishop of Norwich, led an English army to occupy Ypres, 'a nice old town, with narrow, cobbled-stoned streets', and besieged it for four months until French relief arrived.[3] After a French army captured the city in 1678, the engineer Sébastien le Prestre de Vauban installed a series of ramparts to deter further invaders.

In October 1914, the German and British armies eyeballed each other across no-man's-land, locked into trench lines that extended for hundreds of miles on either side, some as little as 50 yards apart. After the Germans had narrowly failed to conquer France within their six-week deadline, there followed a great 'Race to the Sea' – the frantic rush to outflank the enemy that threw a ribbon of trenches all the way to the Belgian coast. A scar of black earth zig-zagged from the Swiss Alps to the English Channel, along which, on this 'Western Front', the contest of the world would now be decided. In the Flanders sector, the town of Ypres took on strategic importance: for the Germans, possessing it would mean a base from which to block British reinforcements across the Channel; for the Allies, it would provide a jumping-off point into Belgium to disrupt the German supply line through Flanders.

And so, by October, British and French forces were concentrating here, to defend the blister of Allied-controlled territory to the east of the beautiful medieval town. On the map, this 'salient' in the front line resembled a half-oval that bulged into the German lines. In the minds of the men, it would become the 'Bloody Salient', a land of screaming shells and hissing gas, waterlogged trenches and scuttling rats. It quickly earned its reputation as the most loathsome place on the Western Front.

Already Ypres had had the bloodiest introduction to the war. On 3 October, overwhelming German numbers had forced the British back to the fringes of the town. On the 18th, the British reclaimed control. On the 20th, the Germans unleashed a fresh offensive all along the front, from Nieuport in the north to Armentières in the south. On both sides, the condition of the troops had severely deteriorated since the start of the campaign. Short of food, especially bread, with nothing hot to eat and only green, polluted water to drink, the German Army had been reduced, according to a diary found on an officer's corpse, 'to the state of beasts'.[4]

Towards the end of October, as Hitler's List Regiment prepared to attack, three corps of the British Expeditionary Force occupied the ancient ramparts of Ypres in an arc running a few miles to the east near the villages of Passchendaele, Broodseinde, Messines and Gheluvelt. In the previous ten days, the Germans had been reinforced. The German Fourth and Sixth Armies, under their respective commanders Albrecht, Duke of Württemberg, and Crown Prince Rupprecht of Bavaria, prepared a fresh offensive, to throw every man who could fire a rifle at the stubborn British defence of the town.

Unknown to Sir John French, commander of the British Expeditionary Force, the Tommies were hugely outnumbered: fourteen German infantry divisions had pulled up in Flanders, against seven British and French (three of which were cavalry fighting as infantry). The Germans had twice as many guns and, later, ten times as many heavy artillery pieces. Both sides fielded two machine guns per battalion. Yet the professional British Army bettered the conscripted Germans in a critical area: their superb riflemen were capable of firing the famous '15 aimed rounds a minute'[5] – a far higher rate than their opponents and with greater accuracy.

The German regiments mounted successive attacks on Ypres, in huge, closely packed masses – easy targets for British rifle fire, which spat round after round into the approaching sea of grey. So dense was this retaliatory fire, some German officers imagined they were advancing on machine guns. Yet despite their terrible casualties, the Germans used their huge numerical advantage to enclose the city in a slowly grinding vice.

On the morning of 29 October several German reserve regiments, containing thousands of young students – middle-class youths straight out of the opening scene of the film *All Quiet on the Western Front* – prepared to charge the British lines near Langemarck, Zonnebeke and Gheluvelt. Among them were older volunteers, such as the skinny twenty-five-year-old private wearing a drooping moustache and baggy uniform, Adolf Hitler.

In a richly self-dramatized passage of *Mein Kampf*, Hitler described what happened in that first attack:

> . . . and when the day began to emerge from the mists, suddenly an iron greeting came whizzing at us over our heads, and with a sharp report sent the little pellets flying between our ranks, ripping up the wet ground; but even before the little cloud had passed, from two hundred throats the first hurrah rose to meet the first messenger of Death.
>
> Then a crackling and a roaring, a singing and a howling began, and with feverish eyes each of us was drawn forward, faster and faster, until suddenly past turnip fields and hedges the fight began, the fight of man against man. And from the distance the strains of a song reached our ears, coming closer and closer, leaping from company to company, and just as Death plunged a busy hand into our ranks the song reached us too and we passed it along: '*Deutschland, Deutschland über Alles, über Alles in der Welt*' ['Germany, Germany above all else, above all else in the world'].[6]

According to witnesses, Hitler's regiment were not in fact singing the '*Deutschlandlied*', the tremendous Haydn melody that later became the national anthem; they were belting out '*Die Wacht am Rhein*' in order to distinguish their positions in the morning mist in the hope of avoiding 'friendly fire' from their own rear gunners.[7] 'Four days later we came back,' Hitler continued. 'Even our step had changed. Seventeen-year-old boys now looked like men.'[8]

This was the start of a terrible series of battles at Gheluvelt and Langemarck. A witness saw Hitler preparing to attack: bent forward, near the front, with a smile on his lips, like an athlete at the start of a race.[9] In his own account, he burst forth without a care for his life, straight into the British guns. In an extraordinary letter to his friend Hepp, Hitler portrayed himself as leading a fresh charge:

The whole thing was getting hotter and hotter . . . Five or six men brown as clay were being led along from the left, and we all broke into a cheer: six Englishmen with a machine gun! We shouted to our men marching proudly behind their prisoners. The rest of us just waited. We could scarcely see into the steaming, seething witches' caldron [*sic*] which lay in front of us. At last there came the ringing command: 'Forward!'

We swarmed out of our positions and raced across the fields to a small farm. Shrapnel was bursting left and right of us, and the English bullets came whistling through the shrapnel; but we paid no attention to them . . . I was right out in front, ahead of everyone in my platoon. Platoon-leader Stoever was hit. Good God! I had barely time to think; the fighting was beginning in earnest! . . . The first of our men had begun to fall. The English had set up machine guns. We threw ourselves down and crawled slowly along a ditch . . and then we were out in the open again.[10]

Hitler and his comrades dashed on, through a swamp and into a forest:

At this time there was only a second sergeant in command, a big tall splendid fellow called Schmidt. We crawled on our bellies to the edge of the forest, while the shells came whistling and whining above us; tearing tree trunks and branches to shreds . . . and enveloping everything in a disgusting, sickening, yellowy-green vapour. We can't possibly lie here forever, we thought and, if we are going to be killed, it is better to die in the open . . .

I jumped up and ran as fast as I could across meadows and beet fields, jumping over trenches, hedgerows, and barbed-wire entanglements, and then I heard someone shouting ahead of me: 'In here! Everyone in here!' There was a long trench in front of me and, in an instant, I had jumped into it; and there were others in front of me, behind me, and left and right of me. Next to me were Württembergers, and under me were dead and wounded Englishmen . . .

An unending storm of iron came screaming over our trench. At last, at ten o'clock, our artillery opened up in the sector. One – two – three

– five – and so it went on. Time and again shell after shell burst in the English trenches in front of us. The poor devils came swarming out like ants from an ant heap, and we hurled ourselves at them. In a flash we had crossed the fields in front of us, and after bloody hand-to-hand fighting in some places, we threw [the enemy] out of one trench after another. Most of them raised their hands over their heads. Anyone who refused to surrender was mown down. In this way we cleared trench after trench . . .[11]

That day and night Hitler's unit attacked four times, he claimed, 'and each time we were forced to retreat. From my company, only one other man was left besides myself, and then he, too, fell. A shot tore off the entire left sleeve of my tunic but, by a miracle, I remained unharmed.' The battle raged without end for four days, Hitler wrote. 'But we were all so proud of having defeated the British!'[12]

Hitler's letter home seems no different to that of any other young man, keen to display his courage. And there is no doubt that the German attacks at Gheluvelt and Langemarck in October 1914 were among the most ferocious offensives of the whole war. As Hitler suggests, a blind, unthinking courage appears to have possessed the Germans who stormed the British trenches. They charged with scarcely a care for their own necks, facing death with suicidal determination. Anything for the Fatherland! They smashed up villages, churches, farms – everything in their path. The skies were red and black with the flames of burning buildings, the fields littered with corpses. The German indoctrination of these young men had been ruthlessly efficient: they were programmed to march straight at the lines of British rifles.

Yet Hitler's letter is unusual in this sense: in drawing attention to his front-line role, in relishing battle and close shaves with death, he writes with the boyish excitement of one of Karl May's westerns. But nowhere does he claim to have killed the enemy or captured prisoners. If he had led from the front, as he claimed, he would certainly have clashed with the British at close range. Modesty cannot explain the omission – that would be at odds with the vainglorious self-portrait he paints elsewhere. The answer is that Hitler exaggerated his role. He was nowhere near the opening assaults of First Ypres.

Other regiments had attacked first and taken the heaviest casualties. At Langemarck those killed included thousands of student volunteers whose loss furnished the legend of the *Kindermord bei Ypern* (the Massacre of the Innocents at Ypres) and who are commemorated in small services today at battlefield cemeteries and at home in Germany. Many were as young as seventeen, boys straight out of school, student dreamers, believers in the glory of the Fatherland and easy prey to war propagandists. Many others were products of the German *Burschenschaften* (university fraternities)[13] – patriotic, blue-eyed, blonde lads, boys of the sort who would later join the Führer's Hitler Youth brigades. Their selfless heroism evoked a nineteenth-century romantic ideal of chivalry. They had no chance in the sights of British rifles.

Although they didn't fight in the battle at Langemarck, the List Regiment's experiences elsewhere in the field of First Ypres were no less bloody. In fact, Hitler could not have survived had he been leading from the front, given the regiment's massive casualties. Nor was he right to claim that 'the Britishers were licked':[14] the German offensive failed to penetrate their opponents' lines further than the village of Gheluvelt, which a renewed British offensive soon recovered.

Notwithstanding the waves of German attacks, the British held Ypres and the eastern edge of the salient. It was an astonishing display of resilience. Their soldiers were, after all, professional, tough-as-nails Tommy Atkinses, as John Keegan writes: '. . . working class, long-service regulars, shilling-a-day men of no birth and scanty education'.[15] They cared nothing for the mystical German patriotism of their young enemy. They were trained to kill, win the war and go home.

The British were astonished at what came at them in those late October battles. Captain Harry Dillon, of the 2nd Oxford and Bucks Light Infantry, beheld 'a great grey mass of humanity . . . charging, running for all God would let them straight on to us not 50 yards off'. He had warned his men what to expect, but no one had anticipated this. He had 'never shot so much in such a short time'. He saw the

Germans fall, veer off course, stagger to the ground, until only 'a great moan' rose in the night, and men 'with their arms and legs off' tried to crawl away.[16]

Private H. J. Milton similarly witnessed masses of Germans 'running into death': '. . . they gave great yells after they started but very few got back. The screams were terrible.' Some British companies fired an average of 500 rounds per man per day: 'This storming, we will never forget as long as we live.'[17]

Within four days the List Regiment had been virtually annihilated, as Hitler wrote in a letter to Popp: 611 of the regiment's 3,600 men had survived the battle; the rest had been killed, wounded or captured, an 83 per cent casualty rate. 'In the entire regiment there remained only thirty officers. Four companies had to be disbanded.'[18] His regiment lost 349, dead, on 29 October alone, with about four times as many wounded, taken prisoner and missing that day. Hitler recounted all this 'without a trace of mourning':[19] his regiment, he wrote, had been cut to 600, as though they were lambs to the slaughter. He would later ostentatiously mourn their loss, from a distance in years; at the time, he regarded them as a necessary sacrifice for the Fatherland.

Hitler's comrades were better able to express the true sadness that struck the Listers. The British stand at First Ypres shocked the German survivors. 'Only a few regiments have had to give such a heavy toll in blood on their first fight,' wrote Adolf Meyer.[20] The carnage left an indelible scar on Oscar Daumiller, a chaplain with the 6th Bavarian Reserve Division. 'It is horrible to see the torments, the indescribable injuries,' he wrote, 'it is horrible to see how the strife . . . has shattered the hearts [of the soldiers].'[21]

Hitler witnessed this horror on his comrades' faces, as he wrote in *Mein Kampf*: 'I remember well my comrades' looks of astonishment when we faced the Tommies in person in Flanders' – but he seemed not to share their fear.[22] There was something boyish, unnatural, in the way he thrilled to the excitement of war, as though the dead and wounded were play-acting in a great human drama staged for his benefit.

*

The slaughter of the German Army at the First Battle of Ypres quickly acquired the aura of a heroic sacrifice. The *Kindermord* inspired the 'Legend of Langemarck'. Though most of the action took place nearer Bixschoote, the more German-sounding name appealed to the folks back home. The legend has it that tens of thousands of these boys were slaughtered as they marched into battle while singing the *'Deutschlandlied'* and other patriotic German songs – a story that would appear on the front page of every German newspaper and which, as we have seen, Hitler would appropriate in his version of the List Regiment's attack at First Ypres in order to identify himself in his readers' minds with this legendary sacrifice.

It later transpired that many of the young casualties had probably died of friendly fire, cut down by their own artillery. And they sang not out of blind patriotism, but – like the List Regiment when they went into action – in a desperate effort to warn the rear gunners of their location, according to General Horst von Metzsch, general staff officer of the XXVII Reserve Corps, who witnessed the 'general panic' as the lines fell apart under fire from the front and rear. The survivors would be 'mentally shattered forever'.[23]

The results of this carnage can be seen today, at the German cemetery near Langemarck, a desolate place where rows of flat black slabs designate the identifiable dead. The remains of 24,917 German troops lie in a mass grave, their names etched on the walls, including some 3,000 student casualties of the *Kindermord*.

Hitler would never forgive or forget the slaughter at First Ypres, particularly the battle at Langemarck. Though he didn't directly participate in the latter, the legend became seared in his mind until he persuaded himself that he *had* fought there. It would haunt and goad him for the rest of his life. For Hitler, Langemarck would for ever be sacred ground, scene of the greatest sacrifice of the young heroes of the Reich.[24] It would hold a similar stature in the pantheon of German heroism as the Battle of Tannenberg, which had taken place two months earlier on the Eastern Front. In years to come, Nazi myth-makers would orchestrate extraordinary annual commemorations of the battle and recast the Führer as a 'Hero of Langemarck'.[25]

Many years later, as conqueror of France and Belgium, Hitler returned to Ypres to erect a memorial and lay wreaths on the graves of the 'Innocents'. In the interim, before his rise to power, his fury at the massacre at Langemarck would stoke his hatred for those he held responsible for Germany's defeat. A vast plan of revenge, as we shall see, took shape in his mind long before he executed it.

Chapter Ten

'You will hear much more about me'

Hitler served four days as a foot soldier. After First Ypres he was transferred to the regimental staff as a dispatch runner (*Meldegänger*, literally 'message runner'). One of ten in his regiment, he was responsible for delivering typed orders from headquarters to battalion and company commanders nearer the front. The runners travelled on foot or by bicycle, rarely as far as the forward trenches, yet often through fields swept with shellfire. They were the only form of communication when shellfire broke the telephone lines, and hence vital.

Hitler soon found himself enjoying a comfortable war, compared with that of front-line infantrymen. The runners received long periods of leisure and far better conditions in the rear areas than their comrades in the trenches. Hitler never spent weeks in a muddy, rat-infested dugout under constant bombardment among men in various stages of nervous breakdown. In the infantryman's mind, Hitler and his fellow runners had it easy, and they mocked the support staff as 'rear-area pigs' (or 'base-wallahs', as the English tended to dismiss those who worked well back from the action).

Contrary to those who dismiss Hitler as a coward, however, he performed a very dangerous job. To run across open ground, in a field exposed to heavy artillery, required great courage. Runners were often forced to 'dart amid flying shrapnel while most soldiers huddled in underground bunkers'.[1] Several, sometimes as many as six, were frequently sent with the same message, in the hope that at least one would get through. On the first day of fighting at Wytschaete, during the Battle of Messines, on 31 October 1914, three dispatch runners were killed and one critically wounded. By the autumn of 1915 Hitler was the only surviving runner of his original unit.[2] A series of near misses would earn him the nickname 'Lucky Linzer'.

Hitler quickly distinguished himself in the role. His commanders and comrades praised his grit and courage at the time, when they had no political motive for doing so. Even in 1932, during Hitler's ascent, a Social Democrat and trade unionist, Michel Schlehuber, who strongly opposed Hitler's politics, described his old regimental comrade as a good soldier who never shirked his duties or avoided danger. If Hitler continued to talk up his performance in letters to the Popp family – 'I have, so to speak, been risking my life every day, looking death straight in the eye'[3] – his accounts were beginning to sound truer to his job, even if he was far from delivering messages every day. In any case, was it not a common trait in young soldiers, to reassure themselves as much as their friends and families?

To the consternation of his comrades, however, Hitler seemed to relish running errands, regardless of the risks. 'I was repeatedly exposed to heavy artillery fire,' he later wrote, 'even though it was nothing but a postcard that needed to be delivered.'[4] Other recollections bear out the truth of this. He never flinched from accepting a new mission and would often volunteer to take the place of married men. 'You don't need to worry about Hitler,' a fellow soldier said, 'he always gets through, even if he has to crawl like a rat up to the trench.'[5]

What interests us – given what happened later – is not whether Hitler was a brave and dutiful soldier (he obviously was), but how he reacted to the war, and how the war affected him. So far, the opening battles seemed to intoxicate, to exhilarate him. His bemused comrades tended to misunderstand the reason for his strange and often irritating enthusiasm. He believed in the cause. Where they fell into cynicism or lost faith, Hitler never abandoned his belief in the sacrifice, for the glory of the German Army and the future of the Reich, a goal for which every man must be willing to give his life. For him, duty to the Fatherland was real and tangible, not mere propaganda. In Hitler's mind, Germany's victory would vindicate everything he stood for: German greatness, racial purity, the Teutonic triumph. To the astonishment of his fellows in the regiment, he even spoke of himself as making a personal and decisive contribution to this triumphant outcome.

For now, however, Hitler was just another runner, albeit one of marked eccentricity. In November 1914 he was promoted to *Gefreiter*, a rank that has no clear equivalent in the British and Dominion armies. Its closest equivalent was 'lance corporal', one up from private and second in charge of a platoon section of ten men. And yet Hitler's new rank gave him no command over other soldiers. His status was more akin to a 'senior private': 'Hitler had merely been recognised as a reliable and trustworthy soldier,' writes Carruthers.[6] His oddness excluded him from serious consideration as future officer material. Nor, in fact, did he seem to want a proper promotion. He liked his job.

To his comrades, in the relative comfort of regimental HQ, Hitler proved a reliable if unusual *Gefreiter*. He had an irritating habit of never grumbling or sharing the soldiers' complaints. He eschewed home leave. He was a prudish, self-righteous loner, obsessed with personal cleanliness. He neither drank nor pursued women. He lived on bread, marmalade and weak tea, plus a dumpling or strip of bacon (he was not yet a confirmed vegetarian). He avidly read the newspapers and was familiar with the inflammatory tracts emanating from home, such as the economist Werner Sombart's widely circulated essay, 'Our Enemies'. Published in German newspapers in November 1914, the essay formed the outline for Sombart's 1915 book, *Händler und Helden* (Merchants and Heroes) and peddled the sort of puerile racial hostility that amused Hitler (e.g. the Serbs were 'mouse-trap peddlers', the Japanese 'clever half-apes').[7]

On 2 December 1914 Hitler was awarded the Iron Cross (Second Class) for his part in helping to save the life of his regiment's new commander, Lieutenant Colonel Philipp Engelhardt, who had stepped out from cover during an attack near Wytschaete. Two dispatch runners reportedly raced forward to shield the colonel and lead him to safety. One was Hitler. Yet his precise role is unclear: a 1915 report gave fellow dispatch runner Anton Bachmann most of the credit; a 1932 report released the year before Hitler came to power not surprisingly gave young Adolf equal credit.

There is no reason to deny the validity of Engelhardt's statement, made at the time of the award, despite the fact that it was dusted down by the Nazis to shore up Hitler's war record. 'I want to stress,' Engelhardt stated, 'when during the attack on the axe-shaped piece of forest (later called the Bavarian Forest), I left the cover of the forest near Wytschaete to better observe the attack, Hitler and another courier . . . the volunteer Bachmann, placed themselves in front of me to protect me from machine gun fire with their own bodies.'[8]

The most persuasive witness was Michel Schlehuber, the future Social Democrat who would reject the Nazis. Called to give testimony in the 1932 inquiry into Hitler's war record by his opponents, who sought to discredit the Nazi leader, Schlehuber destroyed their case. Describing Hitler as a good soldier and faultless comrade, he concluded:

> I have known Hitler since the departure for the front of the Bavarian 16th RIR. I came to know Hitler as a good soldier and faultless comrade. I never saw Hitler attempt to avoid any duty or danger. I was part of the division from first to last, and never heard anything bad about Hitler, then or afterwards. I was astonished when I later read unfavorable things about Hitler's service as a soldier in the newspapers. I disagree entirely with Hitler on political matters, and give this testimony only because I highly respect Hitler as a war comrade.[9]

Clearly both Hitler and Bachmann played a part, as did two other dispatch runners who also received the award. Hitler's decoration was undoubtedly deserved and not the work of 'friends' in high places, as some critics claim. He had no friends in high places. He was overjoyed: 'It was the happiest day of my life.' Ignaz Westenkirchner, a fellow dispatch runner, observed: 'He had now found that for which he had been longing for many years, a real home and recognition.'[10]

The award would also lead to one of the 'worst moments' in his life, with lethal consequences for the officers who nominated him. In a letter to Ernst Hepp, Hitler described the dreadful moment when the award 'saved our lives':

[W]hile they were preparing a list of men recommended for the Iron Cross, four company commanders came into the tent or dug-out rather. To make room for them we had to go outside for a while. We had not been out there more than five minutes when a shell hit the tent, severely wounding Lt-Col Engelhardt and either killing or wounding the rest of the headquarters staff. It was the worst moment of my life. We worshipped Colonel Engelhardt.

The colonel lost his life recommending an award to the man who had helped to save his life.

The trenches near Ypres were barely 50 yards apart in places, and on Christmas Eve 1914 the German and British troops decided to share the festive spirit. Across no-man's-land the Germans shouted, 'Happy Christmas, Tommy!' The British replied, 'Merry Christmas, Jerry!' Above the German parapet a figure then appeared, and another, and another, walking towards the British trenches. The British held their fire and went out to meet the enemy. They exchanged rum and schnapps, and shared photos of their loved ones. Someone played an accordion.

Thus began the famous Christmas truce, one of the most endearing legends of the First World War. Sergeant David Lloyd-Burch, who served with the BEF in No. 10 Field Ambulance, witnessed the German and English troops 'burying the dead between the trenches. Cigarettes and cigars were exchanged. It was so exciting . . . to be above the trenches in daylight. At ordinary times [it] meant sudden death.'[11]

Along the Ypres salient, the Germans and British sang 'Silent Night' together that night, even as the battle raged on in several places. Their generals disapproved of, and later banned, any fraternizing with the enemy. One German runner shared the commanders' view: in fact, the Christmas truce disgusted Hitler, as he sat fuming in the ruins of Messines village, longing to resume fighting. Heinrich Lugauer, a fellow runner, described him as an 'embittered opponent of the fraternization with the English'.[12] Instead, Hitler spent Christmas under a decorated tree, singing 'Silent Night' with a few comrades in emphatic German and taking a macabre interest in two corpses lying near the camp, 'on whom grass was growing', as he told a fellow soldier, Hans Mend.[13]

Hitler never received letters or parcels from home. He claimed that he neither wanted gifts nor allowed his family to send them, a melancholy cover for the fact that he had no family. Indeed, his relatives neither knew nor seemed to care where he was; his sister, Paula, thought him dead. (Paula was then living with their aunt, Johanna Pölzl. In the early 1920s she would move to Vienna, to work as an insurance clerk. The discovery of her private journal in 2005 revealed that her brother used to beat her when she was a child and later refused to allow her to marry Dr Erwin Jekelius, an Austrian Nazi and physician responsible for sending 4,000 of his patients, many of them disabled, to the gas chambers.[14])

Hitler thus cultivated the image of a lonely, defiant figure, an orphaned loner who elicited sympathy: '. . . the poor devil takes part in so much,' Hans Mend wrote, 'yet has no idea for whom in Germany he's endangering his life and risking his health.'[15]

'Haven't you got anyone back home?' Mend once asked. 'Isn't there anyone to send you things?'

'No,' Hitler replied. 'At least, no one but a sister, and goodness only knows where she is by this time.'

Hitler 'just looked the other way,' Mend recalled, 'and busied himself knocking the mud off his boots and doing what he could to clean his shirt.'[16]

His sense of humour was more slapstick than sharp. He saw the funny side to practical jokes, such as when his comrades raised a helmet on a bayonet above the trench parapet to draw enemy fire. 'Even Hitler, who was usually so serious, saw the fun of this,' recalled Ignaz Westenkirchner. 'He used to double himself up with laughter.'[17]

In January 1915 Hitler gave himself a Christmas gift of a fox terrier that had strayed from the British lines. He lavished affection on 'Foxl', as he named the dog, and would remember it affectionately in *Mein Kampf* and later monologues. 'It was crazy how fond I was of the beast,' he recalled in 1942,[18] with genuine warmth:

> I gradually got him used to me. At first I gave him only biscuits and chocolate . . . Then I began to train him. He never went an inch from my side . . . Not only was I fond of the beast, but it interested me to study his reactions. I finally taught him everything: how to jump over obstacles, how to climb up a ladder and down again. The essential thing is that a dog should always sleep beside its master.

Hitler used to tie Foxl up when he went on a mission, and on his return 'He would recognise me even from a distance. What an outburst of enthusiasm he would let loose in my honour!'[19]

Hitler's affection for his dog contrasts sharply with the absence of warm feelings for his old comrades, spoken or in writing. He would remember none of the dead or wounded with any affection in *Mein Kampf*. He told the story of Foxl to a few of the Nazi elite in late January 1942, as part of his 'secret monologues' or 'Table Talk', in which he shared his thoughts for hours with his senior staff on any subject that took his interest, from philosophy and culture to the war, the Jews and religion.[20] At the time of the Foxl anecdote and other playful memories, Germany was entering its most destructive phase of the Second World War and, at the Wannsee Conference on 20 January 1942, Hitler and the most senior Nazis had just ordered the Final Solution.[21]

By early 1915, the war had perceptibly changed every soldier, on both sides. The huge fatalities, indiscriminate slaughter and failure to dislodge the enemy forced every man each day to face a terrible truth:

their bodies were being used in a pure attritional struggle, to plug gaps in the line. They were dying by the hundreds of thousands for little or no gain. In a mechanized war of indiscriminate slaughter that had reduced casualties to 'normal wastage',[22] as the British described their losses, heroism and sacrifice began to lose all meaning. The Germans, like their British and French opponents, daily encountered piles of corpses, ghastly wounds and unspeakable scenes as normative, routine experiences.

Hitler's reaction to all this was unusual. While his fellow soldiers started to bemoan the war, hoping for a mild wound that would send them home, Hitler flew into a rage at such defeatism, scorning their cowardice and want of spine. The hideous scenes of death and destruction made not the slightest dent in his resolution. At the same time, he started to blame Germany's failure to defeat France and Britain on shadowy 'internal' enemies at home, and to disinter the paranoid theories he had absorbed during his Vienna days.

In his long letter to Hepp on 5 February 1915, he referred in writing for the first time to these internal enemies:

> . . . those of us who are lucky enough to return to the Fatherland will find it a purer place, less riddled with foreign influences, so that the daily sacrifices and sufferings of hundreds of thousands of us and the torrent of blood that keeps flowing here day after day against an international world of enemies, will not only help to smash Germany's foes outside but our inner internationalism, too, will collapse.[23]

By 'inner' enemies Hitler meant the social democrats and Marxists, whose names suggested, but were not yet fully synonymous with, the Jews. Here lay the genesis of the myth of the *Dolchstoss*, the 'stab in the back' of the German Army, later espoused by many, which would crowd his thoughts in years to come.

The activities of these 'enemies' on the home front personally affronted him. Whatever they were doing, they were doing this to him and to the German Army, and he made it his personal duty to bring their deleterious work to attention. He fiercely reprimanded defeatist comrades who felt their battle ardour waning. Germany must win the war at all costs, he affirmed.

In time, at every setback, he trained his fury on these shirkers at home, the Marxists, socialists and increasingly the Jews. He shouted down his comrades if they denied forces at home were working to undermine the victory of the Fatherland.[24] On occasions he was heard to blame an 'exploitative system of Jewish bankers' for Germany's problems. According to Hans Mend, Hitler pledged that if he had the power he would 'free the Germanic race from these Jewish parasites and send these racial despoilers . . . to Palestine.'[25]

Mend has been rightly criticized as an unreliable and self-serving witness prone to hyperbole. Yet these excerpts, written in 1931, accord with a few other glimpses of Hitler's frame of mind in 1915 and, as John F. Williams shows, were among the first recorded examples of a more intense strain of anti-Semitism in Hitler.[26] Yet they were fleeting outbursts, at this stage, and not unusual, and certainly nothing like the systematic or obsessive hatred that emerged later. For most of the war, Hitler showed no overt hatred of the Jews, as several other comrades would attest.

'His comrades at the front never heard him talk like this,' writes Toland. 'He appeared to be no more anti-Semitic than they were. Occasionally he would make an innocuous remark such as, "If all the Jews were no more intelligent than Stein [their telephone operator], then there wouldn't be trouble."' Whenever he spoke of Vienna and the influence of Jews, he did so 'without spitefulness'.[27] Nor had he expressed open hostility towards the Jews in his regiment. As we shall see, it would take the confluence of gigantic events and Hitler's hurtling rage to turn this bigoted and bitter young man into the architect of the Holocaust.

In the first half of 1915, perhaps touched by his miraculous survival skills, Hitler began to portray himself to his fellow soldiers as above the common run of humanity, as a 'man of destiny'. Having survived numerous dangerous missions, he felt strangely omnipotent, as if a metaphysical hand had reached down to ensure his survival. In his letters he thanked the miracle, or chain of miracles, that had saved his life when so many around him were falling. He even suggested that he 'enjoyed the special protection of Providence'.[28]

Even though he looked awful, he kept volunteering for missions. His health had rapidly declined. He suffered from a hacking cough but never took home leave and never reported sick. '[N]one of us could convince him to report to the doctor,' recalled Mend.[29] It was as if he were subjecting himself to a trial of strength, testing himself for some future role.

In this terrible state he alluded, in early 1915, to the higher calling that Fate had allotted him, the fulfilment of which would rely on his survival, rendering him, he implied, invulnerable on the battlefield. '[Y]ou will hear much more about me later,' he warned his comrades. 'Just wait until my time comes.' They laughed, but Hitler just shook his head.[30] He would often refer to the day 'his time' would come.

Ever on the watch for someone to blame for Germany's misfortunes, Hitler began to imagine himself as chief inquisitor after the war ended. He would sit silently with his head in his hands, as he had done in the doss houses and cafés of Vienna and Munich, then suddenly jump up and shout that if victory were denied Germany then 'the invisible enemies of the German people would be more dangerous than the mightiest enemy guns'.[31] In revenge, he told his astonished comrades, he would make Germany's leaders 'responsible for these men who have fallen'.[32]

These were the early impulses of a spirit wrestling to break itself free from its apparent destiny, as an obscure runner at the bottom of the German Army, and lunge for a higher calling. These were the first inklings of Hitler's changing sense of himself, as a different man, a leader rising, Rienzi-like, as the saviour of his adopted country.

Chapter Eleven

'At last my will was undisputed master'

Hitler volunteered for several perilous missions between March and May 1915, and witnessed the mutilating impact of new weapons – heavy artillery and machine guns – on lines of advancing soldiers. Near the end of the Battle of Neuve Chapelle, in March, he ran a shocking artillery gauntlet through a rain of shells between the regimental HQ at Halpegarbe and his battalion HQ in the Bois du Biez. His commanding officer expressed amazement that the dispatch runners had survived the onslaught. Hitler later wrote that he had leaped from shell hole to shell hole under hellish fire to deliver his messages.[1]

And on 18 March, he put himself up for another treacherous run, which found him crawling through open country, exposed to English sniper fire. According to the regimental history, the List Regiment's dispatch runners were similarly exposed to open fire during the Battle of Aubers Ridge that May.[2]

Balthasar Brandmayer, then a twenty-three-year-old mason's apprentice from Götting, near Rosenheim, joined Hitler's dispatch unit that month. Brandmayer would never forget his first encounter with Hitler: 'He had come back fatigued after a delivery . . . He was like a skeleton, his face pale and colourless. Two piercingly dark eyes, which struck me especially, stared out of deep sockets. His prominent moustache was unkempt. Forehead and facial expression suggested high intelligence . . .'[3]

The pair got along well, and Brandmayer's memoir, *Meldegänger Hitler* (Hitler the Messenger), published in 1933, admires Hitler's 'iron nature' and unnerving willingness to volunteer for every mission. While the memoir reeks of supplication – Brandmayer had every reason to try to impress his politically empowered old comrade – it holds true in part, when aligned with other witness statements. After one mission, Hitler seemed to be a 'man without nerves', Brandmayer observed:

> Paralysing tiredness weighed like lead on my burning limbs. I threw off my helmet and webbing and sank, dead-tired, into my bunk. I expected Adolf to do the same but how wrong I was! As I turned around I found him sitting near the bed, helmet on head, buckled up, and waiting for the next order. 'You're crazy!' I cried out angrily. 'How would you know?' was his prompt reply. There was no man under his uniform, only a skeleton . . . He had an iron nature.[4]

Other soldiers attested to this scene. Hitler would pace about, weapon in hand, like a wild beast, impatient for action. His reckless courage, his eagerness for another mission, they found unnerving. 'The Austrian never relaxes,' one said of him. 'He always acts as if we'd lose the war if he weren't on the job every minute.'[5]

Hitler did not participate in the Battle of Loos (25 September–13 October 1915). But he heard all about the fate of the British Army in one of its most disastrous offensives of the war. Loos was an Anglo-French attempt to smash the German trenches at Artois and Champagne and break out into mobile warfare. The unspeakable scenes that resulted might have shelved for ever the idea that huge frontal attacks could break the German lines. What happened at Loos revealed a breed of man, the British Tommy, whose courage, unquestioning sense of duty and fear of failure persuaded him to march head-on into enemy machine guns. A German witness, the historian of the 26th Infantry Regiment, famously described the result:

Never had the machine guns had such straightforward work to do . . . with barrels burning hot and swimming in oil, they traversed to and fro along the [British] ranks unceasingly; one machine gun alone fired 12,500 rounds that afternoon. The effect was devastating. The enemy could be seen literally falling in hundreds, but they continued their march in good order and without interruption. The extended lines of men began to get confused by this terrific punishment, but they went doggedly on, some even reaching the wire entanglement in front of the reserve line . . . Confronted by this impenetrable obstacle, the survivors turned and began to retire.[6]

Field Marshal Sir John French, the BEF's serially inept commander, and the then Lieutenant General Sir Douglas Haig were jointly responsible for this debacle.[7] Sir John bore the brunt of the blame for failing to send up reserves in time to hold the British gains, exposing his forward troops to devastating German counter-attacks. The toll was 59,247 British soldiers killed, wounded or missing in the two attacks, including three major generals and eighteen-year-old John Kipling, the only son of the poet Rudyard Kipling. Many of the British inhaled their own poison gas, blown back on to their trenches when the wind changed, killing or incapacitating them. (This was their first use of the gas, which the Germans had used on 22 April that year at Second Ypres.) Sir John was sacked, and he returned to Britain to command the Home Forces, a bitter and resentful man. Haig replaced him. The lessons were clear: something more than artillery, gas and massed ranks of men would be needed to break through the German lines.

Safe in the rear, Hitler and his fellow dispatch runners were enjoying a relatively peaceful year. In the second half of October they followed a leisurely routine of three days on duty and three days off. Hitler, billeted in a warm farmhouse in the tranquil village of Fournes-en-Weppes, spent his spare time reading and drawing dreary scenes of dugouts and French villages. Some days he took a stroll to Fromelles, the ruins of which then contained the German front-line command post and dressing station, where he saw at first hand the effects of modern artillery on the human body: mutilated flesh, multiple amputations, soldiers with their faces and skulls blown off.

He would spend more than a year in Fournes and the surrounding region. He had a lot of time to read, and bought himself a copy of *Berlin*, an architectural guide to the city written by the leading German art critic Max Osborn, a Jew who would later flee Nazi persecution.[8] Hitler greatly admired the book and would carry it with him throughout the war.[9] His respect for Osborn mirrored his admiration for Mahler: striking examples of his capacity – at this point – to admire individual Jewish achievements even as he gradually came to revile the Jewish 'race'.

The arrival of winter rains brought plagues of rats and sickness. Hitler, who had never taken a day's leave, fell ill with a severe bronchial condition, but refused to report to the doctor. He spent Christmas 1915 in a 'surly' mood, alone again and without a word from anyone back home. He neither sent nor received any Christmas cards.

Even in this frigid atmosphere, with his health failing, his conception of himself as the 'man of destiny' had not deserted him. 'By the winter of 1915–16,' he would write in *Mein Kampf*, 'this struggle had for me been decided. At last my will was undisputed master. If in the first days I went over the top with rejoicing and laughter, I was now calm and determined. And this was enduring. Now Fate could bring on the ultimate tests without my nerves shattering or my reason failing. The young volunteer had become an old soldier. And this transformation had occurred in the whole army.'[10]

Whether he actually experienced this internal struggle at the time, as described, is unknowable. But the fact that with hindsight he was determined to anchor to the war years these decisive moments of his life – the mastery of the will, his overcoming of self in the face of hardship – is in itself recognition of the power of the experience.

Around this time he got to know Max Amann, his bullying staff sergeant, who would become the closest thing to a 'friend' that Hitler had. Amann would later head the Nazi publishing house Eher Verlag, publisher of *Mein Kampf*, and take charge of press censorship, closing down newspapers and amassing a fortune through concentrating ownership of the press in his own hands. Amann had a clear interest in flattering his old comrade-in-arms at the 1932 inquiry into Hitler's war record. Yet his remarks bear out Hitler's continuing, extraordinary devotion to the war effort that others had seen. The Führer, Amann said, 'never hesitated in the least in carrying out even the most difficult order, and very often took on the most dangerous duties of his comrades.'[11] Hitler was an isolated, unselfish soldier, he added, who refused extra pay and always seemed to be among the first to volunteer.[12]

The year 1916 would see the List Regiment's greatest triumph – at Fromelles, against the Australian (Anzac) forces; and its worst defeat – on the Somme, the experience of which crushed morale and would ultimately destroy the unit's combat readiness.

With the spring thaw, the List Regiment rallied and the Bavarians and their lucky Linz runner prepared to resume hostilities. A spirit of brutal realism now moved among the ranks. The youthful eagerness to go over the top, so brash and innocent a year earlier, had now yielded in most soldiers to a cold, bestial determination to kill and survive.

At Fromelles, 43 miles (70 km) north of the Somme, on 19 and 20 July, the 6th Bavarian Reserve Division faced an enemy largely made up of the 5th Australian Division, the least experienced of the Dominion units then in France. In the ensuing struggle the Australians stormed the German trenches several times, in reckless displays of bravado that utterly failed. They were driven back, with staggering losses: 5,553 Australians were killed, wounded or taken prisoner, the greatest loss of Australian lives in a twenty-four-hour period.

Hitler took an active part in the battle, delivering orders, 'fleeing grenades' and leaping from crater to crater, according to Brandmayer's exaggerated account.[13] Fromelles was the List Regiment's most decisive victory – and one of Australia's most punishing losses – of the war. Years later, on learning that Hitler had been among the Germans opposing them, Australian veterans of the battle would rue their failure to kill him.

Then came the Somme. The Battle of the Somme began on 1 July, a day that proved the bloodiest in British military history, with 57,470 British casualties by nightfall, of whom more than 19,000 were killed; the Germans lost 40,000 over the first ten days. The ensuing battles, of Albert, Delville Wood, Pozières, Thiepval Ridge, Ancre Heights and many more, surged and flowed over the plains of Picardy, killing or wounding the Allies at the rate of 2,943 men per day.[14]

The Bavarian reserves soon got their turn in hell. On 2–3 October, with their morale high, Hitler's unit moved up to the gently inclining pastures of the Somme valley. By now, the battle had degenerated into one of pure attrition, bleeding hundreds of thousands of lives and involving every available unit in the opposing armies. Rumours of the carnage spread terror in the hearts of soldiers as they headed for the front.

Flung into the Battle of Le Transloy in the sector of Le Barque–Bapaume on the pointless orders of Lieutenant Colonel Emil Spatny, their ineffectual, often drunken, new commander, the Listers were promptly cut down. Within ten days Hitler's regiment had lost 300 dead, 844 wounded and 88 missing. Severely demoralized, the survivors sat in the sodden mud under daily bombardment until 'otherwise peaceful and rational men became irrational', wrote Fritz Wiedemann, the regimental adjutant, who would recommend Hitler for an Iron Cross (First Class) on several occasions and later served as the Führer's personal adjutant in the Nazi Party:

> Despair dug deep furrows in their faces, and also crept into the hearts
> of brave men. Daily they saw comrades dying to the left and right of
> them, they stumbled over their bodies in the fighting and could count
> on the fingers of two hands how many days would be needed until the
> last man in the company would be devoured by the battle and death.[15]

Brandmayer lost his nerve during an attack, and later attributed his survival to Hitler's encouragement: 'My nerve failed. I just wanted to lie where I was. I sank hopelessly into an insupportable apathy. – Then

Hitler spoke kindly to me, gave me words of encouragement, said that someday all our heroism would be rewarded a thousand fold in the Fatherland . . . We returned . . . uninjured. Our faces were no longer recognisable.'[16]

Hitler escaped the worst of the Somme thanks to a shell splinter that struck him in the groin or upper left thigh while on a mission on 12 October near the town of Bapaume. 'It's not so bad captain, right?' he is said to have appealed to Wiedemann. 'I'll stay with you, stay with the regiment?' Wiedemann later recalled the incident:

> There he lay, the man who so badly wanted to be an artist, who loved all newspapers, who philosophized about political and ideological questions in the primitive manner of ordinary people. There he lay, wounded, and had no other wish than to be allowed to stay with his regiment. He had no family and also, if one might say, no homeland. For Gefreiter Hitler, the List Regiment was home.[17]

Hitler was sent to a field clinic at Hermies for immediate treatment of the wound, then to a German military hospital in Beelitz-Heilstätten, in Brandenburg, not far from Berlin. There he encountered, to his disgust, a few 'wretched scoundrels', one of whom boasted 'that he himself had pulled his hand through a barbed wire entanglement in order to be sent to the hospital'. Others ranted against the war, 'with all the means of their contemptible eloquence to make the conceptions of the decent soldiers ridiculous and hold up the spineless coward as an example'. Hitler scorned them all as 'poisonous fellows' who condemned the war and dismissed Germany's hopes of victory.[18]

On the path to recovery and determined to escape his defeatist, bedridden companions, he obtained permission to remain in Berlin for a few weeks, before being transferred to Munich in December. In both cities he witnessed the ravages of the war and winter on the civilian population, whose struggle against poverty and hunger he dismissed as weakness. In *Mein Kampf* he later wrote of this sharp juxtaposition of his battlefield experiences with the 'malingerers' on the home front and, as we shall now see, retroactively apportioned the blame for the ailing German spirit to Jewish 'shirkers'.

Germany's *Kohlrübenwinter*, or 'Turnip Winter', was the harshest in thirty years. The early frost and heavy rains had halved the country's potato harvest. Ordinary Germans were relying on turnips, or swedes, the loathed 'Prussian pineapple'. By late 1916, food was scarce, malnutrition endemic. Food stocks were 40 per cent of pre-war levels, a result of impassable roads and Britain's naval blockade, which had been imposed in 1914 as soon as war broke out and was described in Berlin as the British 'Hunger Blockade'. Food prices soared on the black market. Riots and wholesale theft overrode German loyalty to the war effort. Malnutrition and related diseases – dysentery, scurvy and tuberculosis – were ravaging the cities. Hunger oedema, characterized by gross swelling of the limbs, proliferated among the poor, and long lines of starving women and children were a daily occurrence at soup kitchens. The author Ernst Glaeser witnessed children stealing each other's rations and heard women in food queues talking 'more about their children's hunger than the death of their husbands'.[19] Mobile field kitchens, nicknamed 'goulash guns', rushed to feed the hungriest but did little to assuage the fury of German mothers, who formed a 'new front' against the authorities: in 1916, women committed 1,224 acts of violence against the German police.[20] Thousands were dying, reported an American correspondent in Berlin near the end of 1916:

> Once I set out for the purpose of finding in these food-lines a face that did not show the ravages of hunger. Four long lines were inspected with the closest scrutiny. But among the 300 applicants for food there was not one who had had enough to eat for weeks. In the case of the youngest women and children the skin was drawn hard to the bones and bloodless. Eyes had fallen deeper into the sockets. From the lips all color was gone, and the tufts of hair which fell over the parchmented faces seemed dull and famished – a sign that the nervous vigor of the body was departing with the physical strength.[21]

Most food necessarily went to the armed forces. A single corps of infantry, according to a study by the historian Holger Herwig, devoured 1,000,000 lb (453,592 kg) of meat and 660,000 loaves of bread per month, while their horses needed 7,000,000 lb (3,175,147 kg) of oats and 4,000,000 lb (1,814,369 kg) of hay.[22]

Yet it was never enough. To preserve the food supply, the German government imposed 'meatless' and 'fatless' days. An ingenious array of ingredients replaced the staple diet of bread, milk, sausage and sugar. Black bread, fatless sausage, one egg and a few potatoes and turnips constituted the average weekly diet. Many German people even consumed ground beetles. These measures, however, merely delayed the encroachment of hunger-related diseases. Since the start of the war, the daily calorie intake had fallen by a third, to 1,000, and the civilian mortality rate had increased by 37 per cent. The hardest hit were the weakest – young children, the sick and the elderly – whose mortality rates rose by as much as 50 per cent.

As spring approached, food shortages and soaring inflation led to the breakdown of civic order. Annual domestic wheat production had almost halved, to about 2.5 million tons, and the meat ration was cut to 8 oz (225 g) per week, accompanied by the destruction of a million cows. Starving and exhausted with war, the German people took to industrial action and mass protest against the soaring prices. In April, hunger strikes erupted in about 300 German factories, while around 150,000 Berlin employees in key war industries struck over the lack of food,[23] and thousands of workers in several German cities demanded an end to the war. To offset the wave of strikes, the Berlin government subjected all industries and factories to military law. Anyone capable of working was forced to do so. Social misfits, homosexuals, prostitutes, the mentally ill were pressed into service in factories, hospitals and farms.

Hitler witnessed all this up close, but the miserable scenes of women and children going hungry elicited not a shred of compassion in him, nor any sense of a shared struggle. He felt only contempt for what he saw as spineless civilians on the home front, whose lot was as nothing compared with that of the men at the front. As he wrote in *Mein Kampf*, in Berlin 'there was dire misery everywhere. The big city was suffering from hunger . . . In various soldiers' homes the tone was like that in the hospital. It gave you the impression that these scoundrels were intentionally frequenting such places in order to spread their views.'[24]

Hitler's revulsion at what he saw as defeatism and cowardice on the home front deepened in Munich, where conditions were 'much, much worse . . . Anger, discontent, cursing wherever you went!' Munich was nothing like the place of his happiest memories: 'I thought I could no longer recognise the city.' Among the civilian population, 'the general mood was miserable: to be a slacker passed almost as a sign of higher wisdom, while loyal steadfastness was considered a symptom of inner weakness and narrow-mindedness.'[25] And the idea of a monstrous injustice began to grow in his mind, blending with images of piles of soldiers' corpses . . . and the question, always simmering inside him, of who was to blame.

He would spend most of the 1916/17 winter in Munich, in a reserve battalion, as he recuperated. In December he sent a postcard (unearthed in 2012) to a fellow soldier called Karl Lanzhammer, writing: 'I am now in Munich at the Ersatz Btl. Currently I am under dental treatment . . . Kind regards A. Hitler.'[26]

If the city's poverty elicited no sympathy in him, the collapse in morale and the sight of the wealthy partying in their salons provoked his rage. At the same time, a savage strain of anti-Semitism was at large in Bavaria: Jews were being blamed for profiting from the war, for neglecting their duty to the war effort. And not only there, but all over the country. Wartime anti-Semitism rose to a cacophony in 1916–17, 'when voices blaming the food shortages on Jewish profiteers were on the rise in Germany's urban centres'.[27]

In a notorious passage of *Mein Kampf*, Hitler claimed that feelings of violent anti-Semitism seized him during this period in Munich:

> The offices were filled with Jews. Nearly every clerk was a Jew and nearly every Jew was a clerk. I was amazed at this plethora of warriors

of the chosen people and could not help but compare them with their rare representatives at the front. As regards economic life, things were even worse. Here the Jewish people had really become 'indispensable'. The spider was slowly beginning to suck the blood out of the people's pores.[28]

These tirades, written almost a decade later, grossly misrepresented both the commitment of German Jews to the war effort and Hitler's own attitude to the Jews during the war. In both cases he was projecting backwards the extreme hatred of the Jews that he felt after the war, in the interests of his new political career. Hitler's actual mood in Munich at the time was that of a recovering soldier, exhausted and disillusioned, wandering the city in dismay. Indeed, no such statements of furious anti-Semitism appear in his war letters; nor would his comrades remember him singling out Jews for special hatred in 1916–17.

In any case, the accusation that Jews were shirkers and underrepresented in the German Army was a grotesque lie: a special report of 1916 showed that Munich's small Jewish population was more than fairly represented at the front.[29] After the war, it was revealed that 12,000 German Jewish soldiers had died defending the Fatherland.

By early 1917, aged twenty-eight, Hitler had moved a little closer in spirit to the individual that emerges in *Mein Kampf.* But he had not yet even contemplated a career in politics, far less developed policies or programmes of oppression. He was merely a dispatch runner whose 'wildly articulated ideas' and fulminations against a ragbag collection of enemies (the 'internal threat' in Germany, the Marxists, Jews, Slavs, the ruling classes, English and French, etc.) were mere gusts of rage. The formation of a political movement founded on violent racism, as proposed in *Mein Kampf,* was still six years away.[30]

For now, this strange soldier, with no obvious leadership skills, could only sit and stew in his anger. If he felt the far call of a greater destiny, in which he would realize his Pan-German dream, he still had no idea how he would achieve it or what role he would play.

CHAPTER TWELVE

'For the last time the Lord's grace smiled on His ungrateful children'

Hitler's regiment entered 1917 grimly aware of having failed to distinguish itself in any offensive action except the brief attack at Fromelles. At Ypres in 1914 and the Somme in 1916, they had been comprehensively 'stabbed in the front'. Henceforth, the troops' combat duties were to be confined to 'meandering through quiet sectors'.[1] Morale plunged: twenty-nine cases of serious indiscipline, for absence without leave, desertion, disobedience, self-mutilation and cowardice, were reported in the last months of 1916, among men with hitherto good combat records.[2] The situation was set to worsen.

Hitler did not see the start of this nervous collapse. In January, while still in Munich, he heard that he had been slated to join the 2nd Infantry Regiment, a more aggressive, front-line unit, in recognition of his good soldiering. This he refused to do. He wrote urgently to Captain Fritz Wiedemann, his regimental adjutant: '. . . it is my pressing wish to be with my old regiment and old comrades.'[3] His request was granted. On rejoining the Listers on 5 March, he promptly resumed his duties as a dispatch runner. He seemed to have no ambition for promotion, or for bettering his career in the army. Indeed, asked why Hitler was never promoted, Wiedemann (who later fell out with Hitler) told the Nuremberg war crimes trial that he 'lacked leadership qualities', to an amused audience. Staff Sergeant Amann later claimed that Hitler turned down the offer of a promotion to junior officer, reacting with 'horror' to the idea.[4]

Having not seen his old comrades for five months, on his return Hitler received a rude shock. Rock-bottom morale and deep disaffection with the war greeted his arrival. The Somme had gutted his Bavarians. The better parts of the division were being sent elsewhere, and the better soldiers (including Iron Cross recipients like Hitler) had been offered the chance to join more prestigious units. The residue languished in the rear areas, morosely awaiting orders. The only bright spot was the removal of Colonel Emil Spatny, the regiment's alcoholic commander, who was sent home without a blemish on his service record. He was succeeded by Major Anton Freiherr von Tubeuf, an aggressive young officer who was determined to raise the men's spirit. For now, though, the damage had been done, and the regiment mouldered in demoralized uncertainty.

Not for long. Bloody flashpoints were about to interrupt these protracted periods of inactivity. In April the Listers were thrown into the Vimy Ridge sector of the Battle of Arras (9 April–16 May), soon to be remembered as one of the bloodiest clashes on the Western Front. The British Army sustained its highest daily casualty rate of the war at Arras, which killed or wounded 4,067 men per day.

The Listers' infantrymen withstood several horrendous British attacks during the carnage. They held firm, and the ordeal raised their spirits: the regiment often proved its mettle in defence. As usual, Hitler was champing at the bit to deliver messages, but they were hauled off Vimy Ridge in the second week of April, days before an astonishing Canadian offensive seized the ridge – and sent back to the scene of their worst losses: the bloody salient east of Ypres in Flanders.

On arriving at this loathed place, Hitler's comrades enjoyed a spell of leisure: free beer, sack races, a tug of war and grenade-throwing competitions. As a teetotaller, Hitler shunned beer. And it can be safely assumed that he did not enter the sack race. He longed for the resumption of battle. His impatience was soon rewarded.

In mid-July he and his fellows heard they were to join a fresh attack on the well dug-in British forces to the west of the Gheluvelt Plateau: back to the scene of the *Kindermord*. In fact, this turned into an order to prepare to defend, as news came in of a huge British offensive in the making.

In the trenches, the infantry now endured a nerve-racking wait, sucking through gas masks. Their new commander, Tubeuf, who was proving an arrogant, unpopular officer, described his front-line troops as 'exhausted by nervous strain and constant bodily over-fatigue, worn out from the inhalation of gas-filled air'.[5] Hitler and his fellow runners had limited involvement in the coming action – a few deliveries over ten days. But he would see the shocking results all over the battlefield and in the hospital clinics.

Britain's great Flanders offensive, popularly known as 'Passchendaele' or 'Third Ypres', aimed to capture Passchendaele Ridge, about 5 miles (8 km) north-east of Ypres, swing north to the Belgian coast, and destroy the German submarine bases at the ports of Ostend and Zeebrugge, from where U-boats were waging unlimited war on Allied shipping and any neutral vessel that aided them. That was the initial plan, as Haig, now promoted to field marshal, had presented it to the British War Cabinet. The seizure of the U-boat bases would be the prelude to the total rout of the German forces in Belgium, a war-winning scenario dependent on a run of incredible victories, daunting in their ambition even with the help of brilliant command, fine weather and a lot of luck (none of which was forthcoming or guaranteed). The great French Marshal Ferdinand Foch was not the only commander who had little faith in what he called a 'duck's march' through the Flanders mud.

Haig should have heeded Foch's warning. For one thing, the German lines were far from demoralized, as Haig and his intelligence chief had supposed. By this time the Russians were in a state of collapse. The forced abdication of the Tsar on 15 March had invigorated the Bolsheviks, who violently opposed Russia's participation in the war and whose revolutionary ideas had begun to infiltrate the rank and file. With masses of men now deserting the Russian Army, Germany's vast eastern forces were released for duty on the Western Front. From mid-1917 tens of thousands of fresh German troops were being entrained across northern Europe to Flanders.

Meanwhile, the exhausted French forces – many of whom had mutinied earlier in the year over conditions and what they saw as the suicidal tactics of their generals – were being kept back in a defensive role; they would stay that way at least until August 1917. And if Marshal Philippe Pétain, the new French commander, had exaggerated their state of disrepair, Haig didn't protest: it served his argument that he must attack and attack, to pin the Germans in Flanders and buy time for the French to recover. At the same time, although the Americans had entered the war in early April 1917, they had not yet arrived: the first combat-ready doughboys would not appear until mid-1918.

So Third Ypres (mid-July–10 November 1917) would be a largely Commonwealth campaign, in which hundreds of thousands of British troops and their Australian, New Zealand and Canadian allies (with small French, South African and Belgian units in support) were to be thrown, wave after wave, at the most powerful concentration of German troops on the Western Front.

The opening British bombardment fell on the German lines in the early hours of 15 July – a week before David Lloyd George, the British prime minister, gave Cabinet approval for Haig to proceed. Britain's massed artillery now revealed its terrific power: 752 heavy cannons, 324 4.5-inch howitzers and 1,098 18-pounders unleashed the most powerful bombardment hitherto known in the history of war. For the next two weeks, they would fire 4.5 million projectiles on to the German trenches on the plains beneath Passchendaele Ridge, more than twice the number of rounds that had preceded the Somme.

By the time Hitler's unit arrived in the battle area, around 25 July, Haig's bombardment was well into its final, crushing phase. A hail of shellfire, 'far worse than anything we had experienced on the Somme', fell on the German lines, recalled Sergeant Wellhausen. 'Shells, shrapnel balls and their pots rained down around our heads.'[6] The 'softening up' ranged across the German positions, shattering, cutting down, fragmenting every obstacle, village, house, tree, human, animal caught within 2,000–3,000 yards of the British front. Blankets of British gas interspersed the hail of explosives, smothering the German soldiers' movements and stifling the delivery of relief, rations and ammunition in lethal white and yellow vapour.

The air war roared to life during gaps in the shell and gas storm. Dozens of low-flying British aircraft 'circled our positions', recalled Fusilier Guard Häbel:

> Wherever an individual was seen, British airmen were on hand to direct the fire of their guns onto him. A sentry stood stock still, hidden by a groundsheet so that he could not be seen from the air in front of each dugout. Every few moments someone called to him to see if he was still alive . . . The British were trying to extinguish all signs of life.[7]

The Germans had too few guns to sustain a counter-bombardment. Instead, they directed harassing fire at British troop concentrations: bridges, supply sections, railway lines, billets and munitions depots, unleashing 533,000 rounds during the week beginning 13 July and 870,000 the following week. British firepower was about four times that.[8] The German gunners depended heavily on mustard gas, which brought them some 'relief': between 12 and 27 July, the British lost 13,284 dead, wounded and missing to enemy gas, artillery and aircraft attack.[9]

On the eve of zero hour – when the infantry would go over the top – the bombardment rose to a shrieking, crashing, whizzing pitch. Incendiary grenades, gas, smoke projectiles, heavy mortars, heavy explosives and shrapnel were flung at the German lines in what survivors would recall as 'a hurricane from hell'.[10] It was 'beyond anyone's experience', witnessed General Hermann von Kuhl:

> The entire earth of Flanders rocked and seemed to be on fire. It was not just drumfire; it was as though Hell itself had slipped its bonds. What were the terrors of Verdun and the Somme compared to this grotesquely

huge outpouring of raw power? The violent thunder of battle could be heard in the furthest corner of Belgium. It was as though the enemy was announcing to the world: Here we come and we are going to prevail![11]

The British ground attack started hopefully, on 31 July 1917. Haig's gunners had perfected the creeping barrage, in which thousands of heavy guns fired at once, sweeping the enemy lines with a slowly advancing wall of exploding shells. Clutching the inside arc of this diabolical configuration, tens of thousands of Allied troops swarmed across the field, a technique the Canadians had used to devastating effect during the capture of Vimy Ridge.

On the first day, it started to rain, and the rain kept falling for much of the next two and a half months, in torrential sheets, interrupted by a couple of dry weeks in late September. The heaviest deluge in seventy years reduced the battlefield to a stinking quagmire, in which liquid mud filled the shell craters, creating death traps. The rain turned the battle in Germany's favour: their lines, entrenched along the ridges and huddled inside concrete pillboxes, were free to fire down on an army literally bogged in the mud, helpless without well-grounded artillery.

What followed really went beyond anything hitherto understood as a 'battle'. Harrowing scenes ensued, of men and horses drowning in mud-filled shell craters; of thousands being mown down by German machine guns; of Haig's armies literally shot to a standstill beneath the ridges east of Ypres. It went on and on, for three months. Haig sent wave after wave of young lives into the meat-grinder, to certain death or mutilation, in the name of his attritional strategy of 'wearing down' the enemy.

October was the cruellest month. Haig's decision not to give the Anzacs the time they needed to bring up their artillery enabled nests of German machine guns to mow down thousands of Australian and New Zealand troops in a sea of mud and wire, many blown apart, shot up several times, on a bloody, swamp-like field that was later found to contain a body or body part every square yard.[12]

On 10 November a few surviving Canadians staggered in to claim Passchendaele Ridge, at the cost of almost half a million men – Allied and German – killed, wounded and missing. The ridge held no strategic value in its own right, and a small British force held the village for a few weeks before it fell back into German hands.

In the end, the 1917 Flanders offensive would be remembered as the densest killing field in history, pitching 77–83 German divisions against 50 Commonwealth and six French divisions. In almost four months of carnage, Haig had gained 5 miles (8 km) of front and a strategically worthless ridge, infuriating Prime Minister David Lloyd George, who had sworn at the end of 1916 that there would be no more Sommes.

Estimates of total casualties vary, but the most accurate tallies 271,000 Allied losses (killed and wounded) against 217,000 German.[13] The Germans' defensive strength thus halted the Flanders offensive, forcing an end to Haig's campaign by utterly exhausting his men. They won the war of attrition at Third Ypres, as measured by body count – the capacity to bleed the enemy and crush his morale – the very criteria with which Haig would later try to justify four years of carnage as though it had all been pre-planned.[14]

The List Regiment experienced only the opening blows of Passchendaele. Yet they saw the results. The terrific British cannon barrage preceded their first engagement, followed by the deeply demoralizing appearance of British tanks – the first time Hitler and his fellows had witnessed these primitive monsters in battle. 'Tank fright' seems likely to have caused, in part, the complete collapse of his regiment at Passchendaele.[15]

Hitler's rear position at regimental HQ had no direct exposure to these fat, misshapen vehicles, with their huge tracks, but the sight left an imprint on him. In 1941 he would remark that 'only the heaviest and most thickly armoured tanks had any value', and on other occasions he bemoaned the lack of German tanks at Flanders in 1917, a shortage that would continue into the following year: 'If we'd had 400 tanks in the summer of 1918 we'd have won the war,' he remarked – a rare admission that Germany had been defeated on the battlefield.[16]

The Listers were relieved in early August; further participation in Passchendaele would surely have annihilated them. Despite these trials, the regiment's casualties were relatively light. In the whole of 1917 they lost 478 men dead, or 13.6 per cent of their total number; between 13 and 23 July, they sustained 800 casualties, killed, wounded or captured, according to Tubeuf. Of the 3,754 Listers who lost their lives over four years of war, most were killed in the few weeks at First Ypres in 1914 and on the Somme in 1916 – bombed, gassed and cut down without even setting eyes on an Englishman.

From Passchendaele, Hitler's regiment was relegated to the inactive sector of German Alsace, in the company of enfeebled reserve units deemed unfit for combat, where they would recuperate until September 1917. For Hitler, it was a humiliation; for his comrades, a relief. He was also depressed at the loss of Foxl, his pet dog, which had miraculously survived the Somme and Flanders battles and then gone missing. 'The swine who took him from me doesn't know what he did to me,' Hitler would say during his 'Table Talks' in January 1941.[17]

In late September 1917 Hitler went on voluntary leave, together with a fellow soldier, Ernst Schmidt. It was the first time in the war that he had applied for a period of rest. The pair visited Brussels, Cologne, Dresden and Leipzig, Hitler pointedly refusing to return to Munich, before he travelled on alone to Berlin, where he stayed until 17 October. For the second time in the war, he found himself wandering the German capital, by now a city in the throes of absolute despair. The grief and hunger on the faces in the Tiergarten, the barefoot children on the streets and the sullen mood in the beer halls revealed the utter breakdown in civilian morale during this, the fag end of the German Empire.

By now, the British blockade had reduced Germany, the economic locomotive of Europe four years earlier, into a beggar nation. Her foreign trade had collapsed, from US$5.9 billion in 1913 to US$800 million in 1917.[18] The Treasury was technically bankrupt: tax receipts barely covered the interest on the soaring debt. By the end of 1917, the worst year, the cost of the war topped 52 billion marks, while tax and other receipts were a mere 7.8 billion, creating a deficit of about 44 billion marks.[19]

The Germans could not rely on their main ally, Austria–Hungary: the Dual Monarchy had made no provision for a long, protracted war, and by the autumn of 1917 was on its knees. Supplies of butter, fat, flour, potatoes and grains were exhausted or very low. The available potatoes were 'not fit for human consumption'.[20] As in Germany and Russia, inflation skyrocketed, accompanied by food riots and destitution. On a typical day in Vienna, according to police, 250,000 hungry people could be seen forming some 800 queues outside the food markets and 54,000 people visited the soup kitchens.[21] Members of the bourgeoisie (such as Sigmund Freud) were reduced to buying their cigars and liquor on the black market at huge prices.

From both Vienna and Berlin, many residents flocked to the countryside on so-called 'hamster tours' to steal extra food, provoking a police crackdown. In the face of such shortages, Berlin and other German cities appropriated food and resources from the occupied territories: Romania supplied oil; Serbia cattle, sheep and hogs; Poland grain, potatoes, coal, eggs, horses and wood; and Albania some 50,000 turtles – the bulk of which found their way to the black market or on to the tables of the rich.

By the end of Third Ypres, most surviving German and Austrian civilians were living below the subsistence level and suffering acute hunger or severe illnesses related to malnutrition. Hoarding and ransacking of the rural food supplies were commonplace. German housewives engaged in ferocious rows in queues and often 'brutally snatched' potatoes and fruits from farmers' stalls. Mothers lashed out at an obvious target, the owners of expensive, well-stocked Berlin department stores, many of whom were wealthy Jews. Such German women 'of little means' were indeed 'a potential time bomb' for the Prussian authorities.[22]

Thousands were dying. After the war, British and German official figures estimated the number of German civilian deaths resulting from the Hunger Blockade (and associated diseases) to have been at least 424,000 and possibly as many as 762,796.[23] These figures exclude a further 150,000 German victims of the 1918 influenza pandemic, which 'caused disproportionate suffering among those already weakened by malnutrition and related disease'. By the war's end, the loss of one million foetuses would also be directly attributable to medical conditions resulting from or exacerbated by the British blockade, making it one of the first war atrocities of the twentieth century.[24]

With their sons and husbands dead, wounded or fighting, and their children malnourished and sick, millions of Germans at home were ripe for exploitation by extremists and demagogues. And yet, had they met him then, none would have seen their saviour in the skinny, sick Austrian soldier who passed through Berlin with eyes of scorn for the pathos of the home front, all the while brooding on who should be held responsible.

As before, Hitler looked on this suffering without a shred of compassion. To the twenty-eight-year-old soldier, the complaints of German civilians revealed a weak and coddled people, unable to endure what the troops were going through every day. The distress of others simply failed to move him. He was bereft of any capacity for ordinary empathy. His views were hardening, meshing with the strands of Social Darwinism to which he'd been exposed in Vienna: his fellow human beings were either weak, and as such dispensable; or strong, and therefore exploitable.

And he was enjoying himself, as much as he might, taking himself off to the museums and galleries, riding on the yellow street cars on Unter den Linden, and sending postcards to friends. We know of three to Max Amann, his staff sergeant, and one to Schmidt, in which his tone is upbeat and happy like a tourist on holiday. 'The city is magnificent, a real metropolis,' he told Schmidt. 'The traffic is tremendous, even now. I am out and about almost the whole day. At last I have the chance of getting to know the museums a bit better. In brief: I am short of nothing.'[25]

On his return from leave, in late October, Hitler rejoined his regiment in Picardy, where they returned to brief active duty in the Aisne Valley, soon to be another scene of senseless carnage. The war had come full circle. Back in September 1914, the Germans had dug their first trench lines here, on the north bank of the River Aisne. Now the haggard List Regiment stood guard over the Oise–Aisne Canal, where they would spend a quiet Christmas in readiness for 1918.

While Hitler's unit were rested, and enjoying slightly better morale, the same could not be said for the reinforcements arriving from the Eastern Front, whose spirits were so bad High Command took note. 'Out of two train loads of Prussian replacement troops from the east,' Crown Prince Rupprecht noted in his diary on 3 November 1917, 'ten per cent went absent without leave during the journey.'[26] Many of the arrivals would join Hitler's division, disgruntled older men with little or no battle experience; others were bitter relics of the freezing Eastern Front, relieved to be heading west. All had heard horror stories of the Somme and Flanders, and many believed they were travelling towards certain death or severe wounding. It is understandable that they grabbed a last snatch of life while they felt they had the chance.

Trainload after trainload of such troops whistled and jeered when they arrived at Valenciennes, near the French border with Belgium. A sense of local mutiny was in the air, but no sign, yet, of a complete collapse in morale and mass desertion on the Russian or French scale. Towards the end of November 1917 most of the German Army was ordered to rest and recuperate, to prepare for the first massed German attack in three years, Ludendorff's Spring Offensive, set to begin in March 1918.

By early 1918, more than a million German troops had made the journey from the Eastern theatre to the Western Front, to join the fresh offensive planned by Generals Paul von Hindenburg and Erich Ludendorff. Their sheer numbers boosted waning spirits: here, at last, was the German Army in full, massed in one place for the final onslaught. The two commanders were determined to inflict a final, crushing blow on the Allies, which they hoped would win the war. For the bullet-headed Ludendorff, this had become a question of national (and personal) pride: had millions of German men died for nothing? Would there be nothing to show for so complete a sacrifice?

Heroes of the Eastern Front, neither Hindenburg nor Ludendorff had adequately taken into account Allied superiority in the West – in aircraft, tanks and, with the imminent arrival of the Americans and recovery of the French, a seemingly unlimited reserve of fresh, better-supplied men. Despite these weaknesses, the German commanders saw the chance of a breakthrough, between the demoralization of the British and Dominion forces after Passchendaele and the expected arrival of French and American reinforcements in early summer 1918. It was a window, no more, but a window through which the German commanders hoped to hurl their entire force and crush their enemies. Mars had aligned in Berlin's favour in early 1918, or so it seemed, encouraging Ludendorff to stake all on a massive counter-blow that would grind Haig's men to dust before the Americans and French could tip the scales.

And so, at a meeting on 11 November 1917, the day after the end of Third Ypres, Ludendorff, Hindenburg and their generals had begun planning the first major German offensive since 1915. The Spring Offensive – dubbed the *Kaiserschlacht*, or Emperor's Battle – promised to throw every last man into the mouth of the war. It was scheduled to start in March 1918, by which time Germany would have amassed 192 divisions on the Western Front, opposing 156 Allied divisions. For the first time since October 1914, the Allies would be forced to fight a defensive battle, with far fewer men and guns than Germany – a complete reversal of the situation at the start of 1917.

When Hitler got wind of the plan, in the obscurity of his regimental headquarters, hopes of a German victory spread through him like an intoxicating drug. He was exhilarated, he later wrote. He would bracket his war experience – from his involvement in the first offensives of 1914 to the last in 1918 – as 'the most tremendous impressions of my life', amongst which the launch of Ludendorff's final blow was the most enthralling. For the first time in three years, his beloved German Army was on the offensive, poised to fling everything at the Western Front. Hitler later described a mood of joyful, Heaven-sent deliverance:

> A sigh of relief passed through the trenches and the dugouts of the German army when at length, after more than three years' endurance in the enemy hell, the day of retribution came. Once again the victorious battalions cheered and hung the last wreaths of immortal laurel on their banners . . . Once again the songs of the fatherland roared to the heavens along the endless mortal columns, and for the last time the Lord's grace smiled on His ungrateful children.[27]

Chapter Thirteen

'Since the day I stood at my mother's grave, I had not wept'

On 21 March, in the opening phase of the Spring Offensive, Operation Michael, Ludendorff's mighty arsenal rolled across France in a spectacular reprise of August 1914. The Allied gains of the past two years, on the Somme and at Arras, yielded to the German juggernaut as, initially, the Germans drove the Allies deep into French territory, regaining positions they had not seen since 1914.

Denied the manpower needed to resist this typhoon, the British and Dominion forces fell back, sustaining casualties that 'dwarfed the "butcher's bill" of Passchendaele', as one account claimed.[1] Not quite: some 254,740 British and French soldiers were killed or wounded or missing in Operation Michael, almost 20,000 fewer than the Allied casualties of Third Ypres.[2] German losses amounted to almost the same as those of the Allies.

General Sir Hubert Gough's Fifth Army nearly cracked: in the greatest mass capitulation in British history, 21,000 of his 90,882 casualties were taken prisoner. Gough was sacked, in the richest irony of his career: of all the sackable offences that fastened to his name, March 1918 should not have been one. The Fifth Army's surviving formations bravely held. Had they broken, 'the Germans would probably have won the First World War', notes one historian.[3]

By April, the Allies had retreated as far as Amiens. In Operation

Georgette, the next phase of the *Kaiserschlacht*, Passchendaele fell within three days. Yet remarkably, the British held Ypres – at the *Fourth* Battle of Ypres. Paris trembled under the threat of German occupation for the second time in four years. The British, Dominion and French armies, now fighting under Marshal Ferdinand Foch's supreme command, were staring at the prospect of defeat.

On 11 April, in an emotional departure from his usual granite calm, Haig issued his famous 'backs to the wall' order:

SPECIAL ORDER OF THE DAY
By FIELD-MARSHAL SIR DOUGLAS HAIG
K.T., G.C.B., G.C.V.O., K.C.I.E.
Commander-in-Chief, British Armies in France
To ALL RANKS OF THE BRITISH ARMY IN
FRANCE AND FLANDERS

Three weeks ago to-day the enemy began his terrific attacks against us on a fifty-mile front. His objects are to separate us from the French, to take the Channel Ports and destroy the British Army . . .

There is no other course open to us but to fight it out. Every position must be held to the last man: there must be no retirement. With our backs to the wall and believing in the justice of our cause each one of us must fight on to the end. The safety of our homes and the Freedom of mankind alike depend upon the conduct of each one of us at this critical moment.[4]

Drawing on all their reserves of strength, the British and Dominion forces rallied – and then struck back, with everything they had. The German offensive died hard, over a tortuous retreat lasting several months. Failed tactics, rushed training, demoralization, lack of food and ammunition, and overstretched supply lines caused their eventual collapse – aggravated by the astonishing return to form of the British, Anzac and French forces and the arrival of the first units of the 500,000-strong American Army. The tactical sequence that had

frustrated the British, Anzacs and Canadians for almost three years –
attack, brief success, resistance, counter-attack, then stalemate or defeat
– now dragged down and destroyed Ludendorff's counter-blow.

In March and April, Hitler's regiment was involved in numerous
battles in Picardy and Champagne, chiefly as a support unit, fighting mostly in defence of new ground taken. Yet they sustained huge
casualties, most heavily at the town of Montdidier. By the end of April
1918, the regiment had lost half its strength (with the division sustaining similar losses) – killed, wounded or sick (many from Spanish flu).
As usual, it was the poor bloody infantry who bore the brunt of it.
On the night of 16 April, eighteen-year-old Justin Fleischmann, a new
(and, as it happened, Jewish) recruit, had recorded 'terrible artillery'
and 'heavy gas bombardment' with 'severe losses': 'In the evening we
marched to the most forward line with only 40 men . . .', during which
they got lost and encountered severe shellfire. Fleischmann himself, a
brave soldier, was hit in the head by shrapnel.[5] Food was scarce, morale
sank again to rock bottom and casualties soared.

Yet still they fought on, joining Ludendorff's desperate last stand
at Chemin des Dames in the Aisne Valley – the scene of some of the
bloodiest fighting of the war. By the first week of June, the Listers were
reduced to a quarter of their usual strength, with about 20–25 men per
company.[6]

In one of the bitterest struggles of these final months of the war,
the Second Battle of the Marne – a humiliating re-run of September
1914 – the Germans were literally fought to a standstill in what was to
be their final offensive of the war. The Allies fielded hundreds of tanks
and aircraft; fresh American troops poured into the lines. Staring at the
impossible, many German infantrymen simply turned and fled. Hitler
would later express his rage and disgust at the mass capitulation of his
beloved army, refusing to accept the truth of what he was witnessing.

By now the German Army was exhausted. Its Spring Offensive had
seen it regain a lot of territory, but at the cost of many thousands of
men it could not replace. On 8 August the Allies launched what was

to be their final offensive, known now as the Hundred Days Offensive (8 August–11 November 1918), a series of lightning victories that dealt a death blow to the German war. At last, the Americans were pouring into France: thirty-nine divisions would arrive by the end of September. And a battle-hardened Commonwealth phoenix had risen out of the ashes of Flanders: the Australians were now fighting as part of a stand-alone national army, injecting fresh patriotic zeal into their ranks. The newly formed Australian Corps under General Sir John Monash was about to exceed what anyone could have imagined possible a year earlier, when they lay immobilized in the swamps beneath Passchendaele. (A glimpse of their return to form had been the capture of the village of Hamel on 4 July, a prelude to what lay ahead of great symbolic value.)

On 8 August 1918, the British, Anzacs and Canadians burst out of Amiens, and, along with the French just to the south, broke the German lines, captured 12,000 prisoners and 450 guns, inflicted 15,000 further casualties and advanced 8 miles (13 km), the furthest achieved on the Western Front in a single day (Third Ypres had taken three and a half months to conquer a shorter distance – 5 miles/8 km). Over the next five days, the Canadian Corps defeated or put to flight ten full German divisions, capturing 9,131 prisoners and 190 artillery pieces, advancing 14 miles (22 km) and liberating more than 67 square miles (173 sq. km).

Hitler and his fellow runners were relatively idle during these tumultuous last months, notwithstanding a few moments of terrific action and an instance of personal distinction. He had spent most of 1918 in regimental headquarters, in the rear, awaiting instructions. Earlier in the year his regiment had withdrawn to Comines, for another rest. At the time, Hitler happened to see a letter from his comrade Balthasar Brandmayer's girlfriend and asked, good-humouredly:

'Brandmoari [*sic*], has Trutschnelda written again?'
'Good guess,' Brandmayer replied. 'Have you never wanted a girl?'

'Look,' Hitler replied, 'I've never found time for such a thing. And I don't want to.'

'You're a strange one, Adi! I'll never understand you! There's no hope for you.'

A soldier interjected: 'How would it be if I found a mam'selle for us?'

At which Hitler leapt excitedly up and exclaimed: 'I'd kill myself from shame rather than make love to a French woman.'

Raucous laughter met this remark: 'Listen to the monk!' cried one soldier.

Hitler's face grew serious, as he asked his comrades: 'Don't any of you feel your honour as a German anymore?'[7]

Hitler remained as high-minded as ever, even with the war about to end. His comrades, meanwhile, felt they could afford to relax: they were out of danger, well removed from the ongoing trials of the front-line soldiers.

The German infantrymen returning from the front, however, had been reduced to insensate husks, marked by a 'deadening indifference' to suffering, as one German historian described them: 'Death has lost its terror, since it has been standing next to you as a constant companion every hour of the day and night. The front instinct finds its best breeding ground in that state of "couldn't care less" . . .'[8]

Four years of war had created this 'new type of German soldier', who came staggering back to the rear – one who, resigned or indifferent to his fate, placed little or no value on life, medals or words of praise. Such foot soldiers were affectionately known as *Frontschweine* (front-line pigs). To start with, they had scorned military discipline, hobnobbed with their platoon and company commanders who lay in the mud beside them, and viewed every rear-area soldier with contempt. Hitler felt the sting in their attitude. He shared the comforts of the rear-area pigs, yet his regular appearances as a runner helped to dampen the *Frontschweine*'s criticism: he still served, after all, as a lifeline to the front when the phone lines broke.

By mid-1918, the average 'front-line pig' was in a state of 'mental shock', merely going through the motions of combat. Most had abandoned all hope, epitomized by a wounded German prisoner who sat beside British journalist Philip Gibbs. 'We are lost,' he told Gibbs. 'My division is finished. My friends are all killed.' When Gibbs asked the prisoner what his officers thought, the latter made a gesture of derision with a finger under his nose: 'They think we are "kaput" too; they only look to the end of the war.'[9]

In late July, Hitler's regiment moved to Le Cateau, on the Somme, the scene of nearly four years of bloodshed. Here, his lucky star was about to shine on an action that would greatly assist his later rise to power and cement his reputation as a war hero. Through exceptionally heavy fire, Hitler and another runner delivered messages at great risk to their lives. For this action, both were awarded the Iron Cross (First Class), dated 31 July 1918. Hitler's citation read:

As a dispatch runner, [Hitler] has shown cold-blooded courage and exemplary boldness both in positional warfare and in the war of movement, and he has always volunteered to carry messages in the most difficult situations and at the risk of his life. Under conditions of great peril, when all the communication lines were cut, the untiring and fearless activity of Hitler made it possible for important messages to go through.[10]

Later in his career, Hitler's political enemies would dismiss the award as the favouritism of top brass towards a 'rear-area pig', and more recently Thomas Weber's book *Hitler's First War* is dedicated to making the case that he was a rank coward.[11] It is time to nail the controversy over whether Hitler was a brave soldier or not. The truth is muddied by Nazi propagandists' later claims of the Führer's superhuman battle exploits, of single-handedly capturing prisoners and leading attacks (he did neither).

His officers, however, gave the clearest assessment of Hitler's combat performance and, even though some were biased by their later political beliefs, soldiers tend to stick to an unwritten code: speak honestly about each other or keep quiet. So Lieutenant Colonel Friedrich Petz, who succeeded Engelhardt as commander of Hitler's regiment until March 1916, would describe him in February 1922 as a soldier of 'personal daring' and 'heedless courage', whose 'iron calm and cold-bloodedness never deserted him': 'When the situation was at its most dangerous, he always volunteered to make deliveries to the front and carried them out successfully.'[12] More credibly, given his later falling out with the Führer, Captain Fritz Wiedemann, his regimental adjutant, would recall in 1945 that Hitler had been the 'paradigm of the unknown soldier'.[13]

The fact is, Hitler ranked among those blazing exceptions, on both sides, of soldiers who simply never gave in, who relished war, combat, conquest, action. Such men saw war as the sublimation of the spirit, the highest and most noble sacrifice. In constant affirmation of that conviction, theirs was a form of reckless, insistent courage. Hitler was one such man; so too was the highly decorated future novelist Ernst Jünger. The comparison is intriguing: both men were wounded (Jünger several times; Hitler twice); both returned twice to battles in Flanders, one of the worst sectors of the Western Front; and both received the Iron Cross twice (First and Second Class). Jünger would also receive *Pour le Mérite*, the highest award to German soldiers of his rank. There the comparison ended: after the war, Jünger repeatedly refused to join or endorse the Nazi Party or put his name to any of their works, to Hitler's and the Nazis' fury.

To return to Hitler's new decoration: few Iron Crosses went to ordinary soldiers and very rarely two. So Hitler either enjoyed the patronage of friends in high places (for which there is no evidence) or he'd acted with great courage.

The answer rested with the officer who had first recommended him for the award, First Lieutenant Hugo Gutmann. Gutmann was anything but a pen-pushing staffer prone to minting medals for his mates. He was a brave and highly decorated officer, with long experience of leading his unit in combat. In January 1916 Gutmann himself had received the Iron Cross (First Class) for, as stated in his citation, 'energetic and fearless action' and 'exceptional discretion and great courage' at the Battle of the Somme.[14] For these and other distinctions, Gutmann's fellow soldiers greatly admired him.

Gutmann had promised to recommend the Iron Cross (First Class) for Hitler and another dispatch runner if they succeeded in performing a very difficult mission, which they duly did. Yet, while brave, the action was not 'strikingly exceptional', and Gutmann spent several weeks persuading the regimental commander to confirm the award.[15] Despite this, there can be little doubt that the decoration recognized Hitler's courage.

There was another reason why Hitler's second Iron Cross has drawn close scrutiny: Gutmann happened to be the List Regiment's most highly ranked Jew. The episode shows just how far Hitler had yet to travel before becoming the author of *Mein Kampf.* Had he been a fully formed, vicious anti-Semite during his war years, as he later claimed, Gutmann would surely have known about it and would hardly have fought to secure such a high decoration for the regiment's most notorious anti-Semite.

The truth is, at the time of the award Hitler displayed no outward antagonism towards Gutmann, either on account of his Jewishness or on any other ground, for the simple reason that Hitler was not then an outspoken hater of the Jews. It seems that whatever growing rancour he felt, he kept largely to himself.

The story forms a chilling footnote to his rise to power. As chancellor and Führer, Hitler claimed that he only ever wore his Iron Cross (Second Class), his greatest source of personal pride and political self-confidence; he mysteriously refused to wear the First Class decoration. He later explained, in a 'Table Talk' conversation on 15 May 1942, how he wore the lesser award 'in defiance' of the process that had also decorated the Jew: 'During the First World War, I didn't wear my Iron Cross First Class, because I saw how it was awarded. We had in my regiment a Jew named Guttmann [sic], who was the most terrible coward. He had the Iron Cross, First Class. It was revolting . . .'[16]

Hitler was, of course, lying: Gutmann had been an exceptionally brave soldier. Nor was Hitler consistent about why he wore the lesser award. Before he rose to power, he often proudly wore the Iron Cross (First Class) – for example, during the Munich Putsch – when Gutmann's role was unknown and the higher award served Hitler's political ambitions.

Nazi propagandists later erased Gutmann's name from the record: a Jew could not be permitted such a pivotal role in the Führer's ascendancy. Nor would Hitler's citation remain intact. The Nazis twisted his war record into something superhuman: for example, among the ridiculous stories that, in the party's retelling, appeared in Nazi-era school textbooks was one in which Hitler had single-handedly captured a whole group of British soldiers (or sometimes French *poilus*) at the point of his pistol.

In August the Canadians and Anzacs pulverized the German Army at Albert and Arras. Hitler's Bavarian division took part in the defence, doggedly holding their ground under ferocious attack until forced to retire. They were eventually relieved and sent to the Belgian–Dutch border, where they rested and visited Ostend. Hitler accepted an invitation to take a tour in a U-boat. At the end of September, the Bavarians were ordered back into the fray, to experience some of the final fighting – at the *Fifth* Battle of Ypres. Private Ignaz Westenkirchner, Hitler's fellow dispatch runner, described the events that led to Hitler's last, terrible action of the war – one that would weigh so heavily on posterity:

> For the third time we were back on the old ground, fought over in 1914. Now we had to defend it, inch by inch, all over again . . . On the night of 13–14 October 1918 the crashing and howling and roaring of the guns was accompanied by something still more deadly than usual . . . All of a sudden the bombardment slackened off and in place of shells came a queer pungent smell.
>
> Word flew through the trenches that the English were attacking with chlorine gas. Hitherto the List hadn't experienced this sort of gas, but

now we got a thorough dose of it. As I stuck my head outside the dugout for a quick look round I found myself confronted by a hideous lot of bogies. In the place of men were creatures with visages of sheer horror. At that I shot into my own gas mask! For hours we lay there with this foul stuff poisoning every gulp of air outside.

Suddenly one of the chaps could stand it no longer. He sprang up, wrenched the mask from his head and face, gasping, only to encounter a waft of the white-green poison. It caught him by the throat and flung him back choking, gurgling, suffocating, dying . . .

The gas bombardment continued until dawn, interspersed with heavy explosive, Westenkirchner recalled:

We chaps just hugged the ravaged and shattered ground, lying, indistinguishable lumps of filth and earth ourselves, within the sheltering lip of the water-filled craters torn up by previous shelling. We were practically finished. Only a handful of us yet remained. Most of us lay there, black bundles, never to move again . . .

About seven in the morning Hitler was despatched with an order to our rear. Dropping with exhaustion, he staggered off . . . His eyes were burning, sore, and smarting – gas, he supposed, or dog weariness. Anyhow, they rapidly got worse. The pain was hideous, presently he could see nothing but a fog. Stumbling, and falling over and over again, he made what feeble progress he could. Every time he went down crash, it was harder and harder to drag him to his feet again. The last time, all his failing strength was exhausted in freeing himself from the mask . . . he could struggle up no more . . . his eyes were searing coals . . . Hitler collapsed. Goodness knows how long it was before the stretchers found him.[17]

That was the morning of 14 October, a day after Hitler returned from leave. The Listers had come under a sustained British attack near Comines, south-east of the Ypres salient. Hitler and two of his fellow dispatch runners were gassed with mustard, not the deadlier chlorine.

His eyes were 'burning', he recalled in *Mein Kampf*, '. . . and at seven in the morning I stumbled and tottered back . . . taking with me my last report of the war. A few hours later my eyes were like glowing coals; it had grown dark around me.'[18]

He suffered from mild exposure to mustard gas, the symptoms of which can emerge several hours later: blistering of the skin and painful swelling and tearing of the eyes, accompanied by temporary blindness that can last up to ten days.[19] In other words, Hitler knew he would soon succumb to the gas's effects, so he used the few hours between being poisoned and the onset of the symptoms to fulfil his last duties.

According to a US intelligence report, Hitler was initially suspected of suffering from 'war hysteria' and transferred at first to a psychiatric ward.[20] If so, the doctors had clearly misdiagnosed his condition. The vast majority of historians and contemporary records concur that Hitler was gassed; Hitler himself recounts it, with no reason to lie. Yet even if we accept that some kind of hysteria had simultaneously gripped him (the sources for which are 'speculative'[21]), is it possible that a kind of psychosomatically induced blindness had bizarrely co-incided with, or replaced, the symptoms of his exposure to mustard gas?

A crazier story concerns the treatment Hitler supposedly received for 'hysteria-induced blindness'. According to a theory concocted by Rudolph Binion, the late 'father of psycho-history', Hitler underwent a profound personality change in hospital under the care of a surgeon called Professor Edmund Forster. Forster's treatment reportedly involved placing the patient in a hypnotic trance from which Hitler apparently failed to emerge. The notion of a hypnotized Hitler, eternally spellbound, left to wander the earth to wreak havoc, has been safely dismissed.[22] The truth is less colourful: Hitler suffered the classic symptoms of a mild attack of mustard gas. He was sent by hospital train to a clinic at Pasewalk, in Pomerania, north of Berlin. Highly agitated, if not hysterical, he nevertheless knew his condition was temporary.

Meanwhile, by October 1918 the Allies had forced the Germans back to where their Spring Offensive had begun. Later that month, British forces occupied the Belgian coast and seized the U-boat bases, fulfilling the original goal of Third Ypres the previous year. Blow by blow, the Germans were heaved out of France and Belgium. By November, with terrific losses to both sides, the Allies had regained all the ground lost to the Germans since the start of the year.

Ludendorff would never recover from the nightmare. The opening day of the Battle of Amiens, 8 August, he had labelled 'the Black Day of the German Army', but there had by now been many other black days in the ensuing Hundred Days, during which some of his finest units had been destroyed or utterly broken, the final humiliating blow that ended his war. The German forces surrendered *en masse* or were annihilated. The German Army had been soundly defeated where it hurt most: on the killing field.

On the home front, the socialists, communists and other opposition groups were leading an outcry against the war. In Berlin, left-wing politicians demanded that peace negotiations begin. They variously accused the military commanders of committing national suicide: some 880,000 German soldiers had been killed, wounded or captured between March and July 1918[23] and it would later emerge that 1,621,035 German soldiers had lost their lives that year.[24] The protests were the cries of despair of a battered country.

By the hundredth day Haig's men – the British and Dominion armies – had triumphed, capturing 188,700 prisoners and 2,840 guns, just shy of the combined total of the much larger American and French armies. By this measure, the great Allied counter-offensive of 1918 'was, by far, the greatest military victory in British history', concludes the historian Gary Sheffield.[25]

The crushing impact of the Allied conquests persuaded Hindenburg and Ludendorff to sue for peace. Germany signed the Armistice on 11 November 1918.

As he lay there in the darkness, temporarily blinded by gas, Hitler received the news. On 12 November the hospital's chaplain gathered the patients together: yesterday, he said, Germany had surrendered.

The psychological blow intensified Hitler's anguish. For him, it was a day of infamy. Germany had not been defeated! Germany would never surrender! The home front had killed the army! Such thoughts fed into a river of denial on the part of a humiliated people who refused to accept Germany's military defeat and hungered for an alternative account that would restore national pride.

The great weight of these thoughts, the horror of defeat, the immense repercussions for his beloved Fatherland, racked the mind of the young lance corporal writhing on his bed at Pasewalk. Overwhelmed with grief, Hitler collapsed:

> I . . . threw myself on my bunk, and dug my burning head into my blanket and pillow. Since the day when I had stood at my mother's grave, I had not wept . . . When in the long war years Death had snatched so many a dear comrade and friend from our ranks, it would have seemed to me almost a sin to complain – after all, were they not dying for Germany? And when at length the creeping gas in the last days of the dreadful struggle attacked me, too, and began to gnaw at my eyes, and beneath the fear of going blind forever, I nearly lost heart for a moment, the voice of my conscience thundered at me: Miserable wretch, are you going to cry when thousands are a hundred times worse off than you! But now I could not help it.[26]

CHAPTER FOURTEEN

'What was all the pain in my eyes compared to this misery?'

The bandages on Hitler's face were removed. Slowly, the gassed corporal's eyes came blinking into the light. He looked out on a new world: a defeated Germany, a humiliated people, his beloved army surrendered and broken.

As he lay in his bunk in Pasewalk, in the winter of 1918, helpless and wretched, Hitler received further news: of the army's mass capitulation, the flight of the Kaiser and a Marxist revolution at home. It disgusted him. He shook with rage. He refused to accept defeat. He swore bloody revenge.

Later, Hitler would portray that moment in Pasewalk hospital as a terrible awakening, in which his entire life coalesced around a single, urgent idea: to avenge the German Army against its enemies at home, the 'November Criminals', as they became known – chiefly communists, socialists and Jews – whom he blamed for Germany's defeat. From the depths of his being he believed in the idea of a monstrous and treacherous conspiracy, the famous 'stab in the back' of the German Army. The phrase, first used by the British general Sir Neill Malcolm, head of the British Military Mission in Berlin in autumn 1919, was seized upon by Ludendorff when he first heard it at the time.[1] A few years later, Hitler's party would adopt it as one of their defining political motifs.

Winston Churchill did much to cement Hitler's 'Pasewalk moment'.

In the first volume of his history of the Second World War, *The Gathering Storm*, the British leader anchors Hitler's transformation from 'little soldier' into political hater to the bedridden recovery of his eyesight:

> As he lay sightless and helpless . . . his own personal failure seemed merged in the disaster of the whole German people. The shock of defeat, the collapse of law and order, the triumph of the French, caused this convalescent regimental orderly an agony which consumed his being, and generated those portentous and measureless forces of the spirit which may spell the rescue or the doom of mankind. The downfall of Germany seemed to him inexplicable by ordinary processes. Somewhere there had been a gigantic and monstrous betrayal. Lonely and pent within himself, the little soldier pondered and speculated upon the possible causes of the catastrophe, guided only by his narrow personal experiences. He had mingled in Vienna with extreme German Nationalist groups, and here he had heard stories of sinister, undermining activities of another race, foes and exploiters of the Nordic world – the Jews. His patriotic anger fused with his envy of the rich and successful into one overpowering hate.[2]

In *Mein Kampf*, Hitler would portray Pasewalk as a religious experience, in which divine intervention chose *him* as the saviour of the German people, destined to lead the nation, like Rienzi, out of the darkness and into the light. A new life danced before his sightless eyes, and in the swirling shadows he felt the first, sharp impulse to enter politics – or so he later claimed.

In a passage of rising despair and blistering hatred, Hitler relived his blinded days as a tremendous epiphany, in which he rises as the avenger of Germany, the *Übermensch* incarnate. Note the repeated reference to his war experiences as the driving factor – chiefly the battles at Ypres in 1914 and the 'Massacre of the Innocents' at Langemarck:

> And so it had all been in vain. In vain all the sacrifices and privations . . .
> in vain the hours in which, with mortal fear clutching at our hearts, we

nevertheless did our duty; and in vain the death of two millions . . .

Would not the graves of all the hundreds of thousands open . . . and send the silent mud- and blood-covered heroes back as spirits of vengeance to the homeland which had cheated them with such mockery of the highest sacrifice which a man can make to his people in the world?

Had they died for this, the soldiers of August and September, 1914? Was it for this that in the Autumn of the same year the volunteer regiments marched after their old comrades? Was it for this that these boys of seventeen sank into the earth of Flanders? Was this the meaning of the sacrifice which the German mother made to the fatherland when with sore heart she let her best-loved boys march off, never to be seen again? Did all this happen only so that a gang of wretched criminals could lay hands on the fatherland? . . .

Miserable and degenerate criminals!

The more I tried to achieve clarity on the monstrous event in this hour, the more the shame of indignation and disgrace burned my brow. What was all the pain in my eyes compared to this misery?

The following terrible days [after Germany's surrender] and even worse nights I knew all was lost. Only fools, liars, and criminals could hope in the mercy of the enemy. In those nights hatred grew in me, hatred for those responsible for this deed.

In the days that followed, my own Fate became known to me . . . Kaiser William II was the first German Emperor to hold out a conciliatory hand to the leaders of Marxism, without suspecting that scoundrels have no honor. While they still held the imperial hand in theirs, their other hand was reaching for the dagger.

There is no making pacts with the Jews; there can only be the hard: 'either-or'.

I, for my part, decided to go into politics.[3]

No doubt Hitler sincerely felt the humiliation of defeat and rage on behalf of his fellow men expressed here. Yet the rest of this passage from *Mein Kampf,* written six years after the events at Pasewalk, is a gross distortion to further his political ends. In 1918 he had not resolved on political action or vengeance; he was a wounded soldier with no future. In *Mein Kampf* he retroactively infused his convalescence with transformative power, casting a magician's wand over the genesis of 'the Führer'. This is Hitler the politician projecting back on to his bedridden blindness a moment of 'self-realization' that fed his growing legend and the Nazis' political ambitions. It is the voice, as we shall see, of the self-aggrandizing leader of the failed Munich coup, imprisoned for 'treason' and desperately trying to rebuild his political career.

The coincidence of his sightlessness at the instant of Germany's defeat was, as Kershaw writes, 'a crucial step on the way to Hitler's rationalization of his prejudices'.[4] More than that, Hitler would later characterize the Nazi Party's struggle for power as a response to the 'revelations' that came to him in Pasewalk – many of which were yet to emerge. In *Mein Kampf*, in short, he retrospectively dreamed up a 'messiah' moment in order to unify them.

The timing of Hitler's 'conversion' to a political revolution governed by brutal anti-Semitism may for ever baffle the world, but Pasewalk was not it. A few weeks on an army bunk did not create 'the Führer', whatever myths Hitler and the Nazi legend-factory would like us to think. Germany's newly minted leader did not step out of a gaseous haze to rule the world. The Führer emerged incrementally, as we shall see, from a series of bumbling failures, stunning successes and the application of political skills he had not yet realized he possessed.

That's not to deny that something happened to Hitler in the hospital at Pasewalk: news of Germany's defeat focused his memory on thousands of fellow soldiers killed and wounded – at Ypres and the Somme and other battles. His rage hurtled around for the names of those responsible, crying out for vengeance on an as yet undefined group of enemies – those who had surrendered the Fatherland.

Discharged from hospital on 21 November 1918, Hitler returned to Munich via a month in Traunstein, in south-eastern Bavaria, where he served as a guard in a prison camp. Contrary to his sickbed 'conversion' to politics, he did not seek a political role or even consider politics a viable career at the time, and would not do so for more than a year. Instead, he remained in the army, partly for financial reasons. He joined a replacement battalion, with the hope of staying in the forces as long as possible. There he met several old comrades, some of whom would become prominent Nazis.

He came home to a broken society, wrenched apart by war and destitution: soldiers versus civilians; the extreme right versus the extreme left; militias prowling the streets; and a virulent anti-Semitism rife in the cities. On 7 November, Kaiser Wilhelm had fled into exile in Holland, ending 700 years of Hohenzollern rule; and in Bavaria King Ludwig III had been forced to abdicate. The next day, the Marxist wing of the Sozialdemokratische Partei Deutschlands (SPD), led by the journalist Kurt Eisner, had stormed the military garrisons in Munich and seized power, declaring Bavaria a 'free state' and a republic.

Before plunging into Bavarian politics and Hitler's place in it, let's briefly step back and survey the state of the post-war Reich as a whole. Germany was a fraught land, in utter political, economic and social turmoil. We've already seen the impact of the war on the food supply and economy. Now the apparatus and symbols of the German state were to crumble and fall: the flag and coat of arms were removed and replaced; the Imperial Army, Navy and Air Force dissolved after the sailors' mutiny at Kiel Barracks in late October and early November; and the imperial government collapsed.

The so-called November Revolution of 1918 convulsed the land, in which two parties of the newly empowered left vied for supremacy: the hard-line Independent Social Democratic Party (Unabhängige Sozialdemokratische Partei Deutschlands, or USPD), who wanted a Soviet-style command economy; and the Social Democratic Party (SPD), also known as the Majority SPD (Mehrheits-SPD, or MSPD), committed to a parliamentary democracy.

On 9 November 1918 a leading figure in the MSPD, Philipp Scheidemann, declared the formation of the 'German Republic' at the Reichstag building in Berlin, but within hours his moment of glory was convulsed by the rival proclamation of a 'Free Socialist Republic' at the Berlin Stadtschloss (City Palace) by Karl Liebknecht, co-leader with Rosa Luxemburg of the communist Spartakusbund (Spartacist League), which amounted to the few hundred supporters of the Russian Revolution who had allied themselves with the USPD in 1917.

In the wings of this theatre of chaos lurked the moderate Friedrich Ebert, leader of the MSPD, who, furious at Scheidemann's peremptory declaration of power in the name of the party he (Ebert) led, insisted that the future of the country be decided by a national assembly, which, if the people so desired, might even restore another monarch. The Kaiser would abdicate until 28 November 1918, leaving the country without a head of state.

In the event, Ebert was compelled to take power at the head of a government called the Council of the People's Deputies (*Rat der Volksbeauftragten*), in which the MSPD was forced to share power with their Spartacist and independent enemies on the hard left, and to absorb hundreds of Soviet-style workers' and soldiers' councils set up during the revolution to pursue socialism and dismantle the old regime.

Ebert did so in an atmosphere of extreme peril, brutally expressed in the assassination of Liebknecht and Luxemburg, effectively on his orders, by the *Freikorps* – the new national paramilitary, mainly comprising hardened war veterans – which Ebert deployed to destroy the communist revolution. Captured in Berlin on 15 January 1919 by the Rifle Division of the *Freikorps* Cavalry Guards, Luxemburg and Liebknecht were interrogated under torture and separately shot. Luxemburg's body was thrown into the Landwehr Canal.

The revolutionary tremors from Berlin swiftly reached other German cities. In Munich, having overthrown the Bavarian king, Kurt Eisner became the first republican premier of the socialist state of Bavaria. By Bolshevik standards, Eisner's would be a moderate 'dictatorship of the proletariat'. He offered liberal reforms, such as an eight-hour working day. Nor was it initially violent: Bavaria's Marxist-backed 'revolution' rose against a backdrop of exuberant parties, hysteria, street dancing, sexual indulgence – all the bohemian pleasures that would be beloved of post-war German society and loathed by the abstinent war veteran and social conservative Adolf Hitler. But Eisner's revolution was short-lived. A German Jew, he had few friends and many violent enemies. On 23 November he made the error of admitting German war guilt, leaking evidence of Germany's hand in Austria–Hungary's declaration of war on Serbia, proving, he believed, that 'a small horde of mad Prussian military' men in alliance with industrialists, capitalists, politicians and princes had started the war.[5]

From that moment, in the eyes of the German patriots on the right, Eisner was a marked man and a 'traitor' to Germany. He was murdered on 21 February 1919 by a twenty-two-year-old lieutenant and German nationalist, Count Anton Arco auf Valley, who defended his actions thus: 'Eisner is a Bolshevist and a Jew. He's not German . . . He is a traitor to the country.'[6] The murder inflamed the left: the soldiers who supported the revolution rallied around the creation of a Bavarian soviet (or council), ruled by a Soviet-style provisional government.

The spectre of a Russian-style takeover of Bavaria briefly horrified the conservative rump and sent shockwaves back to Berlin, from where the Council of Deputies dispatched immediate funds to help moderate parties resist the communist uprising that followed Eisner's murder. The mainstream Catholic Bavarian People's Party and a smattering of extreme right-wing groups moved to crush the Marxist bogeyman that had briefly risen to seize control of the state.

In 'liberating' Munich from the Marxists, the Bavarian authorities also relied largely on the *Freikorps*. If initially at the disposal of leaders on both left and right, the *Freikorps* rapidly acquired a reputation for hard-right vigilantism under such early commanders as Ernst Röhm, soon to lead the *Sturmabteilung* (SA) or Brownshirts, Hitler's private army. While destroying Bavaria's brief communist government, the *Freikorps* resorted to savage overkill – revenge for the left's murder of ten hostages (including several members of the extreme right-wing Thule Society) on 30 April 1919. In the aftermath, some 600 left-wing leaders (and many ordinary civilians) were rounded up

Above left: Hitler's father, Alois, flew into a rage at his son's ambition to be an artist, but was no stricter than most fathers at the time.

Above right: Hitler's mother, Klara, was the only person he said he truly loved.

Left: Orthodox Jews in Vienna aroused Hitler's curiosity. He would not become a violent anti-Semite until after the First World War.

Below: Karl Lueger (*left*), mayor of Vienna, and the far-right politician Georg Ritter von Schönerer were 'Pan-German' populists who fiercely scapegoated minorities and strongly influenced young Hitler before 1914.

Above: Hitler rejoices in a Munich crowd at the declaration of war in 1914. A minority celebrated; most people did not want war.

Below: A watercolour by Hitler of the ruins of Messines church, Flanders, in 1914. Vienna's Academy of Fine Arts had not recognized his talent, and he would never forget the rejection.

Left: Hitler (with moustache) as a young 'runner' on the Western Front, with his beloved dog Foxl; and (**above**) in a borrowed pickelhaube. Twice decorated for bravery, Hitler never rose above rank of lance corporal.

Above: German soldiers under gas attack in 1917 use a pigeon to test the gas's strength. Hitler was mustard-gassed just before the end of the war.

Above: Karl Liebknect (left) and Rosa Luxemburg (right), leaders of the communist Spartacus League, were among those Hitler later blamed for the 'stab in the back'. In 1919, however, Hitler served on a Soldiers' council in the short-lived Bavarian 'soviet'.

Above: Food shortages and soaring inflation led to riots in German cities during and after the war. Hitler was disgusted by what he saw as spinelessness on the home front.

Above: The bourgeoisie, especially Jewish financiers, were the targets of Nazi propaganda in the early 1920s.

Right: The Brownshirts, or SA, Hitler's personal militia, were formed in the early 1920s to police his rallies and persecute the Nazis' opponents.

Above: Hitler's speeches inflamed his audiences against 'back-stabbers', the Jews and non-Germans.

Right: *Mein Kampf* (My Struggle), in this rare encased edition, reinforced the message, but most people failed to take it seriously.

Above: Hitler (*left*) with Hess (*second from the right*) in Landsberg Prison, 1925. Lederhosen were one of many privileges granted to Nazi inmates.

Three influential early Nazis (*anticlockwise from the left*): locksmith Anton Drexler, a founder of the party; the poet and society journalist Dietrich Eckart; and the pornographer and anti-Semetic propagandist Julius Streicher.

Left: Cartoons in the late 1920s made clear what the Nazis intended to do with the Jews.

Below: Hitler relaxing with his niece, Angela 'Geli' Raubal, with whom he was rumoured to be sexually involved and who killed herself after he stopped her from marrying a suitor.

Bottom left: After he met Hitler in the mid-1920s, Joseph Goebbels wrote that he could 'conquer the world with this man'.

Bottom right: Hitler with Hermann Göring, one of his most loyal followers, in 1933, the year the Nazis came to power.

Hitler's words were not eloquent, witty or memorable. But his soaring voice and violent hand gestures offered an astonishing visual spectacle, all carefully rehearsed, as shown here.

and slaughtered in a frenzy of domestic bloodletting unprecedented in modern German history.

Hitler did not participate in the crushing of the Bavarian Revolution. In the soldiers' barracks, he spent much of his time subjecting his fellow veterans to angry, indiscriminate tirades against a gallery of 'shirkers' and cowards whom he listed, in no precise order of villainy: parliamentarians, socialists, Jews, Slavs, Catholics, Marxists, internationalists, capitalists. He tossed them all into the pot marked 'November Criminals'.

He blamed the left-wing press and socialist leaders for inciting strikes at munitions plants throughout Germany, which he later branded an 'enormous betrayal of the country'. He blamed capitalists for parasitically preying on the war effort. If he could be war minister for a day, 'within 24 hours the criminals would be put up against the wall'.[7] In this vein, in early 1919, Hitler was merely another angry young veteran, jobless, rootless, venting his fury and frustration at indistinct targets.

At the time, in the minds of a rising minority of extremists, the labels 'socialist' and 'Marxist' tended to be synonymous with 'Jew', simply because Jews had risen to the leadership of the left. Both Kurt Eisner and Rosa Luxemburg had been Jewish Marxist leaders who had strongly opposed the war and led the revolution, making them among the most hated figures in the sights of the far right. Hitler passes over Eisner as 'an international Jew' and doesn't even mention Luxemburg in *Mein Kampf*, an extraordinary omission given their prominence in the revolution and the hatred they engendered on the right.

Yet Hitler's initial targets were not Jewish, partly because the politicians who settled the Armistice and now controlled what was to become (for him) the hated Weimar Republic were not Jewish. The people he most detested at the time, as he identified in *Mein Kampf*, were non-Jews at the less radical end of the social democratic movement: Ebert, for example, who in February 1919 became president of the Weimar Republic and who, in fact, bought into the 'stab-in-the-back' theory when it was politically expedient to do so, telling homecoming veterans 'no enemy has vanquished you'; Scheidemann, from February 1919 chancellor of the new republic; and Emil Barth, an independent Social Democrat and union leader, who played a key part in the German Revolution. All these men were 'ripe for hanging', Hitler would later say: 'I hated the whole gang of miserable party scoundrels and betrayers of the people in the extreme . . . this whole gang was not really concerned with the welfare of the nation, but with filling empty pockets. For this they were ready to sacrifice the whole nation, and if necessary to let Germany be destroyed.'[8]

Also high on Hitler's black list of 'November Criminals' were prominent Catholics such as Matthias Erzberger, leader of the moderate Catholic Centre Party, who had accused the German High Command on 6 July of leading Germany to disaster. Erzberger and Scheidemann had committed the unforgivable crime, in Hitler's mind, of driving a 'peace initiative' of 18 July 1918, which received majority support from Parliament and most German people. Hitler and extreme right-wing cells would brand Erzberger a traitor for signing the Armistice of 11 November. He died of an assassin's bullet on 26 August 1921 while out walking in the Black Forest.

Hitler's own 'conversion' to politics was a messy blend of opportunism, hypocrisy, skill and sheer desperation. In early 1919, he pursued a course in stark contrast to his later account in *Mein Kampf*. Elected his battalion's representative on a 'Soldiers' Council', a kind of military-style soviet that had backed the revolution, his first political role was to speak on behalf of soldiers on a socialist committee.

So despite all his later bluster against the SPD and the Marxists, at the time Hitler declined to join the *Freikorps*, the militia that set forth to destroy them. Nor did he publicly oppose those he later damned in *Mein Kampf*. His role on the Soldiers' Council meant he briefly swam *with* the anti-war left, not against them. His flirtation with the revolution even extended to walking behind the coffin of Eisner, the assassinated Jewish revolutionary. Hitler would excise these episodes from his autobiography, of course, because they tainted the purity of the Nazi legend and gave the lie to his claim that he became a violent anti-Semite in Vienna or Pasewalk.

That Hitler briefly cosied up to revolutionary communists in 1919 should not baffle us. We demand linear correctness in the lives of politicians and leaders even as we ourselves act in inconsistent or contrarian ways. At the time, Hitler wanted a job, influence and a voice. His election to the Soldiers' Council gave him all three. His allegiances at the start of his political 'career' – he had not yet dignified it as such – were confused and chaotic, like those of any political neophyte jostling to find a home in the lower circles of power.

In this sense, Hitler was putting a toe in the water, experimenting. He was a pure political animal, willing to wear whichever suit fitted him best. 'He was like a stray dog looking for a master,' noted Captain Karl Mayr, the closest thing Hitler had to a mentor at the time, 'ready to throw in his lot with anyone who would show him kindness.'[9]

And he soon changed his spots. On 9 May 1919, after the Bavarian Soviet fell, he suddenly joined the counter-revolutionary extreme right, chiefly because they offered him a home. Upon hearing Hitler speak to veterans, in his position on the Soldiers' Council of the 1st Demobilization Company, to which he'd been re-elected on 15 April, Captain Mayr sensed the young man's true vocation and set about inducting him into politics – the politics of the far right. At the time Mayr was an intelligence officer in the Reichswehr, the newly formed and much reduced Weimar Army, a mob of unruly soldiers and a sad shadow of Germany's former military strength. Part of Mayr's job was to weed out Bolshevik sympathies in the forces, and he decided to use Hitler as a kind of 'sniffer dog'. Hitler brought two things to the job: he had been involved in the soldiers' soviets and knew their members; and he had the hunger of the turncoat, a willingness to change his colours to suit his master. Like any political novice looking for a break, a particle of power, he would take any offer going. He was still a political nobody, with nothing to lose. Later, when his flirtation with communists and changing loyalties would have been seen as a blot on his record, he simply glossed over or erased it from *Mein Kampf* – written when he had a lot to lose.

Chapter Fifteen

'I could speak!'

True to his word, in May 1919 Karl Mayr assigned Hitler a role on an 'investigating commission' of the Reichswehr, looking into the causes and perpetrators of the communist revolution. In this role, Hitler would receive his first taste of real political authority: part of his job would be to investigate the political allegiances of his battalion during the revolution, acting effectively as a paid informer against his old comrades or any soldier who had backed the Marxist uprising.

In other words, Hitler's 'first political activity', as he called it, was to denounce fellow soldiers who had dared support the left's anti-war uprising. He was little more than a traitor to the men with whom he served. He would, for example, accuse Georg Dufter, his former colleague on the Soldiers' Council of the 1st Demobilization Company, of spreading propaganda for the Soviet Republic. Dufter, in Hitler's view, was 'the worst and most radical rabble-rouser within the regiment'.[1] So much for soldiers' solidarity.

In Bavaria at this time the armed forces controlled the state administration in the aftermath of the bloody suppression of the communists. The ruling Social Democrats were due to return, in August, and the interim period offered a perfect chance for the far right to seize a filament of power, or at least to harden their grip on the state. They were quick to exploit this unusual opportunity, occupying the power vacuum with unseemly relish: thugs, baton-wielders, paramilitary gangs, extremists of every stripe exercised their muscles, rallying their supporters and harassing their opponents. Far-right political cells proliferated in Munich, in what was a very dangerous time to be a communist or a liberal.

Recognizing Hitler's energy and rousing personality, Mayr, who now headed the intelligence unit of the Bavarian Reichswehr, encouraged his wayward protégé to educate himself, to ground his rampaging mind in the 'national thinking' courses then being held at the *Reichswehrlager* (army base) on the Lechfeld plain, near Augsburg. The lectures promised to advance Hitler's education in capitalism and economics. Yet they began from an extremely skewed perspective: they aimed at fuelling conspiracy theories and fomenting hatred, chiefly against the Jews and Slavs, rather than instructing the audience in basic economics.

Hitler seized on the parts of the lectures that fed his burgeoning sense of himself as a political agitator. If he lacked the critical faculties to analyse what he was being told, he digested what he felt he was supposed to believe, or whatever reinforced his prejudices. He swallowed the lines that the Jews controlled the stock market and that the Jews were spreading Bolshevism. The Jews were everywhere, he heard, controlling the workers, running the markets, poisoning politics – and always acting against German interests. They were 'the enemy of the people'. This was straight out of the script of that paranoid hater of the Jews, the writer Alfred Rosenberg, the closest thing to an intellectual in the early National Socialist movement. Hitler eagerly bought into all this, as though feeding the crystallization of a monstrous theory.

It wasn't a 'eureka moment', of course. Since his Vienna days, Hitler had been exposed to demagogues warning him of secret, Hebraic powers that sought to conquer the Fatherland. Yet he was far more susceptible to their siren song in these years after the war. In Munich at this time there operated a shadowy array of hard-line movements who peddled vast conspiracy theories that conditioned the thinking and mood on the extremist fringe. One was the *Aufbau Vereinigung* (Reconstruction Organization), a Munich-based counter-revolutionary group comprising White Russian émigrés and proto-National Socialists, who aimed to overthrow the governments of Germany and the Soviet Union and install far-right autocratic regimes. The *Aufbau Vereinigung* had a profound influence on the development of early National Socialist ideology and, with the assistance of US car-maker Henry Ford, helped to finance the fledgling movement. According to the historian Michael Kellogg, the *Aufbau*'s ideology helped to persuade Hitler that a Jewish conspiracy involving an alliance of international finance and Bolshevism was determined to crush Germany and dominate mankind.[2]

All these influences played out in the way Hitler perceived the society around him. Convinced that Germany was in the grip of such a conspiracy, he began to see Jews in charge everywhere. There was barely a 'Jew-free' space in Germany, he came to think. In every nook and cranny, prominent 'Chosen People' could be found, manipulating and debauching his beloved Fatherland. He would later blame 'the Jews' for organizing the massive strikes in early 1918 that helped to ensure Germany's defeat,[3] setting aside the fact that most of the German working men who participated were neither Jews nor communists. They were simply employees whose families were hungry and fed up.

Seized by the conviction that a conspiracy of Jewish capitalists and Bolsheviks was working against the German Reich, Hitler could barely restrain himself from speaking out. He felt compelled to share his new 'insight' of a society wholly corrupted by the 'Hebrew race'. In July 1919, he got his chance. While on a training course at Munich University he attended a lecture by Gottfried Feder, an engineer from Murnau who condemned 'Jewish usury' and blamed 'the Jews' for controlling international capital. Feder cast the Jews as the gatekeepers of global capitalism, an outlook that would form the bedrock of Nazi ideology (along with the parallel conspiracy theory that the Jews were behind the rise of global communism).

After Feder's speech, several in the departing crowd paused before a young man with a snub moustache, a flick of black hair and 'remarkably large, light blue, fanatically cold, gleaming eyes', as one observed.[4]

It was not Hitler's appearance that held them spellbound, however, but his extraordinary voice: bellicose, impassioned, unyielding. Young Adolf was in full flight, raging against his enemies. Feder's speech seemed to have inflamed his mind like a torch to tinder.

Hitler's oratorical skills were soon noticed. Feder's brother-in-law and fellow speaker Karl Alexander von Müller mentioned to Mayr after that session, 'Do you know that one of your trainees is a natural born public speaker?'[5] Captain Mayr cast a fresh eye on his furious young protégé, duly rewarding Hitler's 'good work' in ratting on his fellow soldiers and his growing reputation as an impassioned defender of Germany by promoting him to a new 'political' role in the regimental Demobilization Office where his oratorical skills could be used to advantage. This was a job in an 'Enlightenment Squad'[6] at the army base in Lechfeld. In this role, Hitler would serve as one of twenty-six instructors, lecturing returning servicemen in the economic and political conditions at home.

In substance like Feder's, in style far more vitriolic, his presentations were soon the talk of Lechfeld. It was the speaker, not the content of his speeches, that amazed those who heard them: it was *the way he spoke*, on familiar and well-trodden themes, that enraptured his listeners. He appealed to their most basic emotions – fear, envy, blame, hatred – and exhorted them to target the Jews and communists, who, he claimed *ad nauseam*, were responsible for Germany's humiliation. His audiences rapidly grew. Hitler quickly realized that a message of aggressive anti-Semitism struck a chord with many German people, especially the lower-middle classes who had lost most in the post-war economic crisis. By focusing their resentment, like a beam through a magnifying glass, on a single, detested target, Hitler saw that he could unleash the pent-up rage of a people who yearned for someone to blame for Germany's post-war misery.

As such, 'the Jews' served as the perfect scapegoat for this would-be populist and soap-box orator. They were widely unpopular, electorally insignificant and anathema to right-thinking Lutherans. And by stoking Bavaria's latent anti-Semitism into full-blown hatred, Hitler found that he could draw accolades to himself and carve out a new life as a propagandist, an organizer, perhaps a politician. This was not pure opportunism: rather, a potent mixture of the viscerally personal and the brazenly populist, a process by which Hitler's own political ambitions and society's hatred of the Jews became mutually reinforcing.

'Like a sponge, Hitler sucked up popular anti-Jewish sentiment,' writes his biographer Volker Ullrich. 'His turn towards fanatical anti-Semitism, which he would later claim had originated in Vienna, actually took place amidst the revolution and counter-revolution in Munich.'[7]

In fact, Hitler's 'conversion' to extreme anti-Semitism drew on deeper impulses than his exposure to these post-war upheavals. The anti-Semitic mood in Bavaria, which by now had become an autonomous state within the Weimar Republic, ignited his memories of his 'exposure' to Jewish people in Vienna and Munich before and during the war. And these memories acquired a twisted, toxic quality in a mind that would soon identify the Jews as a 'race' of parasites that posed an existential threat to Germany.

Blaming a defenceless minority for Germany's ills distracted attention from the real cause – a world war of unprecedented destructiveness and the impact of the British naval blockade, which hadn't been fully lifted until June 1919. The 'scapegoat' was the crudest political tactic, as old as human organization, relying on lies, disinformation and a primitive appeal to the most basic instincts: hatred, xenophobia, fear.

To succeed, it required a leader, a demagogue, with the charisma and persuasive power to express deep-rooted rage and social dislocation. It also needed a pivotal moment, a catalysing event, that would attract the masses to that leader like iron filings to a magnet.

For Hitler, that moment arrived with the signing by Germany and the Allied powers of the Treaty of Versailles on 28 June 1919. The peace settlement infuriated Germany, chiefly Article 231 – the notorious 'War Guilt Clause' – which required the country to 'accept the responsibility of Germany and her allies for causing all the loss and damage' of the war, itself a direct consequence of German aggression.[8]

All Germany's colonies were to be confiscated, her army reduced to 100,000, her navy to thirty-six ships (including six dreadnoughts), her air force abolished and her imperial ambitions crushed. Parts of her territory were to be handed over to other nations: the Saar coalmines were ceded and Alsace-Lorraine returned to France. In the east, Germany would recognize the independence of Czechoslovakia and Poland, and cede parts of Upper Silesia and Posen to Poland, among other territorial concessions.

The Rhineland would be demilitarized, a measure that fell short of the demand by French Prime Minister George Clemenceau for a French-controlled buffer state against future German aggression. 'America is far away, protected by the ocean,' he told US President Woodrow Wilson. 'Not even Napoleon himself could touch England. You are both sheltered; we are not.'[9]

Cripplingly for the dreams of Pan-Germans like Hitler, the treaty prohibited indefinitely the merging of Germany and Austria. Worse, the German delegates to Versailles, who had no say in the negotiations, were shocked to discover that Germany would not fully share in Wilson's principles of 'self-determination'. These endowed people of the same nationality with the right freely to choose their sovereignty and govern themselves, and that one nationality should have no right to govern another. Would that put an end to the German Reich? Would foreigners henceforth prescribe the form of the German government?

A nation in chains, a slave state: such was the popular German outcry against Versailles. From the Bavarian beer halls to the estates of the Prussian aristocracy, the people railed against a document they feared would make Germany a vassal of Britain and France. 'What hand would not wither that binds itself and us in these fetters?' responded the German chancellor, Philipp Scheidemann.[10] The ferociously anti-Semitic, Pan-German newspaper *Völkischer Beobachter* (which the Nazis would later buy and turn into their mouthpiece) condemned the

Treaty as a 'syphilitic peace . . . born of brief, forbidden lust, beginning with a small hard sore, gradually attacks the limbs and joints, even all the flesh, down to the heart and brain of the sinner.'[11]

In fact, the Versailles Treaty was relatively moderate. It fell well short of the drastic terms Germany had imposed on Russia in the Treaty of Brest-Litovsk (3 March 1918), which forced Russia to relinquish all her obligations to the Triple Entente and cede the Baltic States to Germany, as well as stripping Russia of a large part of her resources. Nor would Versailles prescribe the death of the Reich: Germany would be free to elect its own government and pursue its political destiny. There would be no 'occupying force' of the kind that descended on the divided Fatherland after 1945. And yet, as the historian Michael Burleigh concludes, Germans of all political complexions were united in seeing Versailles as 'the triumph of an Allied conspiracy to enmesh Germany in a network of restrictions and obligations in perpetuity, for the reparations bill was left ominously open-ended.'[12]

In the end, the reparations bill totalled 132 billion gold marks, or about US$30 billion ($400 billion in today's money). The expectation that the Germans would pay this astronomic sum relied on a gentleman's understanding that 'your word is your bond', in an era that had supposedly cast off the notion that treaties were to be fixed in wax lest they be abused, ignored or used to buy time. 'The new attitude,' wrote the historian A. J. P. Taylor, 'corresponded to the "sanctity of contract" which is the fundamental element in bourgeois civilisation. Kings and aristocrats do not pay their debts, and rarely keep their word. The capitalist system would collapse unless its practitioners honoured, without question, their most casual nod; and the Germans were now expected to observe the same ethic.'[13]

Proud, moderate Germans refused to accept the terms. The resurgent centre right believed Germany deserved the magnanimity and respect of a worthy opponent, not the punitive vengeance of victors picking over the spoils. Their defiance arose from the fact that many Germans refused to accept that they had 'lost' the war.

Motivated by their desire to punish their erstwhile enemy, the French and British grossly misjudged the social and economic climate in post-war Germany. The German people were bitter, exhausted, broken: of 13 million Germans who had served in the army during the war years, more than 2 million were dead and 4 million wounded, leaving irreparable scars on parents, wives, families and friends. And now this: the burden of blame and a vast invoice.

Nor were the lofty arguments at Versailles distracted by the Treaty's pernicious effects on the minds of the extremists then proliferating in Germany, such as the then obscure figure of Adolf Hitler. Their rage at Versailles ratcheted up their ache for revenge, and set the world on course for future conflict. Far from making peace, the Treaty prepared the stage for another war.

Bitterness over Versailles became the breeding ground for Hitler the politician. He was a very different animal to Hitler the soldier, though both drew on the same well-spring of rage and defiance. Where the soldier had been content to discharge his duties in a role he relished, the politician manifested a newfound ambition and lust for power. He seethed at the despicable document. For the first time in his life, he sensed that the growing audiences at his lectures were receptive to his tirades. If Versailles infuriated the German people, Hitler would soon give voice to their fury.

He now began to show his mettle as a shrewd, ruthless and strategically minded individual: Hitler the politician quickly grasped the popular appeal of blaming the Jews for Versailles. He reprised the memories of Vienna, most ominously the 'racial' basis for Pan-German supremacy and the lesson of Schönerer's fall: never confuse your followers by dividing your enemies; find a single enemy against whom to rally the masses and focus their ferocity.

So far, Hitler's speeches had been windy rants about German greatness, leavened with hatred of Jews and communists, which appealed to his audiences of soldiers and workers. He had not yet articulated or committed to paper a political programme of violent anti-Semitism.

His fury at Versailles, however, was unextinguishable. Nothing would stand between Hitler and those he held responsible. His first written anti-Semitic statement appeared on 16 September 1919, in his long reply to a soldier, Adolf Gemlich, who had written to ask whether the Jews posed a national threat and, if so, what was to be done with them. Hitler's letter may be read as a kind of psychological pit stop en route to the full-blown expression of his racial creed: it was '*the key document*' in his post-war political life, notes Ullrich.[14] It also marked the point at which he distinguished 'emotional' from 'rational' anti-Semitism, and cast 'the Jews' as complicit in a plan to destroy Germany.

If the letter sounds 'mild' to us, given what was to come, it was in fact Hitler's first written condemnation of *anyone* who shared the Jewish faith, or 'race', as he insisted on calling a religion with ethnic roots as diverse as Sephardi and Ashkenazi, Mizrahi and Ethiopian. Other inconvenient facts had no traction on his mind, such as the fact that the Jews amounted to less than 1 per cent of the German population; that most Jews were neither rich nor powerful nor involved in politics; and that Jewish Germans had fought in the war in proportion to their numbers. No doubt the Jews were, in general, better educated and more prosperous than the average, but, if nothing else, that made them higher per capita contributors to the German exchequer – a benefit, not a hindrance, to society.

'Dear Herr Gemlich,' Hitler wrote:

The danger posed by Jewry for our people today finds expression in the undeniable aversion of wide sections of our people. The cause of this aversion is not to be found in a clear recognition of the consciously or unconsciously systematic and pernicious effect of the Jews as a totality upon our nation. Rather, it arises mostly from personal contact and from the personal impression which the individual Jew leaves – almost always an unfavorable one. For this reason, antisemitism is too easily characterized as a mere emotional phenomenon. And yet this is incorrect. Antisemitism as a political movement may not and cannot be defined by emotional impulses, but by recognition of the facts. The facts are these: First, Jewry is absolutely a race and not a religious association . . . There is scarcely a race whose members belong exclusively to just one definite religion.

Through thousands of years of the closest kind of inbreeding, Jews in general have maintained their race and their peculiarities far more distinctly than many of the peoples among whom they have lived. And thus comes the fact that there lives amongst us a non-German, alien race which neither wishes nor is able to sacrifice its racial character or to deny its feeling, thinking, and striving.

Nevertheless, it possesses all the political rights we do. If the ethos of the Jews is revealed in the purely material realm, it is even clearer in their thinking and striving. Their dance around the golden calf is becoming a merciless struggle for all those possessions we prize most highly on earth.

The value of the individual is no longer decided by his character or by the significance of his achievements for the totality but exclusively by the size of his fortune, by his money. The loftiness of a nation is no longer to be measured by the sum of its moral and spiritual powers, but rather by the wealth of its material possessions.

This thinking and striving after money and power, and the feelings that go along with it, serve the purposes of the Jew who is unscrupulous in the choice of methods and pitiless in their employment. In autocratically ruled states he whines for the favour of 'His Majesty' and misuses it like a leech fastened upon the nations . . .

He destroys the character of princes with byzantine flattery, national pride (the strength of a people), with ridicule and shameless breeding to depravity . . .

His power is the power of money, which multiplies in his hands effortlessly and endlessly through interest, and which forces peoples under the most dangerous of yokes. Its golden glitter, so attractive in the beginning, conceals the ultimately tragic consequences. Everything men strive after as a higher goal, be it religion, socialism, democracy, is to the Jew only means to an end, the way to satisfy his lust for gold and domination . . .

In his effects and consequences he is like a racial tuberculosis of the nations.

The deduction from all this is the following: an antisemitism based on purely emotional grounds will find its ultimate expression in the form of the pogrom. An antisemitism based on reason, however, must lead to systematic legal combatting and elimination of the privileges of the Jews, that which distinguishes the Jews from the other aliens who live among us (an Aliens Law). The ultimate objective [of such legislation] must, however, be the irrevocable removal of the Jews in general . . .

For both these ends a government of national strength, not of national weakness, is necessary . . .

Respectfully,

Adolf Hitler[15]

*

At this point a dour machine-fitter and locksmith called Anton Drexler and a flamboyant society journalist, poet and playwright called Dietrich Eckart entered the stage, and would play vital roles in accelerating Hitler's career.

On 5 January 1919, along with Gottfried Feder and the sports journalist Karl Harrer, the two men had founded a small political party called the Deutsche Arbeiterpartei (DAP, or German Workers' Party). It grew out of the *Alldeutscher Verband* (Pan-German League), which had flourished in the war years and was run rather like a masonic club. The DAP members included a few Bavarian notables and the students Hans Franck and Alfred Rosenberg, both of whom would become prominent Nazis.

Hitler first attended a meeting of this party as an observer (some have miscast his role as 'spy') on 12 September 1919, at the behest of Mayr and the Lechfeld commando unit. At the time the DAP was little more than a Munich drinking club of tradesmen, publishers, students and small-business owners. Yet their political beliefs had two distinctive features: a stringent attachment to the white supremacist

Thule Society (a sort of extreme right, anti-Semitic Rotary Club, which used the sign of the swastika); and a devotion to the ideal of 'national socialism' – championing the working man in the name of Germany.

In the gloomy Sterneckerbräu tavern, later enshrined as a Nazi Party birthplace, Hitler encountered forty-one working men loosely engaged in talk of building a national workers' party loyal to the Fatherland. Their subject: 'How and by what means can we get rid of capitalism?' Near the end of the discussion, Hitler couldn't resist expounding his own, more extreme vision of Germany's political future, provoking Drexler, the party chairman, reportedly to say: 'That one's got quite a mouth on him! We could use that!'[16] At which point, Drexler shoved into Hitler's hands a pamphlet he had written entitled 'My Political Awakening'.

Drexler's 'awakening' cohered with Hitler's own: what Germany needed was a political movement that welded nationalism and socialism – a *German* workers' movement, utterly wedded to the Fatherland, not to Marxism or the siren song of Bolshevism that had destroyed the Bavarian soviet. Hitler was seized at once by the magnetism of the idea: a workers' uprising in the name of Deutschland!

There was nothing new in this: a left-wing pastor, Friedrich Naumann, had set up a similar movement in the 1890s, called the National-Social Association, dedicated to luring workers away from the class war and instilling in them a belief in the German state. It failed, in the early 1900s, at a time when extreme social division made the workers more loyal to class than state.

Yet a very different mood had seized the post-war world, and Drexler's political theories appealed more to the lower-middle classes – the *völkisch* (populist) movement of tradesmen, artisans, ex-soldiers, farmers and clerks, who had lost most in the war and economic crisis – than to the traditional working class.

Many far-right German political organizations, chiefly the Pan-German League, the Thule Society and war veterans' associations, similarly saw the saviour of Germany in the mass power of the *Volk* (people), many of whom were hankering to reassert their economic influence. The German Socialist Party (Deutschsozialistische Partei, or DSP) shared many elements of the same platform – the hatred of 'Jewish' capitalism and the Versailles Treaty – and would later attempt and fail to merge with the Nazi Party.

A few days later, Hitler accepted an invitation to join the DAP, as Member 55 – not Member 7 as he later claimed (in fact he was registered as the 555th member, as the numbering began at 501 to disguise the party's small size) – and agreed to attend a party committee meeting a week later in a tavern in Herrnstrasse. This failed to impress him: the DAP was bereft of organization, slogans, pamphlets, membership cards. It was clubby small-mindedness, in Hitler's view, a mere display of faith and goodwill without any inner order or plan.

While the pathos of this political embryo repelled the thirty-year-old Hitler, its Pan-German ideas attracted him. He applauded the ideal of a 'national socialist' party, which answered his deepest longings for a movement that ran roughshod over the Marxists while elevating the German people. Moreover, the DAP's rudimentary structure offered Hitler a blank slate on which to carve his own programme. 'Never could he,' wrote the American historian Ronald Phelps, 'with his "lack of schooling", have gone to one of the larger parties to face the condescension of their educated leaders and the impossible task of altering their ideas, but in the DAP, "this ridiculous little creation", he could change things and could shine among less than equals.'[17]

Most of all, the DAP offered the structure through which he might express his political fury, chiefly his longing to punish the 'November Criminals' who had surrendered Germany. The party's members shared his burning hatred for these 'internal' enemies, Marxists and Jews. And the party endowed his beliefs with the stamp of officialdom, the imprimatur of authority, to which Germans in need of a leader would soon readily respond.

In the DAP, Hitler found himself a new family, another home, a political society that enabled him to draw together the reins of revenge against his enemies, real and imagined: those who had rejected or impoverished him, surrendered Germany to foreign powers, corroded the purity of the German race (Jews and non-Germans) and signed the Treaty of Versailles.

The DAP leaders immediately welcomed Hitler's ideas and recognized his propaganda skills, and within a couple of weeks of joining the party he was invited on to its executive committee. Hitler moved quickly to reshape the party. An office and a typewriter were set up in the Sterneckerbräu; flyers and pamphlets poured off the production line; volunteers plastered the city in the new ideas. Membership rapidly rose, as did Hitler's reputation. He quickly made himself indispensable, as an organizer and speaker.

On 16 October 1919 the new man in the German Workers' Party took the stage before 111 people in Munich's Hofbräukeller beer hall. Hitler intended to use his first major political speech as a platform for revenge. He didn't disappoint his disciples, flogging the 'November Criminals' with the intensity of a personal crusade. 'For thirty minutes,' according to his biographer Joachim Fest's vivid description, 'in an ever more furious stream of verbiage, he poured out the hatreds that ever since his days in the home for men had been stored up within him or discharged only in fruitless monologues. As if bursting through the silence and human barriers of many years, the sentences, the delusions, the accusations came tumbling out.'[18]

By the end of the speech, Hitler had not only entrenched himself as the front man of the DAP; he had unleashed a new political force. The people in the room 'were electrified', he later boasted: 'I could speak!'[19]

The party agreed. Drexler and Eckart saw in this fiery rabble-rouser a political weapon of unusual emotional power. Hitler should be unleashed on the city. His singular message – denouncing Versailles, avenging German honour and attacking international capital, the Jews, the communists, etc. – exploded on to a world parched of hope and thirsty for vengeance.

Max Amann, the Nazi Party's future publishing magnate, would later comment in amazement at the transformation in Hitler when he fronted a crowd: 'There was an unfamiliar fire burning in him . . . He yelled and indulged in histrionics . . . He was drenched in sweat, completely wet, it was unbelievable.'[20] Hitler honed his scripts and delivery. There was nothing extempore about his speeches: they were all carefully rehearsed. To see him at the podium, pounding his fists, ranting and fuming; to feel the seductive power of this consummate populist was to engender in his audiences a kind of epiphany, awakening them to a new source of hope and power – a new Germany, a mighty Reich, a proud Fatherland. Even the most resistant sceptic fell prey to the allure of his self-belief: here was a man who could express the mood of a nation in the grip of a hitherto inarticulable fury.

During his second public speech, on 13 November 1919, at the Eberlbräu beer hall, Hitler singled out for special disgust the Treaty of Versailles and the man who had signed the Armistice on 11 November 1918, Reich finance minister Matthias Erzberger. Erzberger should be sacked, Hitler shouted, delighting the crowd, several of whom demanded the minister's assassination (within two years Erzberger would be forced from office and murdered).

At the same time, Hitler began to focus the blame for Germany's humiliation on a singular enemy. In a speech on 10 December he elevated the Jews to public enemy number one in his pantheon of villains. The Jews were dividing Germany and profiting from civil war, he insisted, declaring 'Germany for the Germans!' And on 16 January 1920 he called for an end to Jewish immigration, and the closing of Germany's borders to all unGerman elements.

Crowds began to pack into the beer halls to hear this strange, defiant young man, so unpromising in appearance, many agreed, until he stood on the podium – and opened his mouth. Many came out of curiosity, having heard stories of an eccentric ex-soldier turned politician. As many would leave, enthralled, spellbound and signed up to the cause.

Hitler's speeches did not persuade everyone. They followed the same, simple format, of head-pounding repetition. As he himself later admitted, he would ram home a single idea into the brains of his audience until even the thickest member understood him. His bombastic delivery and barking voice could not hide a want of substance, of emotional truth. The themes that bound his speeches together were hatred and defiance, which perhaps explains why he was loath to speak to small groups, or family gatherings, about sensitive or personal subjects. He routinely turned down invitations to address weddings and funerals. 'I must have a crowd when I speak,' he explained, when rejecting a request to speak at a small wedding party. 'In a small intimate circle I never know what to say.'[21]

Professor Daniel Binchy, who would become Irish Minister to Germany from 1929 to 1932, witnessed Hitler speak at Munich's largest beer hall, the Bürgerbräukeller, in 1921. The leader of 'a new freak party' would be speaking, a friend of Binchy's had warned.

'The hall was not quite full,' Binchy recalled, 'the audience seemed to be drawn from the poorest of the poor, the "down-and-outs" of the city . . .' He first set eyes on Hitler as the latter sat waiting his turn to speak. 'I remember wondering idly if it were possible to find a more common-place looking man,' Binchy wrote at the time:

> His countenance was opaque, his complexion pasty, his hair plastered down with some glistening unguent and – as if to accentuate the impression of insignificance – he wore a carefully docked 'toothbrush' moustache. I felt willing to bet that in private life he was a plumber: a whispered query to my friend brought the information that he was a housepainter.
>
> He rose to speak and after a few minutes I had forgotten all about his insignificant exterior. Here was a born natural orator. He began slowly, almost hesitatingly . . . Then all at once he seemed to take fire. His voice rose over falterings, his eyes blazed with conviction, his whole body became an instrument of rude eloquence. As his exaltation increased, his voice rose almost to a scream, his gesticulation became a wild pantomime, and I noticed traces of foam at the corners of his mouth . . . [T]he same phrases kept recurring all through his address

like motifs in a symphony: the Marxist traitors, the criminals who caused the Revolution, the German army which was stabbed in the back, and – most insistent of all – the Jews.[22]

Years later, Binchy heard Hitler deliver a near-replica of the address, and realized that the Führer simply recycled his speeches throughout his career. While his delivery had improved (Hitler practised his gestures in front of a mirror) and his words were tailored to his audience, he always said much the same thing.

Hitler possessed a rare ability to channel hatred and violence into a programme of political action. Like all great political salesman, he appealed to the heart, not the mind – the dark heart of Germany as the 'victim'. It little mattered what he actually said; what mattered was the way he said it. He had mastered the art of delivery, to the point that he was more an actor, an impresario, than a political leader. He knew exactly what the masses wanted to hear, and how to stir them up with violent slogans and images of vast conspiracies.

Yet none of Hitler's speeches conveyed any quotable phrases, great insights or witticisms. If they sometimes provoked laughter, the joke was always at the expense of an easy target, a punchline against Jews or foreigners or others who were unable to respond or protest. '[H]e never succeeded,' observed the historian Percy Schramm, 'as Bismarck, on the basis of his literary culture, was often able to do – in fashioning an enduring phrase or a memorable epigram.'[23]

The newspaper *Völkischer Beobachter*, which the Nazi Party acquired in 1920, published the scripts of Hitler's speeches a few days after he delivered them. To read his words on the unforgiving page is to encounter a puffed-up, paranoid mind, curiously childlike, yet so bloated with self-importance and delusions of grandeur that it was little wonder many people – including most European governments – failed to take him seriously.

The issue of 22 April 1922, for example, published a speech Hitler had given ten days earlier entitled 'The Jew'. 'The Jew,' Hitler told his audience, who responded with laughter:

is slowly bloating up, and if you do not believe this, I beg you to go and look in our health resorts. There you will find two kinds of people: the German, who goes there to catch a breath of fresh air . . . and the Jew, who goes there to get rid of his fat . . . If you go out into our mountains, whom do you find in new yellow boots, with beautiful knapsacks . . . ? The Jews go up to the hotel, generally as far as the train goes, and where the train stops there they also stop. They sit around within a kilometre's distance of the hotel, like blowflies around a cadaver.[24]

The speech then moved on to the more serious matter of the similarities between Hitler and Jesus Christ, in which Hitler portrayed himself as the avenger of Christianity against 'the userers, the vipers and cheats' whom Christ had driven from the temple: 'I recognise with deep emotion, Christ's tremendous fight for this world against the Jewish poison,' he continued:

As [a] man, it is my duty to see to it that humanity will not suffer the same catastrophic collapse as did an old civilisation about 2,000 years ago . . . Two thousand years ago a man was likewise denounced by this particular race . . . That man was dragged into court and they told him: He is arousing the people! So he also was 'agitating'! And against whom? Against 'God', they cried. Yes indeed, he was agitating against the 'god' of the Jews, for that 'god' is money.[25]

His audiences revelled in the comparison: here was a leader prepared to name those responsible for their humiliation, their joblessness and their financial loss. Here was a messiah-like figure, willing to banish the Jews from the Lutheran temple. To a country on its knees, this strangely charismatic speaker offered words that seemed to validate the nation's sacrifice and war record when nobody else would.

It mattered little to Hitler if his enemies – few of whom dared brave the beer halls where he spoke – opposed or mocked him, so long as they never forgot him. Pounded by war and economic failure, Bavarian society swiftly descended to Hitler's level: financial destitution reduced thousands of otherwise sensible people to endorse a man and a programme they would have scorned or laughed off in peaceful and prosperous times. It was a measure of the depths of German despair, rather than any of Hitler's inherent qualities, that he managed to persuade so many.

CHAPTER SIXTEEN

'The movement was on the march'

The path to power unfurling in Hitler's mind at this time involved the seizure and control of the state through brute force and relentless propaganda. He would mould the German nation in his image, impelled by his childhood dreams, his thirst to avenge German military honour and the imperative to 'cleanse' the German race of impure racial elements. With this goal, he focused all his efforts on transforming the DAP into a new party of 'national socialists', to which end they adopted a new name, the Nationalsozialistische Deutsche Arbeiterpartei (NSDAP), on 24 February 1920, under Hitler's pressure. The diminutive 'Nazi', first used derogatorily by their political enemies, became a catchword in Munich's beer halls in the early 1920s.

The party saw itself as the hammer, and the German people the anvil, of a new political forge. And no other member matched the agility and verve with which Hitler saw and exploited opportunities to seize and drive the agenda, from transforming the party aesthetic – vitally important to the artist, who took a close interest in the style of the swastika and uniforms – to cementing the party's '25-point Programme' (see page 178).

Benito Mussolini, leader of Italy's fascist movement, had been the first to exploit the political appeal of a 'national workers' party that welded patriotism with socialism (Tito and Ho Chi Minh would try variants, in Yugoslavia and Vietnam). Under Hitler, however, 'national socialism' would be a different beast, far exceeding the boundaries of the 'nation' and the traditional definition of 'socialism'.

From the outset, Hitler saw the absolute need to differentiate German National Socialism from the Leninist and social democratic breeds he so loathed. The idea of loyalty to class over country was repugnant to him, reawakening the disgust he claimed he had felt for union-ized labour during a brief stint as a construction worker in Vienna. No political system was more abhorrent to him than the Bolsheviks' proletarian paradise then being violently imposed upon Russia (and which would become the Union of Soviet Socialist Republics, the USSR, in December 1922). That explains why Hitler focused his wrath not only on the Jews but also on Bavaria's local communists, whose short-lived soviet, or workers' council, and brief takeover of the state had raised the horrifying spectre of a Russian invasion of Germany.

'The fate of Russia would be ours!' he warned repeatedly in 1919–20. Lenin's Bolsheviks had killed more than 30 million people, he exagger-ated grossly, 'partly on the scaffold, partly by machine guns . . . partly in veritable slaughterhouses, partly, millions upon millions, by hunger; and we all know that this wave of hunger . . . this scourge is approach-ing, that it is also coming upon Germany.'[1] In truth, about 3 million would die under Lenin, chiefly in the civil wars between the Red and White Armies.

Hitler's political purpose was clear: to 'annihilate and exterminate' the Marxist world view, which he would achieve through an 'incomparable, brilliantly orchestrated propaganda and information organization' in tandem with 'the most ruthless force and brutal resolution, prepared to oppose all terrorism on the part of the Marxists with tenfold greater terrorism.'[2] His cheering admirers saw nothing amiss in Hitler calling on Germany to inflict massive violence on their enemies and to use the state as a lawless vehicle for oppression.

Indeed, as well as hatred of the Jews, Marxists and 'November Criminals', Hitler's early speeches contained three related themes that should have rung alarm bells in the wider world: the rejection of democracy; the normalization of vigilante justice; and the gradual dismantling of the system of law and order. All three would define the coming Nazi regime.

The evolving party needed structure and direction in readiness for the mass meeting scheduled for 24 February 1920. Sharing the task, Drexler and Hitler laid down twenty-five principles that amalgamated their ideas – the '25-point Programme' (see Appendix, page 251, for full list) – which they planned to present to the meeting. The first four encapsulated the essence of the NSDAP:

1. We demand the unification of all Germans in the Greater Germany on the basis of the people's right to self-determination.
2. We demand equality of rights for the German people in respect to the other nations; abrogation of the peace treaties of Versailles and St. Germain.
3. We demand land and territory (colonies) for the sustenance of our people, and colonization for our surplus population.
4. Only a member of the race can be a citizen. A member of the race can only be one who is of German blood, without consideration of creed. Consequently, no Jew can be a member of the race.

As well as these demands came a few nods at popular policies, aimed at broadening the Nazis' mandate: social welfare for veterans and the elderly; freedom of religion; and higher education for all. The rest was a prescription for tyranny over a nation emptied of Jews and non-Germans, in which the state would enjoy complete control over the people and the press. The final clause called for 'unlimited authority of the central parliament over the whole Reich and its organizations in general'.[3]

On 24 February 1920, in the upper hall of Munich's Hofbräuhaus, Drexler and Hitler unveiled the programme to a crowd of 2,000 of the party faithful. Hitler worked them into a frenzy with his attacks on the Jews and Versailles. 'How shall we protect our fellow human beings against this band of bloodsuckers [the Jews]?' he roared. 'Hang them,' the crowd shouted back.

Hitler would remember that speech in the Hofbräuhaus as one of the high points of his early political career; and the Nazis would later cherish it as a founding moment of the movement. He claimed that he had converted the hall to National Socialism and kindled the fire that would sharpen the 'German sword of vengeance', 'restore freedom to the German Siegfried' and 'bring back life to the German nation . . .' He felt that the 'Goddess of Vengeance was now getting ready to redress the treason of the 9th November, 1918 [the date of the proclamation of the German Republic by Philipp Scheidemann, but Hitler was probably also alluding to the hated Armistice, two days later].' He concluded: 'The hall was emptied. The movement was on the march.'[4]

Opposition taunts of 'Down with Hindenburg, Ludendorff and the German Nationalists!' drowned out part of his speech, according to a cursory report in the next day's newspaper (in fact, the mainstream German press barely reported the event, so little credibility did they accord the new party on the extreme right, whose members they tended to dismiss as upstarts and freaks).[5] But Hitler had achieved what he had set out to do: win notoriety as the most provocative spokesman of the extremist parties in Munich. It all seemed so easy, because his most valuable political asset came naturally to him, as Kershaw observes: '. . . to stoke up the hatred of others by pouring out to them the hatred that was so deeply embedded in himself.'[6]

Around this time, early in 1920, Dietrich Eckart, one of the founder members of the DAP, a heavy-drinking poet and playwright who subscribed to a mystical notion of German supremacy, began to exert a powerful influence over Hitler. Eckart, on first hearing Hitler speak in 1919, was at once drawn to the raw energy of the man's voice and had been one of the first to recognize his potential.

Eckart saw that Hitler's ideas needed a more solid grounding, and his brawling style refashioning to appeal to a wider German audience. He now appointed himself as the Nazis' Pygmalion, carving his protégé into the kind of man who would be presentable to families, wealthy matrons and their daughters. He introduced Hitler to powerful people, showing him off in the city's fashionable salons. Most of all, Eckart helped raise funds for the fledgling Nazi Party.

His most important influence on Hitler was to cement in the latter's mind a connection between Marxism and Judaism. Eckart achieved this by drawing on the 'intellectual' racism of Alfred Rosenberg, an émigré from Estonia who had supported the counter-revolutionaries against the Bolsheviks in Russia, and a committed anti-Semite, who met Hitler around this time and was soon to become the Nazi Party's chief ideological thinker.

Hitherto none-too-subtle code words for each other, 'Marxism' and 'Judaism' were now routinely used synonymously, conflating in one vast conspiracy the principal enemy of the German state: a Jewish Bolshevik. According to this 'analysis', Jews were communists and communists were Jews (when they weren't being capitalists). Hitler had often made the connection; now he shared Eckart's and Rosenberg's pseudo-scientific certainty.

Eckart also offered Hitler an instruction in 'racial theory'. Spurring him on was the publication, for the first time in Germany, of *The Protocols of the Elders of Zion*, a bogus document purporting to reveal the existence of a Jewish plot to foment war and revolution and to conquer the world. It had first appeared in Russia in 1903 and circulated throughout many other countries in the early part of the twentieth century; Rosenberg too had been profoundly influenced by it. Its sensational appearance in Germany in 1919 could not have come at a worse time for the Jewish people. The NSDAP not only believed it, they also commandeered it as part of their ideological arsenal. Eckart frequently invoked *The Protocols* in declaring an apocalyptic war on the Jews. 'When light clashes with darkness,' he wrote, 'there is no coming to terms! Indeed, there is only struggle for life and death, truth and lies, Christ and Antichrist.' In Eckart's mind the First World War had not ended; it continued, as a holy crusade against the perpetrators of Germany's humiliation.[7]

Eckart's lurid biblical imagery portrayed Germany as a nation more sinned against than sinning, martyred by a Jewish cabal who would be severely punished: 'These Pharisees . . . whine about their wretched nest eggs! The liberation of humanity from the curse of gold stands before the door! It's not simply a question of our collapse – it's a question of our Golgotha!'[8]

Hitler drained the cup of Eckart, Rosenberg, Feder and other anti-Semitic 'evangelists' in damning the Jews as the common element that bound Germany's enemies together. The Jews were not only active leaders on the left; they were the dominant force on the capitalist right. They were damned whatever they were, or wherever they happened to be. In Hitler's mind, Marxism, capitalism and Judaism now coalesced as a monolithic movement, menacing the national polity and threatening to infect and destroy the Germanic race itself.

Hitler later claimed that he 'became an out-and-out anti-Semite' at this time.[9] Vienna, Pasewalk and Versailles, of course, had elicited similar 'life-changing' statements. In truth, as we've seen, his 'conversion' resulted from cumulative memories and experiences, ambition, hatred and vengeance, shaped by Mayr, Drexler, Eckart, Rosenberg and others, and, most acutely, his long memory of the war.

In the next two years, Hitler's emerging, savage anti-Semitism and raw political ambitions would serve and mutually reinforce a common goal: the seizure of power. With his oratorical skills and organizational flair, he was seen in the party as the coming man, an indispensable political asset. The rank and file increasingly embraced him as their mystical leader, the prophet of the movement; a few of the better-read Nazis saw him as their long-awaited *Übermensch*, the Nietzschean superman.

Standing in a crowded beer hall one night in the summer of 1920 was a tall, striking young man with the swagger of a war hero and an expression of delighted recognition on his face. This was Rudolf Hess, a twice-wounded former soldier who, like Hitler, had served in a Bavarian division during the war. He had taken part in the First Battle of Ypres, Verdun and the Somme, and then trained as a fighter pilot. Like Hitler, he was twice-decorated, receiving the Iron Cross (Second Class) and the Bavarian Military Medal for bravery.

That night Hess listened, transfixed, as his fellow war veteran addressed the Sterneckerbräu: 'Hitler stood in the tobacco haze in a grey soldier's uniform, crying out that the day would come "when the banner of our movement shall wave over the Reichstag in Berlin, over the Berlin Palace, indeed, over every German home".'[10]

Hess fell swiftly into a state of awed devotion. He shared Hitler's belief in the 'stab in the back'; he blamed the Jews and Marxists for Germany's defeat; he decried Germany's humiliation at Versailles. Yet nobody had rolled them all together, into one grand political case for German defiance, like Hitler was doing. Here was the man who could save Germany, Hess thought. He joined the NSDAP in July 1920, as Number 16.

In Hess, Hitler found a trusted friend, fundraiser and collaborator. Both had survived the near-annihilation of their regiments, in 1914 and 1916, and both 'felt themselves entitled to speak of destiny's special protection'.[11] They became inseparable companions on the long march to power.

Hess and Hitler, according to an incisive essay by Konrad Heiden, became 'intellectually conjoined to a degree that is possible only in abnormal personalities. Indeed, they had grown into one person-ality consisting of two men.'[12] Hess's mind was, in a sense, 'grafted upon Hitler'.[13] Hess even acted as Hitler's stand-in bodyguard, on 4 November 1921, injuring himself while protecting Hitler from a bomb that exploded in the Hofbräuhaus.

Throughout the 1920s their relationship deepened into one of mutual 'admiration and love', in which Hess became Hitler's amanuen-sis and personal secretary, the man to whom the Führer would dictate *Mein Kampf*.[14] In the years to come, Hess would rise on the wave of Hitler mania, eventually rewarded for his loyalty with the post of Deputy Führer.

*

For the time being, Hitler was still little more than a beer-hall rabble-rouser and 'drummer boy' for the movement, as he himself would say. His methods were those of the political bully and grassroots thug. His comrades made no secret of the party's brutal origins. Like most of the early Nazi members, Hitler enjoyed a good beer-hall brawl. And while he rarely participated directly, he relished ordering the party's militia, the *Sturmabteilung* (SA) – literally, Storm Detachment or storm troop (the name derived from small, lightning attack units in the First World War) – to smash up his political enemies: the flying steins (beer mugs), the smashed jaws, the blood on the floorboards – all announced the arrival of Hitler and his movement.

The SA, known as the Brownshirts on account of their light khaki uniforms, acted as Hitler's personal police force and were initially deployed to control crowds and beat up protestors. They swiftly and violently made their presence felt in the beer halls and at party rallies, and on the streets. Gangs of SA prowled the city, threatening anyone who struck them as Jewish or homosexual or somehow not acceptable to the Nazis. They rapidly became one of the best-organized, largest and most brutal examples of an assortment of private militias spurred into being by their leaders' defiance of the Versailles Treaty, which had banned paramilitary armies. Any budding Führer worthy of respect would boast a detachment of 'bodyguards', or whatever euphemism he chose to describe his personal thugs.

Such was Hitler's popularity, the Brownshirts attracted waves of loyal adherents and rapidly grew into a private army that would play a powerful role in his rise to power in the 1920s and 1930s. Hermann Göring, a once-dashing former air ace, who joined the Nazi Party in 1922 and was to become one of Hitler's closest henchmen, was one of the earliest and longest-standing SA commanders, on whom Hitler lavished praise: 'I made him the head of my SA. He is the only one of its heads that ran the SA properly. I gave him a dishevelled rabble. In a very short time he had organised a division of 11,000 men.'[15]

Another notorious future Brownshirt commander was Ernst Röhm, an early party member, a rotund 'hard man' and (later) open homosexual. He was first given command of the Brownshirts in 1924, after the Munich Putsch (see Chapter 18), but his ideas failed to impress and he resigned. Recalled from a foreign posting in 1931, Röhm was again given command of the SA, and this time he built it into a rival power base that proved to be his undoing. He would be executed on 1 July 1934, during the 'Night of the Long Knives', on charges of treason.

With such men in command of his protection, Hitler was free to roam the city and speak wherever he chose. His popularity rose in parallel with his fame as a war hero and far-right revolutionary. Word of his charisma and the passionate reaction to his speeches was drawing hundreds to the beer halls to hear him. By late 1920, the NSDAP had enlisted more than 3,000 members. Hundreds were applying daily. Every time Hitler spoke, more signed on to the Nazi programme. The party had become the 'recognised force in the Bavarian ultra-right'.[16] Within a year it would be the leading *völkisch* party,[17] largely due to Hitler's skill as a propagandist, organizer and orator, fronting audiences that attracted as many as 3,000 people (6,000 heard him speak at Munich's Zirkus Krone on 3 February 1921, his largest rally of the early 1920s).

He had become the party's public face, chief spokesman and, in many eyes, its de facto leader. He put his personal touch on every aspect of the party's operations and propaganda. The Nazi presence began to proliferate throughout Munich, and into Bavarian towns, marked by the visually striking swastika flags and armbands, the stomping groups of Brownshirts and the adoring fans of the 'Hitler cult'.[18] Rudolf Hess, in his new role as Hitler's secretary, wrote of the party's growth that year: 'A terrible day of judgement dawns for the traitors of the nation before, during and after the war . . . Some day it will arise, this Greater Germany that shall embrace all who are of German blood.'[19]

Yet Hitler still had little recognition outside Bavaria. He himself later acknowledged that he was 'nobody' at this point in his career. And he would have stayed that way, as Kershaw persuasively argues, if not for the support of powerful sponsors and the desperate conditions of the post-war Reich.[20] What he needed now was a platform, a power base that would catapult his burgeoning political ambitions on to a larger, national stage – and he needed to exert complete control over his party. But not even Hitler would anticipate the pace of his rise to head a movement that would seriously consider overthrowing the leadership of the German state.

Around mid-1921, Hitler set his mind on taking over the party leadership. It would be a desperate lunge for power, to shore up his rising status in the party and thwart attempts to merge the NSDAP with the German Socialist Party and another *völkisch* movement, the Deutsche Werkgemeinschaft, led by Dr Otto Dickel, a remarkably charismatic speaker (who was even seen as a rival to Hitler) with a mystical faith in the German worker.

To Hitler's mind, the NSDAP's incumbents had exhausted their usefulness. Drexler, the chairman, lacked the energy and vision to fulfil the party's ambitions, yet Hitler had hitherto delayed making a bid for the top job because he lacked the numbers. But now, in early July 1921, soon after his return from a trip to Berlin, he woke up to a threat to what he regarded as 'his' movement. Furious at the talk of mergers, which would have diluted his power, and disdainful of Dickel's *völkisch* idealism, he could wait no longer.

Like any giant political ego that feels itself thwarted, Hitler moved to highlight his importance and indispensability in brazen style. On 11 July 1921, at a meeting of the NSDAP leaders with Dickel and his party to discuss a loose confederation, he threw a tantrum, tore up his membership card and stormed out. It was less a calculated move (as Hitler's later, carefully timed tantrums would be) than the reaction of a cornered bully, shouting and screaming until he got his way. It was a pattern of behaviour that would recur throughout his leadership: he recognized no compromise, no halfway point. He would have all or nothing, and punctuated his demands with angry threats and a refusal to listen to advice or competing interests.

At first, the party's leadership were furious. Hitler's behaviour was unacceptable. Several even accused him of being in the pay of Jews and a supporter of the ousted Austrian emperor. Anonymous pamphlets attacked him as an enemy of the party. But senior Nazis – Eckart, Drexler and Rosenberg – realized that the loss of their finest speaker would be a body blow to the movement. Eckart intervened, and on 13 July Drexler asked Hitler to suggest terms that would persuade him to reverse his decision.

Hitler bided his time. He went ahead with a speech at the Circus Krone, Munich's largest hall, on 20 July, which drew a capacity crowd. It was a resounding success. Then he won an ovation from exultant party stalwarts at a special members' meeting in the Hofbräuhaus on the 29th. Firmly in charge of the agenda, Hitler let Rudolf Hess do the rest. His loyal number two brought the party leadership to their senses. 'Are you really blind to the fact,' Hess wrote, 'that this man alone possesses the leadership personality capable of carrying out the struggle for Germany?'[21]

Hess's intervention, and the party's anxiety to have Hitler back on board, encouraged him to lay down his terms. He would settle for nothing less than dictatorial control over the party's direction, the first of a string of all-or-nothing gambles he made throughout his political career. If he were to rejoin the NSDAP, he insisted, the party must be led and organized in a way that would make it 'the sharpest weapon in the battle against the Jewish international rulers of our people'.

To this end, he must be elected as first chairman with 'dictatorial powers'.[22] The NSDAP's committee grudgingly agreed. From that moment, Hitler would no longer be the party's 'drummer boy', content to whip up the masses for the satisfaction of an idle leadership. He would be its voice, chief propagandist and dictator.

As chairman, Hitler moved quickly to elevate his own men and remove or relegate the NSDAP's former leaders. Anton Drexler was made the party's honorary life chairman, a sop to his powerlessness. Hitler thus set in motion, as early as mid-1921, a political movement personified by him and answerable to his will, whose primary, stated goals were the rejection of Versailles and the oppression and eventual eradication of the Jewish people from Germany.

He aimed to transform the Nazi movement into a properly structured political party that would command mass appeal.[23] In working to this end, he deployed another face of his many-faceted character: the organizer. He proved himself an exceptional party agitator and a political lightning rod. He reformed the party's internal structure. He banished its democratic ethos and solicited new members who would be loyal to him rather than to the original leadership.

And he met the leaders of Munich society. Eckart continued showing off his protégé to wealthy political donors and local aristocrats. Hitler leapt at the chance to meet his social superiors, and his wealthy donors found it amusing and charming to entertain a street radical, a beer-hall ruffian, and fawned on him as if he were an exotic species. He revelled in charming wealthy old women. His manners were extravagant, bowing and scraping to disguise his social awkwardness, a caricature of a gentleman. His apparent vulnerability lit their maternal affections. Helene Bechstein, of the piano fortune, was not the only rich heiress who declared, 'I wished he'd been my son.' Hitler would return their compliments; in his 1925 Christmas message to Frau Carola Hoffman he wrote 'To my beloved true little mother.'[24] Winifred Wagner, the composer's daughter-in-law, was 'full of reverence' whenever Hitler visited the family in Bayreuth. Such women mothered and fed him, chose his clothes, guided his taste and decorum, as though he were a lost and lonely orphan in search of love (which in a sense, he was). And as he rose to the status of a political celebrity, these impressionable dames found themselves venerating and adoring him. Several dared entertain the thought that young Adolf might be a future husband to their daughters.

Hitler used them as tools for his advancement. He tended to exaggerate his obsequiousness in order to extract the devotion of powerful people who could serve him. The party needed their patronage and their money. And while the Bechsteins, the Hanfstaengls (owners of a fine-arts publishing house) and other wealthy Bavarian families warmed to this shy, suddenly excitable young man, whose 'almost comic servility' amused them,[25] they little realized they were in the play of just one of Hitler's personas, adapted to his audience and purpose.

In the beer halls he played the role of a barking revolutionary; at the lectern, a ranting demagogue; and in the salons of the rich, a schmoozing sycophant. In time, as a famous politician, addressing captains of industry, he would come across as a staunch conservative and economic rationalist. And while he loathed the conventional morality of the Church and the bourgeois hypocrisy behind the notions of 'tolerance' and 'decency', Hitler was adept, when his audience demanded it, at pretending he shared these sentiments.

His personas served several functions: to shield his past, enhance the Hitler 'mythology', and free him to perform as he saw fit, to bully, persuade or charm. Nobody quite penetrated Hitler's many masks, not even his closest companions or the people who worked beside him. Ernst Hanfstaengl and his family were not alone in thinking Hitler a friend, but one who would soon become 'more secretive than friendly'.[26]

CHAPTER SEVENTEEN

'The world of the woman is the man'

Hitler's local success emboldened him to dream beyond Bavaria, to project the NSDAP as a true 'national' party, and to think of himself as a leader of the German state. His icy character thawed a little. He lowered his defensive shield. Secure within the orbit of his personal bodyguards – the *Stosstrupp* – he agreed to be photographed in his habitat for the first time (hitherto, he had threatened or seized the cameras of anyone who dared try to photograph him without permission).

His adoring crowds liked what they saw. Here was their saviour, their battle-hardened war hero who had returned from the trenches to knock Bavaria into shape and avenge Versailles; here their warrior-leader, who proudly flaunted his war record where so many veterans were ashamed or never spoke of theirs.

Hitler turned thirty-two in 1921, yet he seemed possessed of the spirit of an adolescent. He swaggered around Munich in his tight-fitting suits, a revolver on his hip and a whip in his hand. He looked more like a gang leader, a streetwise youth, than an aspiring politician. His snappy gait and menacing countenance suggested a gangster, not a serious contender for high office. He even took his gun to dinner parties.

As his fame grew, he became more self-conscious of the way he dressed and tended to adapt his uniform to his audience. Around town he wore plain dark suits, unremarkable ties and perhaps a trench coat or greatcoat, depending on the season. At beer-hall rallies he often wore a military uniform and sometimes his Iron Cross. In the salons of his wealthy donors, he occasionally put on lederhosen and a feathered cap, though his knobbly white knees did not encourage him to make a habit of wearing the Bavarian leather breeches.

Even at this early stage of his political career, in appearance, habits, views and personality Hitler was already stamped with the hallmarks that he would exhibit as Führer of Germany. His complexion was pale and 'almost girl-like', as the German historian Percy Ernst Schramm – who, as the official diarist of the Wehrmacht during the Second World War, observed Hitler at close range – would note:

His mouth was relatively small, his chin not well developed. His lips were thin and pinched. He had a high forehead but it did not stand out because it was covered by his forelock. He had few eyelashes on his lids, but his eyebrows were thick, and above them slight bulges appeared in his forehead . . . The man's head seemed to dominate his entire body; torso, arms, legs – all seemed to hang down from it.[1]

This unflattering portrait jarred with the image Hitler intended to convey, of the solitary predator, the 'lone wolf' and ruthless operator, orchestrating the events that bore his party's name.

It was around this time that his little toothbrush moustache made its permanent and most fastidious appearance. Bavarians nicknamed it a *Rotzbremse*, or 'snot brake'; in Britain and America it was chiefly associated with the comedian Charlie Chaplin. Though fairly common in Germany in the years after the war, Hitler's facial hair was not fashionable and repelled his comrades. When Ernst Hanfstaengl advised him to shave it off, Hitler replied, 'If it is not the fashion now, it will be later because I wear it.'[2] The toothbrush moustache never caught on, despite Hitler's confidence. Its true purpose, in his case, was to disguise his flaring nostrils, which he thought unappealing.[3]

In his personal habits, young Hitler was a model of 'normality'.

He lived modestly and had bland tastes. Haunted by the memory of dirt and squalor in his days on the streets, he bathed regularly and cared meticulously for his few remaining teeth. As the historian Roger Moorhouse notes, 'Adolf Hitler had very bad teeth – *catastrophically* bad teeth. It is not clear precisely why – bad genes, bad diet or poor personal hygiene – but some among his entourage would later claim that his halitosis was sometimes so bad that they involuntarily took a step back when talking to him. By the last year of the war, his teeth had deteriorated to such a state that only 5 of his 32 adult teeth were his own.[4] In his domestic regime, Hitler was self-disciplined and organized, shunning alcohol and red meat, though he was yet to become a fully fledged vegetarian. He loved being near animals, pretty women and children.

A marked trait of Hitler's personality was his childish sensitivity. He took any slight personally, reacting with extreme aggression. He never tamed his hypersensitivity to personal criticism or controlled his rages, as Kershaw observes. His resort to 'extraordinary outbursts of uncontrolled temper' and his 'extreme aversion to any institutional anchoring' would manifest themselves to the end of his days.[5] He personalized every enemy, as Alan Bullock has observed: not only the Jews, but the 'November Criminals', modern artists, Slavs . . . all were somehow acting against *him*, debasing his vision of an Aryan world.[6] He used anger and garrulity to political advantage, to bully, obfuscate or disorientate his opponents.

Hitler continued to 'educate' himself, as he had done in Vienna, by selecting information and 'ideas' that reinforced his 'world view'. 'Hitler's thought,' Schramm observed, 'is rather to be understood as a huge collection of the most diverse origins, upon which he sought to impose his own order and logic.'[7] He seized on whatever information helped to enhance his image and rise to power, regardless of whether it was true or factually sound. He swallowed whole Hanns Hörbiger's absurd World Ice Theory (which promoted the idea that ice was the basic structure of the cosmos and underpinned the whole development of the universe); and, as we have seen, appropriated the essence of Social Darwinism as the basis for his ideas on 'race'. He had little interest in literature, read neither contemporary fiction nor the classics. Even his love of opera waned as his authoritarian impulses took control.

As such, his mind resembled a junk yard of ideological clutter, packed with conspiracy theories, pseudo-science, hated enemies and methods of revenge, which he pummelled into place in his speeches. 'Facts' and 'truth' were useful to Hitler only insofar as they fed his propaganda machine. 'Truth' meant what he said it meant. He was the ultimate 'populist' politician, 'the greatest demagogue in history,' concluded Alan Bullock.[8]

Those who sought 'reason' or intellectual consistency in Hitler's words would come away gravely disappointed: he would say and do anything to achieve power, and jettison any doctrine or policy in the pursuit of it. His only consistent position, from 1921 on, was his violent hatred of the Jews. He refused to be impressed by complexity, insisting that the 'human will' could solve any problem, no matter how difficult.[9] He was, as a result, utterly, terrifyingly unpredictable.

Wilful ignorance is no barrier to self-confidence. Flush with the arrogance of a man for whom political power validated any action, however odious or criminal, Hitler barged around party offices, dispatching orders, serving judgements and issuing long sermons on the party's ideological mission and the importance of propaganda. At other times he would do little, whiling away the hours in cafés, listlessly sipping tea and eating sweet cakes.

This was the same pattern of behaviour, of great energy interspersed with inertia and indecision, that he had displayed in Vienna. This time, however, people noticed, people listened. His followers hung on his every word. In the ingratiating company of his Nazi comrades, Hitler's mind hardened; the parade of 'traitors' he sought to punish lengthened. He nursed titanic grudges.

He spent a great deal of time noting down the names of Jewish painters and writers with a view to imposing an absolute ban on 'degenerate' (i.e. Jewish) art and ordering the burning of 'unGerman' books. Disgusted by their 'decadence' – and embittered by his own failure as an artist – Hitler would justify any action that suppressed modern artists on the grounds that the leading lights were Jews. Once in power, he would outlaw 'Jewish' artists and 'Jewish' scientists, and ban their 'decadent' work. Those who failed to escape would be dispatched to death camps.

Hitler's character, too, acquired a range of careful poses, or political personas, which he rehearsed and perfected. He was in this sense a consummate performer, and yet few knew when the 'real' Adolf was performing. Those close to him saw a true and loyal friend, a hard worker, a leader of destiny, who 'could and did command respect', as Schramm later observed.[10] Schramm, who would study him at close quarters, detected an array of guises or 'characters' in Hitler: the brave war veteran of uncommon will and self-discipline; the puritan who neither drank nor smoked, shunned sexual intimacy and stuck to a strict vegetarian diet; the gangster and popular curiosity in the salons of the rich; the tireless party worker and 'loyal comrade'; the prankster who loved to imitate the characters and accents of his enemies; and the brooding ideologue and political revolutionary, always on the edge of a tantrum.

Yet Schramm saw another face to Hitler that eluded Bavaria's great and good at the start of the 1920s. Had they been able to see that face, Schramm believed, 'even the most loyal and devoted of them would have turned to stone.'[11] Writing at the time of the Führer's 'Table Talk' discussions, in 1941–2 at the height of the war, Schramm was shocked to discover that Hitler could joke and laugh over lunch and then, in the afternoon, order the mass execution of civilians, contemplate the starvation of Leningrad and set in motion the systematic annihilation of the Jews.

Much of what Schramm saw also applied to Hitler in the 1920s. 'Whenever anyone tries to understand Hitler,' he wrote, 'the final result never adds up correctly. His contact with children and dogs, his joy in flowers and culture, his appreciation of lovely women, his relationship to music were all quite genuine. But no less genuine was the ferocity – morally uninhibited, ruthless, "ice-cold" – with which Hitler annihilated not only real but even potential opponents.'[12] Similarly, Helmuth Greiner, who would later join Hitler's circle of dinner companions, observed, 'I have never heard a word come over his lips, which even suggested he had a warm or compassionate heart.'[13]

Hitler's sexual relations were, for much of his younger life, 'arms-length' or non-eventful, partly because he was afraid of contracting venereal disease and partly because the human body disgusted him. During the war, as we have seen, he shunned sleeping with Frenchwomen as contrary to the honour of a German soldier. He seems to have been a virgin at least until the Armistice. And while he later made 'passionate declarations' to society beauties, he rarely dared touch them beyond a furtive grope or a kiss.

Ernst Hanfstaengl, who observed him closely over fifteen years, described Hitler as 'impotent, the repressed, masturbating type':[14] 'I do not suppose he had orthodox sexual relations with any women.' Hanfstaengl's wife, Helene, agreed: for her, young Hitler inhabited a sexual no-man's-land. That was not unusual at the time for a certain kind of ascetic who dressed up his fear and avoidance of sex as self-discipline and personal strength. Hitler later explained that he refused to marry because he was too busy and would have neglected his wife: 'It is much better to have a lover.'[15]

As for his virility, Hitler had two testicles, according to a report by the family doctor, Eduard Bloch. His penis 'was completely normal', Bloch wrote, dismissing stories that it was outlandishly small or diseased, as his enemies liked to say.[16] Nor had a goat bitten off half of it when he was a boy, as a fellow pupil, Eugen Wasen, later claimed. 'Oh yeah, Adolf!' Wasen told a post-war tribunal. 'He'd made a bet that he could pee into the mouth of a goat . . .' As one German doctor later noted, either the goat had very good aim or Hitler had 'no reflexes'.[17]

There is no evidence that Hitler was homosexual or 'sexually perverted', by the standards of either Weimar Germany or today.

Nothing has appeared to validate claims that, in the late 1920s, he indulged in sado-masochistic sex and 'golden showers' with his beloved half-niece, Angela Raubal, known as Geli, or that he urged her to urinate and defecate on his face. His enemies would circulate many such stories after he came to power. (It is heavily insinuated, however, that he engaged in a sexual relationship with her after she moved into his apartment in Munich, in 1929, as a medical student. When he discovered that she was involved with his then chauffeur, the SA leader Emil Maurice, he terminated the relationship and sacked Maurice. She then became his virtual prisoner. Jealously possessive, Hitler later forbade her to marry another suitor, from Linz – an episode that seems directly linked to her suicide. Her body was found in Hitler's Munich apartment on 19 September 1931, shot through the lung with Hitler's own pistol.[18] She was twenty-three.)[19]

As for his popularity with women, Hitler certainly drew many to his rallies. He was ever-alert to feminine beauty, his well-known roving eye tending to alight on the prettiest girls in the room. As he grew into middle age, his few intimate relationships would be with women. And no doubt many thousands of women persuaded themselves that they adored him, rather as an adolescent loves a pop star. They flocked to hear him speak, lavishing him with praise and soliciting his company at any chance.

The admiration was not mutual. Hitler's actual view of the role of women adhered to the sternest biblical precepts of the nineteenth century. 'The world of the woman is the man,' he would say. 'Only now and then does she think of anything else . . . A man has to be able to stamp his imprint on any woman. As a matter of fact, a wife does not want anything else!'[20] Women were unable to discriminate between reason and emotion, he argued, disqualifying them from politics or any serious occupation. A woman's duty to society, he believed, was to look pretty, preferably blonde, and breed his Aryan race.

Hitler's health has been the subject of endless speculation. As a young man he did not exhibit any obvious mental disturbances or psychological damage (crude though the diagnoses then were). For what it's worth, Hitler's future personal physicians, doctors Theodor Morell and Karl Brandt, thought their patient of perfectly sound mind, displaying not the slightest signs 'of even the beginning of any form of mental illness'.[21] They would say that, of course. And yet, no independent diagnosis of insanity has stuck:[22] Hitler was not schizophrenic, depressed or bipolar.

A fascinating study of Hitler in October 1943 by Dr Henry Murray, a prominent Harvard psychologist, and other experts for the US Office of Strategic Services (OSS – the precursor to the Central Intelligence Agency) draws a compelling portrait of a 'megalomaniac' who worshipped 'brute strength', 'purity of blood' and 'fertility', and felt contempt for 'weakness, indecision, lack of energy, fear of conscience'. However, their summary of Hitler's personality – a concatenation of 'war neurosis', 'hysterical blindness' (his blindness was caused by mustard gas), 'bad conscience', paranoia and sexual masochism – falls short of explaining the Führer-in-full.[23] These traits were common enough, and hardly marked you out as a future tyrant. In fairness, the authors were writing before Germany's surrender, so the full extent of the Nazis' war crimes was not yet known.

If Hitler suffered from 'war neurosis', or what we call post-traumatic stress disorder, as Dr Theo Dorpat also argues, his condition was no different from that of millions of former soldiers who got on with their lives after the war without recourse to acts of violent revenge. If his mind was a textbook case of 'narcissistic personality disorder' or extreme sociopathy, as others have claimed,[24] he was no more or less afflicted than millions of distempered individuals who crowded the post-war cities, many of whom rose to prominence and pursued relatively normal lives.

The definitive inquiry into Hitler's health, *Was Hitler Ill?*, by the distinguished German medical professor Hans-Joachim Neumann and historian Henrik Eberle, published in 2012, set out to establish once and for all whether or not Hitler was mentally or physically unwell, and, if so, whether that might help to explain the Holocaust. They confirmed that, towards the end of his life, Hitler suffered from high blood pressure, irritable bowel syndrome and stomach cramps, as well as the symptoms of Parkinson's disease, which first appeared in 1941 and are thought to have arisen from his contraction of *Encephalitis lethargica* during his service on the Western Front.[25]

In his final years, Hitler's doctor prescribed heavy doses of drugs to relieve stress, skin rash, cramps and 'extreme agitation'. Yet he neither took powerful drugs nor suffered from these conditions as a young man. He was never a drug addict, as suggested in a 'dangerously inaccurate' history of Nazi drug use published in 2016.[26] Nor would he display manic, sociopathic or paranoid disorders, concluded Neumann and Eberle in their exhaustive study: 'Hitler seethed with hatred, but he was always capable of synchronising his desire to exterminate the Jews with public opinion . . . He was well aware of what he was doing at all times during his political career.'[27]

This bears out the verdict of British historian Sir Robert Ensor, writing in his 1939 pamphlet 'Who Hitler Is': 'There are psychologists who consider him a paranoiac. Certainly, when he lets himself go in anger, he raves like a madman. But he does so in order to achieve a desired result, namely terror. The baffling torrents of mere verbiage [have] their calculated utility.'[28]

In sum, Neumann and Eberle found 'no scientific medical proof that Hitler suffered from a mental illness'.[29] Their study demolishes the 'psycho-historical' explanation for the Holocaust – that to commit such a monstrous crime, Hitler must have been insane, drugged or traumatized. 'The answer to the question "was Hitler ill",' they conclude, 'is therefore as follows: the leader of the NSDAP, chancellor of the German Reich and commander-in-chief of the German Wehrmacht, was healthy and accountable.'[30]

Are we to conclude, then, that he was 'normal', a proposition from which conventional morality recoils? Perhaps we should look to Hitler himself for the clearest guide to his character. Obviously he saw himself as exceptional, in many ways. In the early 1920s he described himself as 'ice-cold', with a will of iron. What this meant was he had overcome 'weakness', suppressed within himself any trace of the voice of conscience or compassion, of basic human decency. He was desperate for the world to take him seriously (of European politicians, only Churchill would). His plans for vengeance against the 'November Criminals' were deadly earnest. When he spoke of massive retaliation against the Jews, the Marxists, or anyone who opposed him, he meant it. He planned to act on his threats. He regarded his coming programme as morally and politically sound, a true reflection of the will of the people.

And as he grew into the role of political leader and ideological crusader, his character became more rigid, his ego more imperious. The impact of his personality could quite overwhelm those who had not been exposed to it, as Schramm saw: 'Such could be its strength that it sometimes seemed a kind of psychological force radiating from him like a magnetic field.'[31] Others, however, experienced the opposite effect: one colonel, for example, felt 'a steadily rising aversion' to the very presence of Hitler. Such was his fabled 'sixth sense' – to detect who was with him or against him – Hitler felt this at once and had the colonel removed.[32]

Many were sacked for displaying the slightest whiff of disagreement; actual dissent led to their removal, imprisonment and probable death. Hitler demanded absolute loyalty. He interpreted criticism as insubordination and disobedience as treachery. He also had a particular and inveterate distrust of 'experts', whom he dismissed or refused to consult. He always knew better, a trait that stayed with him until the end. General Ludwig Beck, chief of the German General Staff for much of the 1930s, claimed that he never once had the chance properly to advise Hitler on defence.

He lived in a realm of violent threats and false promises. Ensor observed:

[H]is tactics have always conformed to a few plain gangster precepts. Remember the value of threats, but remember that it is conditional upon their always being executed. When you are planning to attack a man, take away his character first; overwhelm him with a 'drum-fire of lies and calumnies'; then, when even his friends are ready to jettison him, strike him down. If you want to gain time or ground, promise the moon; only, so use what is gained that you never need redeem your promises.[33]

Hitler's 'promises of the moon' – an expanded Reich, a society rid of Jews and other undesirables, the abrogation of Versailles – seemed realizable in a society so desperate that it was willing to suspend disbelief in the agent of their delivery. His political magic flourished in a world as debased and fractured as his own mind.

The source of his future power was already plain to him in his early days as leader of the NSDAP. 'For to be a leader means to be able to move the masses,' he wrote.[34] And as he entered 1922 he planned to build his influence and popularity beyond his Bavarian base. His personal militia, the Brownshirts, were rapidly expanding into the state regions. Most of all, his vision of a Greater Germany ruled by a 'Master Race', a phrase that started to infuse his speeches, intoxicated his followers. Chief among them at this point were his personal myth-maker and ghost-writer Rudolf Hess; his media maestro Max Amann; his ideological guru Alfred Rosenberg; his private militia commander Ernst Röhm; and his favourite war hero and flying ace Hermann Göring.

In early 1922 Hitler won a new and devoted acolyte, the ferocious anti-Semite and publisher of violent pornography Julius Streicher, an all-round abomination who specialized in fabricating images of Jews degrading German women and who would later be known as 'Jew Baiter Number One'. Streicher, whose excesses drew the condemnation even of senior Nazis, later claimed that he became a disciple of Hitler while hearing him speak in a beer hall that winter:

Thousands of men and women jumped to their feet, as if propelled by a mysterious power . . . they shouted, 'Heil Hitler! Heil Hitler' . . . Here was one who could wrest out of the German spirit and the German heart the power to break the chains of slavery. Yes! Yes! This man spoke as a messenger from heaven at a time when the gates of hell were opening to pull down everything. And when he finally finished, and while the crowd raised the roof with the singing of the 'Deutschland' song, I rushed to the stage . . .[35]

If each of these men had 'some flaw in the weave', as the architect and future Nazi minister Albert Speer would later observe, with calculated understatement, all were utterly devoted to the man they saw as the saviour of Deutschland. Hitler ruthlessly played them off against each other, but won their adoration and loyalty. They would act on his every instruction. Hess prophesied admiringly that Hitler would have to 'trample' people to achieve his goal.[36] The trampling was about to begin, with a Nazi uprising in Bavaria.

CHAPTER EIGHTEEN

'You must fight with me – or die with me!'

The 'King of Munich' was how Hitler's enemies derided him in 1922. As his popularity rose, his disciples took the epithet literally. The trouble was, their hero's ego outran his actual appeal: at this point, he overestimated his popularity outside Bavaria, making his next leap into the unknown reckless and politically naive.

Inspired by Mussolini's triumphant March on Rome in late October that year, which saw a transfer of power in Italy to the Fascist Party, Hitler rashly conceived of a mass march on Berlin, the crucible of German power. The roots of this hubristic folly lay in his rising political confidence, which persuaded him that his popularity meant he could dispense with democratic channels. Elections were a tedious irrelevance to a man set on establishing a dictatorship. Not that the Weimar government, a series of chaotic centre-left coalitions that inspired little confidence, helped itself: while Weimar culture brimmed with intellectual and artistic excellence, the Berlin leadership was perceived as corrupt and decadent, to the extent that Hitler and his henchmen decided they could overturn Germany's democratically elected state and seize power by brute force.

This went beyond mere party-political ambition: Hitler's every action manifested a will that sought to concentrate total power in himself. And his movement swam in nourishing waters. The Bavarian state government, virtually decoupled from the authorities in Berlin, had swung aggressively to the right under Gustav von Kahr, elected prime minister in March 1920. Kahr was a monarchist who had pledged to restore order in the wake of the Marxist uprising and its bloody suppression, rid Bavaria of communists and stem the 'tide' of immigration, especially eastern Jews.

Kahr liked what he saw in the youthful Hitler, who professed (in a meeting between the two men in May 1921) that his only goal was to convert the workers to National Socialism. The appearance of the 'modest man, the ordinary ex-soldier' was one of Hitler's more effective disguises. This affectation of humility presented him as a reasonable man, a man you could work with. The fact that this pose was in stark contrast to what you had expected helped to authenticate it.

Kahr responded helpfully: he welcomed 'converts' to Nazism over communism; and besides, Hitler was proving useful to the prime minister. His Pan-German rhetoric served to fasten the people's minds on patriotism, not socialism, and love of country over class chimed with Kahr's nationalist-monarchist agenda. With the nightmare of the Bavarian soviet still high in the public mind, the social glue of a shared national purpose – to revive German greatness – stuck faster than the workers' calls to unite.

All this meant that Hitler and his party were winning adherents. The National Socialists were *working* as a populist force. They had hit the ground running at the most opportune time. They offered hope at a time of despair; they preached defiance at a time of submission; and they were turning socialists into nationalists, pleasing Kahr's government. That was a critical reason for the Nazis' special treatment in Bavaria – and their post-war popularity. On a personal level, Kahr praised Hitler's energy and self-discipline, not suspecting for a moment that the latter's ultimate goal was to rise up against the Bavarian state, seize power, destroy his rivals and opponents, topple the German government and purge his party and nation of 'impure' elements. Kahr was scarcely a mote in the eye of that diabolical vision (and for opposing the putsch, he would be executed on the Night of the Long Knives, on 30 June 1934, in Dachau).

For now, though, his regime was a beacon of hope to hundreds of little lights on the far right, drawn to this oasis of extremism where bigotry and racial persecution were officially tolerated. By 1921 scores of such militant groups had congregated in Munich, of which the National Socialists were among the largest and most visible. Their local power derived not from any democratic mandate, but from their private armies, such as the Nazis' SA. Concerned by the power of these citizens' militias, the German government passed a decree designed to protect the Republic against right-wing extremists and Kahr was ordered to disband them in return for Berlin's support.

Kahr failed to do so, and resigned on 1 September 1921. He was replaced by Hugo Max Graf von und zu Lerchenfeld, leader of the Bavarian People's Party, who tried to suppress the far right and defuse the tension that threatened to rupture the state, but lost the confidence of his party and was forced to resign on 2 November 1922. The elderly, ineffectual Eugen Ritter von Knilling succeeded him but, as we shall see, would soon be forced to recall Kahr and endow him with near-dictatorial powers to confront the explosive events of November 1923.

During Lerchenfeld's brief tenure, some paramilitary units folded or consolidated; others refashioned themselves as security forces. But Hitler's SA expanded: ignoring the Bavarian government, the Brownshirts seized the chance to fill the power vacuum in Munich. Under the leadership of Emil Maurice, an early party member (and one of the rare *Mischlings*, Nazis deemed to have both Aryan and Jewish ancestry), the SA unleashed bursts of violence in the city's streets and beer halls. Coercion trumped the letter of the law in those virtually lawless days, and pressed the state authorities into submission.

Insurrection was in the air. Armed men and lynch mobs prowled the streets of Munich, united by their hatred of Versailles, Jews and the Weimar government. Almost every week during 1921–2 the NSDAP held speaking events in the city's beer halls, or assaulted rival gatherings, which usually descended into brawls. Hitler delighted in the violence that resulted: the crashing chairs and flung beer steins, the cries of

'Murder!' and 'Hang them all!' It was all great, menacing fun. During these fracas the belligerents tended to shorten 'National Socialist' to 'Nazi', a name easier to shout. From the outset, the Nazis' chief opponents, mostly communists, liberals and social democrats, associated the word with violence and bloodshed. 'Nazi' quickly became synonymous with 'oppose us and expect a fist in your jaw'.

Young Adolf would stand at the centre of these tumultuous elements, dressed in a beige trench coat and a grey velour hat, brandishing his silver-handled whip and sneering at his enemies from behind his bodyguards like the junior don in a Mafia family. He was now recognized as a leader of 'gangster ruthlessness'.[1] His singular goal was to ensure people never forgot him or the Nazis. 'Who cares whether they laugh at us or insult us, treating us as fools or criminals?' he later wrote in *Mein Kampf.* 'The point is that they talk about us and constantly think about us.'[2]

Hitler actively participated in inflicting violence on occasion. On 14 September 1921, for example, he, prominent NSDAP members Hermann Esser (who would later edit the Nazi newspaper *Völkischer Beobachter*) and Oskar Körner, as well as supporters and Brownshirts, burst in on a meeting at the Löwenbräukeller, where Otto Ballerstedt, the popular leader of the Bayernbund, a rival movement that sought Bavarian autonomy, was addressing the crowd. Hitler personally assaulted and severely injured Ballerstedt, who was dragged from the beer hall (and would later be murdered in the Night of the Long Knives, in a terminal act of vengeance: Hitler never forgot a rival). At their trial in January 1922, Hitler and Esser were convicted of a breach of the peace, public indecency and assault, and sentenced to 100 days' imprisonment, of which Hitler served barely a month (24 June–27 July 1922).

This pattern of violence continued at numerous rallies during 1922, most seriously at Coburg, northern Bavaria, on 14–15 October, where 800 SA men entered the city in closed ranks, sparking a bloody confrontation with socialist groups.

After his spell in prison, Hitler's voice rather than his fists or pistol became his most effective weapon in this fiery atmosphere. He had honed his rich baritone into an instrument of mass control, often inciting his audiences to commit violence.[3] Unamplified before 1928, his speeches now followed a clear pattern, observed Ernst Hanfstaengl: they began softly, almost haltingly, luring his listeners in; they then rose into a quivering vibrato, appropriate to his themes of a people betrayed; and they climaxed with shouts, almost screams, accompanied by the violent chopping of his hands, like 'the approach of a cleansing thunderstorm'. At the end of these displays of furious indignation his audiences were 'irresistibly swept into mass ecstasy'.[4]

Hitler's disciples would also kill for him, so persuasive were his ringing denunciations of politicians he loathed. His attack on the Weimar government's liberal Jewish foreign minister, Walter Rathenau, helped to accelerate the latter's assassination in June 1922 – echoing the fate of Reich finance minister Matthias Erzberger, murdered the previous August – by members of an extreme right-wing cell called Organisation Consul, which the Nazis later absorbed.

Meanwhile, the worsening state of Germany played directly into the NSDAP's hands. The Nazi Party's fortunes rose with the collapse of the economy, which reached its post-war nadir in the early 1920s. An ever-accelerating cycle of printing money, fuelling inflation and devaluing the mark was ruining the middle classes. Since the outbreak of war, prices had been constantly rising while the currency collapsed: in 1914, 4.2 marks equalled US$1; by 1919, there were 8.9 marks to the dollar. Very soon, hyperinflation put the mark:dollar rate at hundreds of millions to one.[5] And it was set to get much worse.

Hitler had no immediate solutions, but he knew who to blame. Week after week, he preyed on the victims of this economic shambles by ramming home the promise of vengeance against the 'perpetrators', the Jewish capitalists, who had rigged the system against the people. His message won over rising numbers, thirsty for a scapegoat.

The NSDAP grew rapidly throughout 1922, rising to more than 20,000 members by the end of the year and almost tripling that number twelve months later, to 55,000. Most were small businessmen, shop-keepers, tradesmen, artisans, students and farmers; just 9.5 per cent were unskilled labourers. The Nazis were never a traditional working-class movement, although substantial numbers of workers backed them. They were, like their leader, largely from the lower middle classes, the white-collar workers or *Mittelstand*, a type caricatured as a Bavarian man with a pot belly.[6]

It was around this time that Hitler's supporters started openly worshipping him as their 'Führer', greeting each other with a stiff, out-stretched right arm (which they copied from the Italian Fascist Party) and shouting, '*Heil Hitler!*' – the same greeting Schönerer had used in Vienna. They wore the swastika – the *Hakenkreuz*, or hooked cross – with pride, though few knew the symbol's provenance. It is in fact a Hindu and Buddhist religious symbol dating back more than 11,000 years; it still emblazons the walls of villages in India and Nepal. The Nazis appropriated theirs from the Vedic Indians (1500–500 BC), a warrior 'race' who provided, according to Alfred Rosenberg and his Nazi ideologues, the Aryan model of racial purity. Hitler had personally chosen it as the party emblem in 1920, writing later, 'After innumerable trials [including a 'good design' submitted by a dentist from Starnberg] I decided upon a final form – a flag of red material with a white disc bearing in its centre a black swastika.'[7]

And so, attired in their brown uniforms, with armbands sporting an old Hindu cross in red, black and white, Hitler's private army of stormtroopers set forth to enact his revolution. All they needed was the signal to rise and put down their opponents.

In January 1923 France appeared to give them one. In a vindictive twist of the knife inserted by the Versailles Treaty, French and Belgian forces occupied Germany's coal-rich Ruhr valley as punishment for late payment of reparations, infuriating Berlin. Nowhere was this humili-ation more palpable than in Bavaria, whose local firebrands rushed to denounce France and called for an armed response to their old enemy.

Unusually, Adolf Hitler urged restraint. He argued that it was point-less to challenge French troops from a position of weakness; he was also well aware that a sudden, violent reaction to the occupation would send the unhelpful message that Hitler couldn't control his people. His immediate enemy, for now, he said, was the 'Berlin Jew government', led by that rancid mob of 'November Criminals', the back-stabbers whose destruction he sought as a prelude to the Nazi takeover of Germany.

This was consistent with what he had always affirmed as the party's chief priority: the destruction of the Weimar government – and democracy itself. Hadn't he demanded as much as early as 1919? A government of power and authority, led by a man of iron, he had said, must replace the Berlin mob and 'ruthlessly clean out the pigsty'.[8] Only then would Hitler turn the power of a renewed Reich, under Nazi control, on its erstwhile foreign enemies. So, much to their irritation, he urged his jumped-up supporters to bide their time.

Rumours of a coup abounded, however, instilling fear in the moderates in the Bavarian government, who called for new curbs on the Nazis' excesses. In reply, Hitler threatened violently to defy any official constraints on his movement. He went further, reconstituting the SA at the centre of the 'Working Association of Patriotic Fighting Organizations' – a streamlined assortment of paramilitaries founded by Röhm in February 1923 – whose mission was to seize political power, 'cleanse' the Fatherland of its internal enemies (Jews, communists and other undesirable elements) and rebuild the nation. It would soon be subsumed within the *Kampfbund*, a broader league of far-right militias formed in Nuremberg that September, of which the SA was the most powerful and whose ultimate leader was Adolf Hitler. The SA began their newly invigorated crusade by raiding bookshops and kicking Jewish pedestrians, while senior Nazis whipped up public fury against any Jews who retained good jobs or positions of influence.

Hitler and his henchmen staged a series of mass demonstrations. Their followers still hoped and expected these actions to spur an insurrection, but they were again severely disappointed: Hitler twice pulled back from the brink, at party rallies on 27 January and 1 May. By resisting the pressure to launch a putsch, he caused several in his trigger-happy ranks to question his leadership. Yet Hitler knew a pitched battle with the Bavarian state police would fail. Even if he won the fight, he would lose the propaganda war, imperilling his long-term plans.

It was not that the Nazis were weak: at several points, the SA virtually held Munich in the palm of its hand. Hitler had the weapons, and the military power, to occupy the city (as they virtually did during the January rallies). In the May demonstrations, Röhm even seized arms from the Munich barracks and distributed them, ready for an attack. In a humiliating capitulation, however, Hitler bowed to the authorities' demands and returned the weapons, igniting further questions over his leadership.

The Bavarian government tolerated the Nazis' violent incursions on public order through clenched teeth. Ministers feared they would lose their popular mandate if they offended the state's fastest-growing political movement. So rather than crack down on 'Hitlerism', they merely sent prosecutors to investigate whether the Nazis had incited armed insurrection. No charges were laid.

After a holiday in a mountain village near the Berchtesgaden – his future alpine retreat – Hitler returned to Munich in the summer of 1923 to scenes of economic devastation and political gridlock. Food riots, strikes and hyperinflation gripped the country. The million-mark note was worthless. The billion-mark note soon yielded to a trillion-mark note. The mark:dollar rate was more than 100 billion to one; by late November it would peak at 4,200,000,000,000 (four trillion two hundred billion) marks to a single dollar.[9]

People's homes, in which they'd invested their life's savings, were suddenly worth no more than a pound of butter. Those unable to repay their loans were forced on to the street. 'It was simply inconceivable,' a Nazi Party member recalled, 'for the old people that this bale of banknotes in their hands was simply worthless.'[10] A spirit of nihilism and despair prowled the cities. Unemployment soared. Social chaos erupted. Hunger and misery were etched on the faces of many who had been wealthy, or at least comfortable, before the war. An obsession with 'them' and 'us', with the question of whom to blame, besieged the public mind.

In such a world, in their fury at Berlin's decadence and incompetence, otherwise moderate conservatives joined the calls for an insurrection, a putsch that would seize the levers of power. The Nazis were hustling for pole position in a revolution every pundit assumed was coming. Hitler had pledged to clean out the pigsty; his chance was now imminent.

In September, the Bavarian prime minister, Eugen von Knilling, declared martial law and brought back Gustav von Kahr as *Staatskommissar* (state commissar) with almost dictatorial powers to suppress the 'Hitler movement'. Along with General Otto von Lossow, commander of the Reichswehr in Bavaria, and Colonel Hans Ritter von Seisser, the Bavarian police chief, Kahr formed a right-wing triumvirate that in effect controlled the state government. On 26 September, fearful of revolutionary pressures, they launched a state of emergency and banned political rallies throughout October. This had the effect of ratcheting up the tension and infuriating the Nazis.

Letters poured into NSDAP headquarters, urging action. 'Now may the Almighty make your arm as strong as your words are beautiful so that the day of liberation will be upon us,' a once-affluent woman told Hitler.[11] The beer halls were packed to the rafters, the crowds craning to hear their new 'messiah', as many of his fans now openly called him. In a speech on 30 October 1923 he declared that victory would be theirs after Berlin's Marxists and Jews were stabbed through the heart, and the black, red and white swastika flew over the nation's capital.

Hitler specialized in excess, Kahr knew, but this was going too far. How dare these upstarts in swastikas presume to rule all Germany?

The Bavarian state crackdown placed Hitler under immense pressure to respond and now, to his party's relief, he acted. First, he secured the backing of two powerful people: Ernst Pöhner, Munich's former police chief, an extreme anti-Semite who had attempted to expel all eastern Jews from Bavaria in 1919 (Hitler offered him the post of Bavarian president if the coup succeeded); and General Erich Ludendorff, Germany's most famous military commander and war hero, who had allied himself with the Nazis and had himself called for a march on Berlin.

Hitler also ensured that the Brownshirts would procure the necessary weapons. And he reset the time. Originally the putsch was planned for 11 November, but rumours of a monarchist resurgence under Kahr made Armistice Day seem the perfect occasion for putting Crown Prince Rupprecht on the Bavarian throne – a possibility that infuriated the Nazi leader, whose dreams of power now transcended the House of Wittelsbach. He brought forward his plans to 8 November.

The Beer Hall Putsch of 8–9 November 1923, later to be enshrined in Nazi folklore as the *Hitlerputsch* and its victims eulogized as 'blood witnesses' to the party's birth pangs, was more a farce than a failure. Hitler's aim was recklessly ambitious: to seize power from the state government, declare a Bavarian dictatorship and march on Berlin, sweeping the country – and the Bavarian leadership – with him. He was confident the Reichswehr would rally to his cause.

Hitler kicked off the revolution in theatrical style, by barging into the offices of the *Völkischer Beobachter*, riding crop and pistol in hand, and telling Hanfstaengl and Rosenberg that the revolution would begin that night. And so, at 8 p.m. on 8 November, around 2,000 of the party faithful set off for the Bürgerbräukeller, where Kahr was to give a speech to a packed room of 3,000 prominent locals, including heads of industry and government agencies. Hitler travelled to the scene in his private Mercedes, with Rosenberg, Hess and Göring in tow. His black tailcoat made him look more like a waiter than a revolutionary. Anton Drexler came along for the ride, thinking he was heading for a country meeting. When told the truth, he refused to participate, sealing his dismissal from the party leadership.

A large crowd had surrounded the entrance to the Bürgerbräukeller. On Pöhner's orders, the Munich police dispersed them, clearing Hitler's path to the entrance. More than 600 SA men had secured the building without interference and placed a machine gun near the auditorium.

At 8.45 p.m., Hitler entered the hall. With a stormtrooper on either side and his Nazi henchmen surrounding him, he smashed a beer stein on the ground, took out his revolver and muscled his way through the crowd. They barely noticed him at first; nobody seemed to realize that a revolution was taking place.

Firmer measures were needed. Hitler jumped up on a table, fired a shot into the ceiling and yelled: 'The national revolution has broken out! The hall is filled with six hundred men. Nobody is allowed to leave.'[12] A machine gun was aimed at anyone who disobeyed, he warned. The Reich and Bavarian governments had fallen, he shouted, and a provisional government led by himself and Ludendorff had replaced it. The army and police barracks were in his hands, he lied.

He ordered Kahr, Lossow, Seisser and their aides to a side-room, at gunpoint. Göring took charge of the hall, as Hitler followed his captives. Waving his gun in the triumvirate's faces, Hitler demanded their support for his revolution in return for key positions in his new regime. He threatened to kill them if they disobeyed; and then, apologizing for threatening such extreme action, he adopted a softer tone: would they agree to be deposed if he reinstated them under his own regime? 'You must fight with me, triumph with me – or die with me,' he pleaded. 'If things go wrong I have four bullets in this pistol: three for my collaborators should they desert me, and the last bullet for myself.'[13]

Kahr, a seasoned politician, sensed at once the vulnerability of Hitler's situation. He stalled, daring his adversary to shoot him: 'Herr Hitler, you can have me shot, you can shoot me yourself. But whether or not I die is of no consequence to me.'[14]

Hitler implored Kahr to change his mind. Would the role of Regent of Bavaria interest him after the revolution? '[T]he people will kneel at your feet,' Hitler cried, but to no avail. The prostration of the nation meant nothing to Kahr (but the offer said a lot about what mattered to Hitler); nor was such a role in Hitler's gift.

A little earlier, several putschists had been dispatched to collect Ludendorff, whose personal prestige was seen as vital to the uprising's credibility. Meanwhile, Ernst Röhm and members of the private militia he founded in 1923, the *Bund Reichskriegsflagge*, now SA men, were waiting in the Löwenbräukeller when he received an order (via a phone call from the beer-hall kitchen) to seize vital fixtures in the city, including the army barracks. The cadets at a nearby Officers' Infantry School were similarly dispatched.

At around 9 p.m., the granite figure of Erich Ludendorff strode into the Bürgerbräukeller, amazed to find himself in the eye of a revolution and its figurehead: the old general had not been fully briefed on the plan. Yet he admired Hitler and rallied now to the insurrection. His recognizable features – the bullet-shaped head and bejowled face – reassured the crowd and weakened the triumvirate, who, encountering Ludendorff in their little ante-room, began to concede defeat under the general's withering frown. Pistols were put away and peaceful negotiations began. If Kahr backed the coup, Hitler assured his hostage that he would stand by him 'as loyally as a dog'.[15]

Back in the beer hall, the crowd had lost patience with this violent interruption to their evening's enjoyment and had degenerated into an unruly mob of hecklers. Göring had become a figure of fun. The former flying ace and SA commander seemed to lose his nerve in the presence of so many highly placed civic leaders who scorned his boorish, cowboy antics. The coup put them in mind of a South American farce.

Hitler's reappearance quickly restored order. Seeing his comrade's discomfort, he swung into action, grabbing the audience's attention with a speech of astonishing piquancy. He appealed for their support for a 'nationalist' movement against 'the Berlin Jew government and the November criminals of 1918'.[16] He appealed to their unity: 'Outside are Kahr, Lossow and Seisser. They are struggling hard to reach a decision. May I say to them that you will stand behind them?'[17]

The crowd's first reaction was to laugh and roar their approval, seeing the episode as something of a vaudeville show. Hitler silenced them with a bloody ultimatum: 'You can see that what motivates us is neither self-conceit or self-interest, but only a burning desire to join the battle in this grave eleventh hour for our German Fatherland . . . One last thing I can tell you. Either the German revolution begins tonight or we will all be dead by dawn!'[18]

To a stunned hall, with the memory of the war uppermost in his mind, Hitler then reprised his 'Pasewalk moment':

Now I am going to carry out what I swore to myself five years ago today when I lay blind and crippled in the army hospital: neither to rest nor to sleep until the November criminals have been hurled to the ground, until on the ruins of the present pitiful Germany has been raised a Germany of power and greatness, of freedom and glory! Amen.[19]

The crowd was deeply moved. 'I cannot remember in my entire life,' recalled Dr Karl von Müller, a professor of modern history at Munich University, who witnessed the scene, 'such a change in the attitude of a crowd in a few minutes, almost a few seconds . . . Hitler had turned them inside out, as one turns a glove inside out, with a few sentences. It had almost something of hocus-pocus, or magic about it.'[20]

Ludendorff led the response, pledging his support. Kahr, too, who had reluctantly re-entered the hall behind Hitler, offered his loyalty, followed by Lossow and Seisser, all of whom now gave the impression that they had conceded defeat. In fact they were still 'playing along' with Hitler (as they had whispered to each other earlier in the fracas). Hitler, too, entered into the spirit of the 'game', responding by delightedly shaking their hands.

The hall then sang the national anthem while Prime Minister von Knilling and several Bavarian Cabinet members were 'arrested', in a token gesture to the revolution. The delighted audience dispersed. The beginning of the putsch had ended bloodlessly.

Then Hitler mis-stepped. Called away to a disturbance at the army barracks, which had not been seized, he left Kahr, Lossow and Seisser in the care of Ludendorff. The old general, easy prey to arch politicians, agreed to liberate his prisoners if they gave their word of honour to support Hitler's new regime.

With the coup unravelling around him, Hitler returned to the Bürgerbräukeller, where to his dismay he found Ludendorff, the man he'd once worshipped, now alone and minus his three important prisoners. Ludendorff met Hitler's scepticism over the freed prisoners' avowals of loyalty with angry astonishment. He would not endure doubts being cast on a German officer's word.

Hitler had a surer grasp of the politicians' minds. Freed at around 10.30 p.m., the triumvirate at once reneged on their word. They ordered the seizure of the radio station and barracks, which the Nazis had mysteriously failed to secure, and prepared an address to be broadcast to the city. At around 2.50 a.m. on 9 November, Kahr announced on air that he firmly rejected the coup leaders' terms and disowned any agreement extracted at gunpoint. The coup was over, he declared.

The Bavarian government spent the night strengthening its forces and rounding up Hitler's men. Kahr ordered the police to arrest the ringleaders and the SA commanders. The Brownshirts had not, and never would, seize the city's vital buildings, as instructed, but Röhm and his men did manage briefly to occupy Lossow's defence commando. They spent much of the night immersed in their first pogrom, busy destroying shops and, in the city's wealthier areas, arresting and beating up Jews, whom they accused of profiting from the war. For the targeted Jews it was a terrifying precursor of the Kristallnacht attacks that would come fifteen years later, on 9–10 November 1938. One eager participant was an unemployed student of agronomy called Heinrich Himmler, then twenty-three, for whom the putsch was the catalyst for his political career and the start of his rise to become the second most powerful man in the Third Reich (and one of the few Hitler would authorize to speak to the party elite about the Final Solution). In fact, had the *Hitlerputsch* succeeded, Munich's Jewish community would have been the first to die, and their possessions confiscated, as Hitler had threatened.

The coup continued unravelling into the early hours. At around 3 a.m., the local garrison of the Reichswehr ambushed Röhm's men as they left the beer hall. Shots were fired, but there were no fatalities. Röhm's forces retreated. Before dawn, realizing he was losing control, Hitler ordered the taking of the Munich city councillors as hostages and dispatched Max Neunzert, the communications officer of the *Kampfbund*, to ask Crown Prince Rupprecht to mediate between Kahr and the coup leaders. Neunzert failed to reach the prince, and so, too, did the putsch.

The sun dawned on a city of failed dreams, recriminations, anger and exhaustion. All seemed lost and Hitler's mood blackened. Cornered and furious, he succumbed to 'a strange alternation of moods, first apathy, then violent despair, histrionics that anticipated the convulsions and rages of later years.'[21]

At which point, it took an old soldier to rally the troops. Sensing a disaster looming for Hitler and the Nazis, Ludendorff dusted down his heavy frame, raised himself to his full height and barked, '*Wir marschieren!*' ('We will march!') The general's defiant, parade-ground voice salvaged a little dignity from the fiasco: the Nazis would march through the streets in a show of intransigence and in the coming days would hold a huge rally. Hitler enthusiastically declared, 'Propaganda, propaganda . . . now it all depends on propaganda!'[22]

Around mid-morning on 9 November, some 2,000 party members, led by Hitler, Ludendorff, Göring, Röhm and other senior Nazis, marched out of the beer hall with no specific idea where they were heading. On an impulse, Ludendorff decided to lead them to the Bavarian Defence Ministry. They marched through cheering crowds, in the direction of the Odeonsplatz, breaking a police cordon near Ludwigs Bridge.

Nearing the Odeonsplatz, loudly singing an old military song, the marchers encountered a larger security cordon, of 130 soldiers under the command of State Police Senior Lieutenant Baron Michael von Godin. Tensions rose and shots were fired. In the street fight that ensued, fourteen members of the Nazi Party were killed and several wounded, including Göring, who was shot in the hip; four police-men also lay dead. The enraged Ludendorff, wearing civilian clothes, a green felt hat and a loose loden coat, marched through the melee like a returning Caesar, untouched: nobody dared fire on the national hero.

At this moment, Hitler was walking arm in arm with Max Erwin von Scheubner-Richter, a senior Nazi. He carried a slouch hat, and wore the collar of his trench coat turned up against the cold. Suddenly, Scheubner-Richter took a hit: a bullet pierced his lung. As he fell dead, the weight of his body wrenched Hitler's right shoulder out of joint, badly dislocating it. Despite the acute pain, Hitler got up and ran, abandoning his dying comrade. He fled down a side alley and leapt into a waiting car that rushed him to the home of his wealthy friend Ernst Hanfstaengl, outside Munich. He later lied that he had run from the scene in order to carry a child to safety.

Hanfstaengl had himself fled Munich, but his wife Helene was home that night when Hitler knocked. Supported by comrades, he stumbled in covered in dirt, with his arm hanging at an odd angle. A doctor reset the shoulder the next day. In agony, Hitler threatened suicide and reached for his pistol. Helene snatched it away and hid it.

On the afternoon of 11 November, the police surrounded Hanfstaengl's house. Seeing that all was lost, Hitler gave himself up. Arrested and charged with high treason, he presented a miserable sight at Landsberg Prison in the south-west of Bavaria. Again, he indulged in the histrionics of the self-anointed martyr, asking for his pistol. When this was refused, he went on a brief hunger strike, which soon landed him in the infirmary.

Among his senior comrades who were also captured and similarly charged were Ernst Röhm, Emil Maurice, Wilhelm Frick and Ernst Pöhner. Göring was smuggled to Innsbruck and his wound treated (it was here that he began his lifelong addiction to morphine). Ludendorff had surrendered, and would soon be released, pending trial. Hess fled to Austria, but decided to return and was arrested. The NSDAP and SA were both outlawed, the Nazi press banned, and yet, despite a crackdown on its activities and a search of its newspaper office, the party continued to operate underground under the dubious leadership of Alfred Rosenberg (it seems Hitler had selected the man least likely to upstage him). The Munich public were, in any event, firmly on the side of the putschists, and several rallies would soon hail Hitler and condemn Kahr.

In his early days in prison, while awaiting trial, Hitler moaned that his life was over, his movement finished. He feared the end of his political future. He gave not a thought to his fellow revolutionaries, several of whom were dead or imprisoned. It seemed the only person who had lost something that day had been Adolf Hitler: nothing and nobody else mattered. The man who had shown not a scintilla of concern for the civilian victims of the First World War, who had betrayed his comrades-in-arms after it, and who had run away from the uprising he'd led, revealed his true nature again: that of a violent, egocentric criminal, who treated humanity as his personal plaything and the world as his to conquer.

The trial of ten putschists – the most prominent of whom were Hitler, Ludendorff, Hess and Röhm – opened on 26 February 1924 to a packed room in Munich's First District Court. Hitler arrived with a confident swagger, wearing his Iron Cross, First Class, the one he had received on a Jewish officer's recommendation. His bearing impressed the court reporters: unintimidated, unbowed, he glared around the chamber, filing away the names of the prosecutors and witnesses in his powerful memory.

Accused of masterminding the operation, Hitler, who had chosen and been allowed to defend himself, confessed to leading the putsch but not to the charge of high treason. He was avenging the betrayal of Germany in November 1918, he claimed, and acting in his country's interests. The presiding judge, Georg Neidhardt, who had supervised Hitler's previous court appearance, sympathized, as did most of the pro-Nazi magistrates. Neidhardt gave Hitler full rein to speak for as long as he wished and to cross-examine witnesses as he pleased.

Hitler quickly turned the courtroom into his personal political platform. Any pretence of independence swiftly evaporated, and the trial became a political circus, a 'carnival', wrote one journalist. He was allowed to expound on Nazi dogma and even cross-examine witnesses for the prosecution.

Among those witnesses, only Lossow went on the attack, subjecting

Hitler to a blistering character assassination. Hitler was not only a serial liar, the army commander said, he was 'tactless, limited, boring, sometimes brutal, sometimes sentimental, and unquestionably inferior.' Lossow sneered that Hitler had come a long way from being merely the 'drummer' in a patriotic movement. Now, his followers addressed him as the 'Chosen One'. Lossow unwittingly drew public attention to what Hitler's disciples already thought: Hitler was more than a 'German Mussolini' (as Hitler had promoted himself, according to a psychiatric report); he was indeed the coming 'German messiah'.[23]

Lossow's words resonated with only a small minority.[24] Almost everyone present believed Hitler a war hero, a great man and their future leader. He had been unfairly accused. The trial was high vaudeville and merely served to buttress Hitler's popularity. In his closing speech, he was given the time to grandstand, to bask in his popularity and turn the tables on his accusers, Kahr, Lossow and Seisser. In reply to Lossow's demeaning attack, Hitler laid out a vision of himself that might have sounded grotesquely self-delusional were his audience not so enamoured of the speaker. Certainly, he would be far greater than a drummer boy, he told the court:

> How petty are the thoughts of small men! Believe me, I do not regard the acquisition of a minister's portfolio as a thing worth striving for. I do not hold it worthy of a great man to endeavor to go down in history just by becoming a minister. One might be in danger of being buried beside other ministers. My aim from the first was a thousand times higher than becoming a minister. I wanted to become the destroyer of Marxism. I am going to achieve this task, and if I do, the title of Minister will be an absurdity so far as I am concerned.

He would follow the example of his hero Richard Wagner, who had eschewed all titles on his gravestone: 'I was proud that this man and so many others in German history were content to give their names to history without titles. It was not from modesty that I wanted to be a drummer in those days. That was the highest aspiration – the rest is nothing.'

He felt himself destined for greatness: 'The man who is born to be a dictator is not compelled. He wills it. He is not driven forward, but drives himself . . . The man who feels called upon to govern a people has no right to say, "If you want me or summon me, I will co-operate." No! It is his duty to step forward.'

He appealed to the magistrates' patriotism, to the greatness of Germany, to the will of the people: 'I believe that the hour will come when the masses, who today stand in the street with our swastika banner, will unite with those who fired upon them.'

The army was not to blame. Their old flags would one day wave again, he told the courtroom. And with defiance in his eyes he turned on the judges:

> For it is not you, gentlemen, who pass judgment on us. That judgment is spoken by the eternal court of history. What judgment you will hand down I know . . . You may pronounce us guilty a thousand times over, but the goddess of the eternal court of history will smile and tear to tatters the brief of the state prosecutor and the sentence of this court. For she acquits us.[25]

With a single speech, Hitler had turned his trial into a condemnation of his enemies and a judgment on the state. At his sentencing on 1 April, he was found guilty of 'high treason' – as the magistrates were bound by law to find him, despite their sympathies – and sentenced to five years in prison, of which he was expected to serve only a few months. Others received similarly lenient punishment. Röhm was given a suspended sentence and was conditionally discharged. Hess received eighteen months. Ludendorff was acquitted. The defendants had acted out of selfless patriotism and deserved praise, not condemnation, the verdict concluded. The deaths of four policemen went unremarked. These were April Fool's jokes, some muttered; but they were a minority: the light sentences for such a serious crime provoked laughter and delighted the packed courtroom, which resounded with cries of 'Heil Hitler!' 'It was the moral equivalent of an acquittal,' comments Ullrich.[26] It was also a resounding propaganda victory for the Nazis that resonated well beyond Bavaria's borders.

The Beer Hall Putsch taught Hitler the hard lesson that the violent overthrow of the state was futile, and that he had neither the following nor the means to pull it off. From now on, he would pursue a peaceful, if no less illegal, path to power: rigging the democratic system, threatening his opponents and 'cloaking his illegal acts in the guise of legality,' as Fest concludes.[27] The end he sought was power, whatever the means. And so he settled into a leisurely confinement in prison, during which he would plan the Nazi Party's next act and write his personal manifesto. He was about to celebrate his thirty-fifth birthday.

Chapter Nineteen

'If fifteen thousand of these Hebrew corrupters had been held under poison gas . . .'

Incarcerated in Landsberg Prison, 40 miles (65 km) west of Munich, Hitler was able to rest and reflect. He enjoyed all the creature comforts of home. His cell was more like a drawing room, nicely furnished, with a relaxing view of the countryside. Surrounded by fellow Nazi inmates, he formed and led a discussion group in the low-security fortress. As well as Hess, they included the *Kampfbund* leader Hermann Kriebel; Friedrich Weber, leader of the *Bund Oberland* (another of the *Kampfbund* groups); the SA leader Emil Maurice, and members of the *Stosstrupp*, Hitler's bodyguard unit.

The prison officials looked kindly on Hitler's 'special needs', exempting him from labour details and allowing the chief Nazi to dress in lederhosen, stroll in the fortress grounds and dine – from a vegetarian menu, if he chose – under a swastika banner.[1] Hitler was permitted many visitors – politicians, fans, society ladies, soldiers, lawyers, clergymen, aristocrats and workers – who sat by their idol, sometimes for up to six hours a day, the maximum allowed per week for ordinary inmates. At least five visitors a day came to his room in April and May 1924, and more than 330 during his entire 'stay'.[2] The most famous were Ludendorff, Rosenberg, Amann, Streicher, the piano heiress Helene Bechstein, the socialite Elsa Bruckmann and Hitler's half-niece Angela 'Geli' Raubal.

In Landsberg, Hitler enjoyed the respect and deference accorded a Mafia boss. His comrades basked in the reflected glory of sharing their prison terms with their leader, on whom they lavished attention. On 'comradeship evenings', a military band struck up when Hitler entered the common room, his worshippers standing to attention behind their chairs until he reached his place. Outside the guards would assemble to hear their famous prisoner speak. The cult of the Führer was taking shape in the most unlikely place.

Hitler eschewed exercise and sport, making him one of the few prisoners who gained weight. His excuse offered a glimpse of his self-image at this time, that of the brooding dictator-in-waiting. 'A Führer can't afford to be beaten by his followers, even at gymnastics or games,' he solemnly explained.[3]

His decision later to adopt a vegetarian diet has been attributed to his weight gain in prison.[4] He began to eat less meat in Landsberg, because 'meat and alcohol harm my body', he told his friend Hanfstaengl. He had therefore 'decided to summon the will-power necessary to do without both, as much as I enjoy them.'[5] At other times, he explained that he chose a vegetarian diet because meat made him 'sweat tremendously' during his speeches.[6] (In coming years the vegetarian teetotaller would cut a lonely figure at the tables of the rich and powerful, heavy with joints of beef, legs of lamb and bottles of wine. At times, he was known to refer scornfully to his carnivorous companions as 'cadaver eaters'.)

In prison, with much spare time, Hitler sat and read, continuing his 'self-education'. The guards delivered whatever books he requested; 'Landsberg was my state-paid university,' he later remarked.[7] In the comfort of his room, deep in his books, he drew on new reserves of self-knowledge, he claimed: 'the level of confidence, optimism and faith that could no longer be shaken by anything'.[8] Rudolf Hess was utterly persuaded. In his eyes, Hitler grew in stature in Landsberg. To Hess, he became the saviour of Germany, with 'faith enough to move mountains'.[9]

On his thirty-fifth birthday, 20 April, Hitler received hundreds of gifts and letters from well-wishers and devoted fans. One came from a PhD graduate in philology who, agog with admiration, ascribed to his newfound hero a famous quote by Goethe: 'To you a god has given the tongue with which to express our suffering'.[10] The correspondent's name was Joseph Goebbels.

Adjusting to the title of *'Führer vom Volk'* ('Ruler of the People'), to which the putsch had raised him, Hitler felt moved to write the story of his life. On 7 July 1924, he announced his decision to step down from the leadership of the (then banned) NSDAP in order to commit himself to this autobiographical work.

His timing was auspicious: in his absence, the party had fallen apart, riven with internal disputes and petty power struggles that underlined the Nazis' reliance on the Führer. These intimations of his indispensability fired Hitler's ego and emboldened him to write more than a memoir: this would be a political and racial manifesto.

Hitler seized the time afforded by his prison sentence: he shut himself away, refusing to see all but essential visitors, and dedicated himself to the story of his life and the rise of the National Socialist movement. He dictated the draft to Hess, who, with Emil Maurice's help, transcribed and polished it, then Hitler helped to type the final version. No idle amanuensis, Hess probed and primed the Führer all the way.

In *Mein Kampf* (My Struggle) we encounter the core text of the Nazi Party's ideology and Hitler's full-blown *Weltanschauung* (philosophy of life). Many have branded the book bombastic, banal, derivative and pretentious. In parts, it is all these things. It is also often tediously repetitive and grindingly dull. To read *Mein Kampf* is to subject your brain to an incessant verbal hammering: 'Submit to my will or die!' Hitler's sentences shout.

There is no denying that the book has flashes of clarity, even lyrical beauty; yet for the most part Hitler's 'autobiography' is a document of savage banality, striking for its dearth of human decency and any sense of humour.

The Führer would typically start a passage in a portentous, pseudo-academic voice and soon lose himself in a welter of denunciations, rank prejudice and the usual vitriol, against the Jews, Marxists or whoever happened to enrage him, as if goaded by some malign troll sitting on his shoulder. Readers hoping for a powerful argument, or simply common sense, came away shaking their heads with disappointment. Many found it difficult to take seriously a man who could write of 'the hissing of the Jewish world-hydra' and the coming of the 'Jewish world dictatorship'.[11]

Hitler often resorted to ludicrous neologisms – the 'Jewification of our spiritual life', the 'mammonization of our mating instinct', etc. To call this stuff 'paranoid' would be to dignify sheer silliness as a medical condition. Even his Nazi editors silently despaired of their Führer's draft, written in the sneering tone of an embittered man who refused to accept criticism or instruction (just as Hitler the schoolboy had done). According to one psycho-historian, *Mein Kampf* is redolent of a mind under siege, its author an adolescent who refused 'to surrender to the domineering father and insisted on protecting the loving mother'.[12] While this may sound like psychobabble, the theme of the heroic son defending his mother from a brute resonated in the psyche of the 'beaten underdog' that characterized post-war Germany.

In the final analysis, *Mein Kampf* is simply, astonishingly vicious. A 'curiously nasty, obscene odour' emanates from its pages, observed Joachim Fest. It was the stench of the author's memory of poverty, war, bloodshed and death, preying on a mind disgusted by 'the images of puberty: copulation, sodomy, perversion, rape, contamination of the blood.'[13]

And that is why so many liberals and left-wingers dismissed Hitler as a bad joke, a violent criminal whose time was up, a marginal player who hadn't a hope of gaining power. They misread the national mood and Hitler's will. Which is to say, they misread *Mein Kampf*.

What of its 'content'? *Mein Kampf* was conceived as a personal and political manifesto. Much more than this, it maps a path to power; prophesies the rise of the Thousand Year Reich; describes the racial composition of 'Aryan' Germany; prefigures the seizure of *Lebensraum*, 'living space', to the east; and outlines a vision of the Fatherland led by a strong and powerful leader, a veritable superman (of whose identity no German reader was left in any doubt). And it prescribes, with awful precision, the punishment that awaited the Jewish people once the National Socialist movement had seized power.

In *Mein Kampf* Hitler synthesized, consciously or unconsciously, a multitude of sources: the ruminations of pseudo-academics, the ramblings of 'racial theorists', and the decontextualized lines of a few brilliant minds. Much is derived from other works without attribution or care for their authors' intent or context.

Among Hitler's chief influences were: the nineteenth-century French diplomat Arthur de Gobineau's theory of the Aryan Master Race; journalist Wilhelm Marr's pamphlet 'The Victory of Judaism over Germanism', which blamed 'Jewish financiers' for the crash of 1873; *The Protocols of the Elders of Zion* (1903), the fabricated conspiracy theory of world Jewish domination; the nineteenth-century historian Heinrich von Treitschke's vision of a German colonial superpower from which the Jews would be excluded; the works of the English 'racialist philosopher' Houston Stewart Chamberlain, who posited that the Jews were a 'race', not a religion, so regardless of whether they converted to Christianity they were still 'Jews' (a distinction the Nazis would later use to condemn converts to the gas chamber); General Friedrich von Bernhardi's military theories, chiefly drawn from his book *Germany and the Next War* (1911), which ennobled war as a 'divine business' and a 'biological necessity'; Martin Luther's polemical outburst, *The Jews and Their Lies* (1543); Friedrich Nietzsche's philosophy of the 'Superman', the hyper-evolved 'great man' of the future; and Arthur Schopenhauer's classic work, *The World as Will and Representation* (1818–19). Hitler took Schopenhauer's remark 'The Jew is the great master of lying'[14] out of context and gave it an odd, folksy twist: 'His mode of life,' Hitler wrote, 'compels the Jew to lie, and to lie always, just as the Northern man is compelled to look for warm clothing.'[15]

These influences and sources mingled with Hitler's personal experiences, which he weaves through the book: his life in pre-war Vienna and Munich; the lessons of Lueger and Schönerer and the Pan-Germans;

his poverty and rejection as an artist; the love of his mother and his fear of his father; all the way back to his childhood memories of Wagner, and of Karl May's stories of the Old West.

Yet the most pervasive influence on *Mein Kampf*, which hangs over everything like a dark cloud, was his memory of the Western Front: the 'Massacre of the Innocents' at Ypres; the battles of the Somme and Flanders; his disgust with Versailles and the 'November Criminals'; his ache for vengeance against the back-stabbers; and, above all, his murderous hatred of those he held responsible – the Jews.

All this culminated in his ideology of the Master Race, ruled by the archetypal Nazi superman – the blonde, blue-eyed beast who would prosecute a divinely inspired war of revenge against those who had perpetrated the humiliation of 1918. Under this programme the Third Reich would reconquer Europe, enslave its people, occupy Russia and the East, rid the occupied lands of Jews and other despised minorities, and rule for a thousand years.

Propaganda would be crucial to the success of the Nazi programme, Hitler had always insisted, so he devoted a chapter of *Mein Kampf* to the dark arts of mass indoctrination. His recipe for winning over the masses would rely on their ignorance and gullibility: he portrays the people as little more than useful idiots, on whose support he temporarily relied for his rise to power: 'The receptivity of large masses is very limited. Their capacity to understand things is slight whereas their forgetfulness is great. Given this, effective propaganda must restrict itself to a handful of points, which it repeats as slogans as long as it takes for the dumbest member of the audience to get an idea of what they mean.'[16]

Equating political power with the dominating of women, he continued:

The psyche of the great masses is not receptive to anything that is half-hearted or weak. Like a woman, whose psychic state is determined less by grounds of abstract reason than by an indefinable emotional longing for a force which will complement her nature, and who, consequently, would rather bow to a strong man than dominate a weakling, likewise the masses love a commander . . .

They are equally unaware of their shameless spiritual terrorization and the hidden abuse of their human freedom . . . All they see is the ruthless force and brutality of its calculated manifestations, to which they will always submit in the end . . . Terror at the place of employment, in the factory, in the meeting hall, and on the occasion of mass demonstrations will always be successful unless opposed by equal terror.[17]

In other words, where propaganda fell short, the state would use brute force and the will of a 'strong man' to persuade the people.

Mein Kampf defines the 'philosophy' of Nazism chiefly by what Hitler despised. What he despised started and ended with 'the Jew', those 'parasites' and 'leeches', he variously wrote, who were responsible for the evils of the world.[18] In *Mein Kampf* we encounter the full-blown, violent strain of his anti-Semitism, a visceral hatred of the Jewish people that would accompany him for the rest of his life and riddle every corner of his coming rule. We have seen his paranoia grow by increments. Now *Mein Kampf* confirmed its vast reach. In Hitler's mind, Judaism, Marxism and international capital had merged into a monolithic traitorous and poisonous alliance against the German people.

According to this reading, 'the Jew' was at once 'a cowardly Pacifist', 'a vicious warmonger', a 'scheming wheedler of the proletariat' and 'an overstuffed plutocrat', concludes one assessment.[19] The Jews should have been rooted out and destroyed long ago, Hitler wrote: 'All the implements of military power should have been ruthlessly used for the extermination of this pestilence.'[20]

'Judeophobia' more accurately described Hitler's ceaseless, all-consuming obsession with the Jews, observes one historian.[21] If so, his 'phobia' had been brewing for years, as we've seen, from the streets of Vienna, to the war-torn cities of post-war Germany, to the beer halls of Munich. Its full, murderous form now lashed out against a group of people with nothing in common except their religion, on whom Hitler now heaped not only the responsibility for Germany's defeat, economic collapse and artistic 'decadence', but also the miseries and failures of his own life.

He had often in the past attacked the exponents of Modernism, in dance, theatre, design, cinema and cabaret, as well as physicists, philosophers and psychologists who peddled 'unGerman' ideas, as a Jewish cabal. They included, at various times, Otto Dix, Bertolt Brecht, Ernst Bloch, Walter Gropius, George Grosz, Max Ernst, Max Beckmann, Paul Klee, Thomas Mann, Max Reinhardt, Ernst Toller, Herbert Marcuse. Not all were Jews, though Jews were prominently represented in German culture. And now, noting their prevalence, Hitler compared their influence to a kind of contagious disease, an epidemic, writing in *Mein Kampf*:

> In my eyes, the charge against Judaism became a grave one the moment I discovered the Jewish activities in the Press, in art, in literature and the theatre . . . One needed only to look at the posters announcing hideous productions of the cinema and theatre, and study the names of the authors who were highly lauded there to become permanently adamant on Jewish questions. Here was a pestilence, a moral pestilence, with which the public was being infected. It was worse than the Black Plague of long ago.[22]

His mind was now set on a course that led inexorably to the destruction of an entire people whom he regarded as an existential threat to Germany, as *Mein Kampf* reveals: 'If,' he wrote, 'the Jew is victorious over the other peoples of the world, his crown will be the funeral wreath of humanity and this planet will, as it did millions of years ago, move through the ether devoid of men.'[23]

Yet the racial bludgeoning of the Jews was also popular and opportune, as Hitler's keen political antennae had detected. By blaming the Jews for *all* of Germany's miseries, he 'directed the frustrated rage of the German people against a convenient and defenceless victim'.[24]

In fomenting a monolithic Jewish conspiracy, Hitler's paranoia was in full accord with the populist will and his own political plans.

In this context, the Führer's views on 'leadership' carry the darkest intent:

> The art of leadership consists in consolidating the attention of the people against a single adversary and taking care that nothing will split up that attention into sections. The more the militant energies of the people are directed towards one objective the more will new recruits join the movement, attracted by the magnetism of its unified action, and thus the striking power will be all the more enhanced. The leader of genius must have the ability to make different opponents appear as if they belonged to the one category . . .[25]

A lesser known source for the hate-filled language against the Jews in *Mein Kampf* was the work of the leader of the Reformation, Martin Luther (1483–1546). Hitler revered Luther as one of the greatest Germans, along with Frederick the Great and Bismarck, and when he branded the Jews 'vermin', 'liars', 'vipers', 'belly worms' who were 'devouring the nation's body', Hitler was taking his cue from the great theologian. This lexicon is traceable to Luther's 65,000-word denunciation of the Jewish people, *The Jews and Their Lies*, published in 1543.[26]

To put this in context, and in fairness to the fiery priest from Wittenberg, Luther was not an 'anti-Semite' or 'racist' in the modern or Hitlerian sense, of course. As a younger man, Luther had preached tolerance and kindness towards the Jews, for instance in his essay of 1523, 'That Jesus Christ was Born a Jew'.[27] He turned violently against the Jewish people late in life, when he was very ill, on religious, not racial or political grounds, for their persistent and, to him, dumbfounding refusal to convert to Christianity and follow Christ's teaching. This he deemed the act of a devil-led people, and in the last few years of his life Luther savagely attacked them in print.

The Jews and Their Lies calls for the burning of Jewish schools and synagogues, the destruction of Jewish homes and the confiscation of their money. Those 'poisonous envenomed worms', Luther wrote, should be enslaved or exiled. *Mein Kampf* echoes that verdict: 'the Jew' must be expelled from Germany. Luther even helped the local authorities drive the Jews from their Saxon villages, an act the Nazis would repeat on Kristallnacht in 1938. In a final rage at their recalcitrance, Luther damned the 'Chosen People' as 'the Devil's People' and the 'anti-Christ', concluding: 'We are at fault in not slaying them'[28] – words that haunt *Mein Kampf* and gave the Nazis a religious authority for the Final Solution.

Hatred, political opportunism and a sixteenth-century theological authority do not alone explain Hitler's singling out of the Jews for persecution and destruction. Another motive overpowered the rest: race, as he explained in *Mein Kampf*. The Jews were 'racially inferior', a category into which he bundled anyone whose 'race' failed to conform to his Nordic, or Aryan, ideal.

There is nothing new in the idea of breeding a Master Race; it has been around since Plato suggested the stronger citizens of Athens should reproduce the 'Guardians' of his idealized Republic. In *Mein Kampf*, Hitler took the idea to its terrifying conclusion. According to his 'biological race theory', human 'races' were condemned to fight it out until the 'fittest' won – a notion as demented as it was widely accepted at the time.[29] 'Man must kill,' he concluded: 'Whoever wants to live must fight, and whoever does not want to fight,' he wrote, 'does not deserve to live.'[30] He repeated this message many times, telling a crowd at Essen on 22 November 1926: 'Only force rules. Force is the first law.'[31]

In a world of masters and slaves, the weak, the sick, the defenceless were not only doomed; they *deserved* to die, Hitler continued. This outcome was not only scientifically determined, it was the will of God, he insisted. In a speech that expanded on *Mein Kampf*, he later declared that 'the stronger has the right before God and the world to enforce his will.'[32]

In this light, the Jews, more than any other 'race', posed a unique menace to Hitler's vision of Aryan rule. He feared the Jews as much as he hated them. He saw 'Jews here and Jews there and Jews everywhere'. If allowed to procreate, they would realize 'the Pan-Jewish prophecy that the Jews will one day devour the other nations and become lords of the earth.'[33]

Despite their tiny numbers – the Jews made up less than 1 per cent of the German population when Hitler became Chancellor in 1933[34] – the Führer would always insist, to the dismay of his less monomaniacal followers, that he would make the removal and destruction of Jewry the party's chief priority. *Mein Kampf* is explicit about this.[35]

Mein Kampf contains a litany of errors and fabrications. We haven't the space to correct them all, but it is worth drawing attention to a few basic flaws given the programme of genocidal murder the book inspired.

Drawing on his favourite 'racial theorists' – chiefly Rosenberg, de Gobineau and Chamberlain – Hitler argues that the 'human race' contained several subsidiary 'races', such as Aryan, Teuton, Anglo-Saxon, African, Asian, Slav, Jew and so on. Whether they liked it or not, these 'sub-races' were doomed to an eternal life-or-death struggle for survival.

He explicitly opposed breeding between them (and would ban it as Führer), in case the 'weak races' poisoned the genetic purity of the 'strong'. In making this case in *Mein Kampf*, he offers a list of 'successful' examples of pure-bred creatures from the animal kingdom: 'Every animal mates only with a member of the same species. The titmouse seeks the titmouse, the finch the finch, the stork the stork, the field mouse the field mouse, the dormouse the dormouse, the wolf the she-wolf . . .'[36] The lesson being that the Aryan (or 'wolf', to extend the analogy) should breed only with the Aryan, and never with the Jew or Slav (the birds and mice of the analogy). 'There is no cat,' Hitler goes on to explain, 'with a friendly inclination towards mice.'

It is worth restating a biological fact known to most schoolchildren, and which Hitler and his racial theorists had overlooked (as have the neo-white supremacists of our own time): there is only one human race. It is a species called *Homo sapiens*, to which all human beings belong, and have done for almost 300,000 years (according to fossils recently discovered in Morocco[37]), regardless of their appearance, religious belief or skin colour, which are the long-term differences arising from environment, climate and culture.

The fittingly Nordic botanist Carl Linnaeus first coined the name *Homo sapiens* in 1758 to describe the only extant human species, to distinguish us from six extinct species of hominids, such as *Homo erectus* and *Homo neanderthalensis* (Neanderthals). *Sapiens* is a member of the taxonomic genus *Homo*, itself part of the family *Hominidae*, itself part of the order of primates. (For a recent history of the only extant human species, see *Sapiens: A Brief History of Humankind*, by an Israeli historian, the fittingly Jewish Yuval Noah Harari.[38]) The finch family, on the other hand, to extrapolate Hitler's comparison, contains no fewer than 218 species, and the stork more than a dozen. Whether these species inter-breed, Hitler doesn't make clear.

Nor does he discuss the existential struggle for survival between *Homo sapiens* and rival species within *Hominidae*, which include three other genera of great apes. Their continuing existence leads us to the awkward conclusion that a scientifically accurate Nazi race law would have banned interbreeding between *Homo sapiens* and gorillas, and sent chimps and macaques to the death camps.

In other words, being members of the human 'race', 'racists' unwittingly attack themselves and their own species when they attack other humans, of different skin colour or culture. The simple truth is: we're all *Homo sapiens* and we're all in this mess together.

Another basic error in *Mein Kampf* arises from Hitler's use of the term 'Aryan'. It appears forty-nine times in the Mannheim translation (and fifty-eight times in the Nazi-approved translation), with reference to the Master Race that would emerge from the Nazis' 'Aryanization' of Germany – that is, the extermination of 'lesser races', homosexuals and the disabled.

Though their provenance is unclear, the 'Aryans' appear to have been a nomadic Indo-Iranian people who spread over northern India between 1500 and 500 BC and worshipped Vedic deities. 'Aryan' loosely defined their shared language and religious beliefs, not their 'race'. In sum, the blonde, white supermen and -women of the Nazi imagination were modelled on a 'race' that never existed; and the Vedic Indo-Iranians from which the word 'Aryan' derives were as far removed as can be imagined from Hitler's pot-bellied Brownshirts.

The perversion of the term exemplifies the destructive power of words when repeatedly harnessed to bogus ideas through official propaganda. Hitler popularized the 'Aryan ideal' in speech after speech to ordinary beer-swilling Germans, who were delighted to find themselves anointed the torch-bearers of human civilization. To a packed Munich beer hall on 2 April 1927, he would announce:

> We see before us the Aryan race which is manifestly the bearer of all culture, the true representative of all humanity ... Our entire industrial science is without exception the work of the Nordics. All great composers from Beethoven to Richard Wagner are Aryans, even though they were born in Italy or France. Do not say that art is international. The tango, the shimmy and the jazz band are international but they are not art. Man owes everything that is of importance to the principle of struggle and to one race . . . Take away the Nordic Germans and nothing remains but the dance of the apes . . .[39]

In the murderous sweep of his mind, Hitler had not forgotten homosexuals, transgender, Roma, Sinti, the disabled, chronically sick and mentally ill, who were deemed similarly flawed, genetically inferior, racial weaklings who served no useful purpose. All should be prevented from breeding with healthy German stock, he believed. In power, the Nazis would dispatch tens of thousands of these people to the death camps, along with the Jews and other 'non-Aryans'.[40]

Hanging over *Mein Kampf* is the memory of the episode by which Hitler measured everything else in his life: his recollections of the First

World War. The passage of time had not diminished his fury. The 'great injustice' of the Armistice, the stab in the back of the army, supercharged his titanic grudge against the Jewish people who, he claimed, had 'perpetrated' Germany's humiliation.

This monstrous delusion poisoned everything Hitler said and wrote in the book. In a passage of staggering self-deception, he persuaded himself that 'Jewish treachery' had killed the German Army, and that Germany might have won the war had these 'traitors' been slaughtered in 1914:

> If at the beginning of the war and during the war twelve or fifteen thousand of these Hebrew corrupters of the people had been held under poison gas, as happened to hundreds of thousands of our very best German workers in the field, the sacrifice of millions at the front would not have been in vain. On the contrary: twelve thousand scoundrels eliminated in time might have saved the lives of a million real Germans . . .[41]

Hitler thus prefigured, as early as 1924, how he would try to destroy the Jewish people: with a far more lethal variety of gas than the mustard gas that had left him temporarily blinded in Pasewalk. Henceforth, he would dedicate his life to the destruction of a 'race' whose 'guilt' and 'crimes' he conflated with the mounds of German corpses on the Western Front. He also alluded to the purpose and scale of a coming Holocaust. The first job of the Nazi Party, he wrote, must be 'to wipe out the Jewish state'.[42] The Nazis would survive only through 'a vast plan of extermination' of the exponents of rival 'ideas' and beliefs.[43]

Almost a decade before the German people elected Hitler their chancellor, the world had been warned. Nobody who bothered to read his book should have been surprised or shocked by what followed. In *Mein Kampf* Hitler laid bare the Nazi programme of conquest, persecution and genocide.

*

The first volume of *Mein Kampf* appeared on 18 July 1925, seven months after Hitler's release from Landsberg Prison. He had initially titled it *Four and a Half Years of Struggle Against Lies, Stupidity and Cowardice*, but his publisher, Max Amann, fearing readers would shun such a lugubrious title, recommended the shorter one.

Mein Kampf would sell 10,000 copies by the year's end, after which sales flagged. Hitler was still, after all, a minor politician and ex-prisoner, despite his international fame as the leader of the Beer Hall Putsch. It would take the revival of his political fortunes, in 1930, to interest readers in his book. By the end of 1932, sales would reach almost 230,000; and by 1944, 12.5 million copies had been printed, obligatory reading in schools and among Nazi Party members. *Mein Kampf* would make Hitler a wealthy man a year before Germany lost the war and he killed himself.

On first publication it received 'mixed' reviews, if it was reviewed at all, outside Germany. Some readers drew the right conclusions about it. One was the British historian Sir Charles Grant Robertson, who had read the book and heard Hitler speak. In 1936 Robertson reflected:

> No one can read *Mein Kampf* without amazement at the shallowness of its 'philosophy', the travesty and superficiality of its historical interpretation of the past, or the demagogic crudity of its anti-semitic appeal to all the basest and fiercest of human motives – fear, jealousy, greed – and above all to the most invincible of all national passions – the purging of defeat by the expulsion of a national scape-goat on whom the misery of an innocent people, deceived into sin, can safely be put.[44]

*

On 19 December 1924, Hitler stepped out of prison to relaunch his political career. If the beast had been 'tamed' in prison, as the *New York Times* wishfully reported at the time,[45] Hitler showed no such restraint on his first public appearance, in the Bürgerbräukeller, the scene of the Putsch. He took the stage as a newly minted 'democrat', apparently willing to campaign peacefully for power. But nothing else had changed: he began his speech by branding the Jewish people the tools of the devil who must be eliminated from the earth.

One man taking a very close interest in Hitler's career at this time was the student who had written to him in prison, Dr Joseph Goebbels. To Goebbels, Hitler was Germany's only hope, the saviour of the country, the God-sent 'sweet' messiah and 'coming dictator', as he wrote on 20 November 1925.[46] In his diary in June the following year, Goebbels relished the prospect of working with him: 'One could conquer the world with this man.'[47]

The Führer was ready to start.

The making of the Führer

Through the late 1920s and well into the 1930s, foreign governments, journalists and the intellectual 'elite' ignored or ridiculed the threat of Hitler. He was simply laughable, beyond the pale.

Stefan Zweig, the bestselling Austrian writer of the time, admitted in his memoir that he and his fellow intellectuals had failed utterly to apprehend the coming maelstrom. 'The few among writers who had taken the trouble to read Hitler's book, ridiculed the bombast of his stilted prose instead of occupying themselves with his program,' he wrote. Well into the 1930s, 'the big democratic newspapers, instead of warning their readers, reassured them day by day, that the move-ment . . . would inevitably collapse in no time.'[1] 'They took him neither seriously nor literally,' concluded George Prochnik in an article in the *New Yorker*.[2]

In *Mein Kampf,* Hitler meant what he said. His words were not the ravings of a poser or mere populist, such as Lueger or Schönerer, or any number of fanatics in Bavaria at the time. In *Mein Kampf* Hitler warned the world what to expect when he seized power: war, persecu-tion, revenge, mass death. He laid it all down with a visceral fury that European governments failed to heed, even after he came to power in 1933.

Among foreign politicians, only Winston Churchill accurately assessed in advance the threat of Hitler. In the Führer, Churchill detected the paranoia of a tyrant and the lawless destroyer of European culture. During his 'wilderness years' (1929–38), the British leader repeatedly tried to warn the British government of the malign spirit at large in Germany, notably in his radio broadcasts of November 1934:

> Only a few hours away by air there dwells a nation of nearly seventy millions of the most educated, industrious, scientific, disciplined people in the world, who are being taught from childhood to think of war as a glorious exercise, and death in battle as the noblest fate for man. There is a nation which has abandoned all its liberties in order to augment its collective strength. There is a nation which, with all its strength and virtue, is in the grip of a group of ruthless men, preaching a gospel of intolerance and racial pride, unrestrained by law, by Parliament, or by public opinion . . .'[3]

In the transcript to a broadcast the previous night, he had written: 'In that country all pacifist speeches, all morbid books are forbidden or suppressed, and their authors rigorously imprisoned. From their new table of commandments they have omitted "thou shall not kill".[4]

If Hitler's political ideas scarcely rose above the level of a beer-hall rant, his multifaceted character was far from ordinary. He possessed a will of iron, a forensic memory, a gift for mass manipulation, and fixative charisma as a public speaker. His violent hatred of the Jews stoked the fires of racial hatred in Germany and around the world, fuelling fascist movements from the Balkans to Great Britain. Though largely a lower middle-class movement, Nazism attracted followers from all social backgrounds; soft-brained English aristocrats found Hitler unusually seductive.

To this day, some claim Hitler was a great, if flawed, leader, crushed by the machinations of others. The historian Joachim Fest asserts that had Hitler died of an assassin's bullet in 1938 most Germans would remember him today as one of the greatest statesmen their country had produced.[5] This astounding remark fails any objective test of 'greatness' if the term means a just and enlightened leader.

The inconvenient fact is that by 1938, on Hitler's orders, the Nazis had viciously consolidated their power, dismantled the legal system, killed off parliamentary democracy, assembled a huge war machine, oppressed 'non-Aryan' minorities and erected a one-party dictatorship.

Nor was Hitler the tool of others. Both Marxists and capitalists sought to portray him as the puppet of their opponents, failing to see that Hitler was always his own man, impelling his audiences in the direction he chose through the sheer force of his voice and his irrepressible will.

That is not to say that millions of ordinary Germans approved of the Holocaust – most were unaware of the extent of the Nazis' crimes, and many of those who knew were indifferent to what they found out;[6] it is to say that feelings of violent nationalism and hatred for easily scapegoated minorities were so ingrained in post-war Germany as to facilitate the rise of a politician who articulated, and would later act on, those feelings.

The brutalization of a people, rather than any inherent qualities in Hitler as a man, brought him to power. The First World War debased German society so completely that racist cranks and fascist rabble-rousers were considered 'rational' and 'normal'. As Fest rightly observes, Hitler's rise to power 'depended not so much on his demonic traits as on his typical, "normal" characteristics . . . He was not so much the great contradiction of his age as its mirror image.'[7]

The First World War did not 'change' Hitler; it drew him out. It extrapolated him. And he ran with the memory, distilling and exploiting its essence, as far as it would take him. At every level – psychologically, emotionally and politically – the war acted like a forge for his character, hammering his embittered mind into a vengeful political machine. Insofar as he personified the forces of hatred and destruction, he personified the war.

His inchoate loathing, his unfocused aggression, his hunt for a culprit, his longing for a role, a 'fit', in a world that had rejected him, all coalesced with his fury at Germany's defeat and its aftermath. Even strategically, the First World War influenced his judgement – in the Second he would disastrously misapply the strategic lessons of the First and grossly underestimate the strength of the Red Army.[8]

The memory of the humiliation of November 1918 travelled with him like a weeping wound, unhealable, an ever-present reminder of an experience that shaped his thought and action. He was not like most soldiers, of course: Hitler had constantly thrilled to battle, later describing his regiment's last, doomed offensive action in 1918 as the most 'stupendous' experience of his life.[9] He passionately loved soldiering, as he always said. He saw something at First Ypres that eluded his fellow men: for Hitler, the soldiers' sacrifice was not only heroic, it was also necessary, noble and *natural*.

For young Hitler, the First World War was the final act of 'the fittest' in the great drama of the human race, the re-enactment of a vast Teutonic legend from which the Nibelungs would emerge victorious and inherit the earth. When the Germans failed to do so, Hitler identified those he held responsible for the soldiers' humiliation, and would even describe, in *Mein Kampf*, their coming punishment.

The war and its aftermath threw him into politics. His memory of the *Kindermord*, his wounds and gassing, his contempt for the complacency on the home front, his rage against Versailles, his intense idea of himself as a man of destiny and avenger of the army – all served to recast this flint-hearted individual on a political career driven by vengeance and fomented by millions of fellow travellers who had found a man willing to act on their darkest prejudices.

Above all, in mourning the loss of thousands of 'beardless youths' at Langemarck in 1914, Hitler would never forgive those he held responsible for Germany's defeat: the 'shirkers', the Jews and socialists who, he claimed, had 'cunningly dodged death'.[10] In largely blaming the Jews, in 1919, for Germany's 'stab in the back', Hitler refused to accept what had been palpably clear to any soldier at the Armistice on 11 November 1918: Germany had lost the war at the front.

The memory lived with the Führer until the very end. In his Berlin bunker he looked back on the First World War as the defining event of his life. He wore his Iron Cross (First Class) at his marriage to Eva Braun on the night of 28/9 April 1945, forty hours before the newly-weds would kill themselves.

The collapse of any society brings forth monsters, to adapt Goya. In this sense, there was nothing uniquely 'German' about the Nazis. Hitler and the party he created could have happened anywhere. It is fair to say that Britain, France, America, or any other nation for that matter, left in the same brutalized state as Germany in 1918, would have found their own 'Führer', preying on their humiliation and social chaos, and blaming it all on a defenceless minority.

In this light, Hitler was Europe's creation as much as Germany's: he sprang from the broken world of Flanders and the Somme, Versailles and hyperinflation. The First World War ploughed a field so barren of hope that Hitler's murderous manifesto fell on hearts and minds so utterly fraught they were willing to believe in it.

In sum, Hitler was more than the creation of the First World War. In his mind, he was its will and representation, a miracle of survival who imagined he gave voice to the dead, that his howl of hatred spoke for the remains in the mass graves at Langemarck, after a war that had killed 2.5 million German people.

A question often asked is: how could the Nazis have committed their shocking crimes? The conventional moral outrage implicit in the question suggests the Nazis were exceptional – outliers, monsters, freaks, insane. The truth, as we've seen, is that Hitler was medically 'normal' and completely accountable.

So, too, were most of his staff and the bureaucrats who ran the Nazi instruments of power: ordinary people, in the main, tradesmen and unionists, clerks and bankers, journalists and businessmen, farmers and councillors. Millions of them were persuaded to believe, or were frightened into believing, in the Nazi programme of conquest, racial persecution and German 'greatness'. When they heard Hitler railing against the Jews, observes Ullrich, 'hardly anyone seems to have disapproved'.[11] Most Germans were not the genocidal automatons of Goldhagen's book *Hitler's Willing Executioners*, who fell into step with the mass slaughter of their own people. Most conformed to the portrait given here, and in Kershaw, Ullrich and elsewhere, of a broken nation of vengeful soldiers, indifferent functionaries, and a cowed and hungry people.[12]

The Nazis acted as they did because they genuinely believed in the word of their Führer. The rank and file thought they were building a new society ruled by a higher race, a supreme people. And they did so *because they could*: the rule of force, party propaganda, European appeasement and, above all, the will of their charismatic leader, legitimized and *normalized* the hell of Hitler's Germany.

A more disturbing question is: what could have stopped Hitler? Nothing – not political opposition, foreign intervention, religious forbearance, popular resistance, compassion or the voice of conscience – exerted any restraint on his rise to power.

The tragedy is that Hitler and the Nazis acted with the appeasement, or the complicity, of the world. Encouraged by the blind eyes turned by the few opposing nations and the zealous participation of collaborating ones, the National Socialists reckoned they had received the nod of history. They felt they were acting with political and moral impunity. Goebbels' outlandish propaganda persuaded a majority of otherwise sentient Germans to think they were part of a quasi-religious movement, on an eternal mission to build a new nation, a *good* nation.

Without wading too deeply into the thickets of commentary about the 'normalization' of the far right in 2016–17, a few points are worth making about Hitler's legacy.

Were Hitler alive today, it's a safe bet he would find millions of brawling adherents in the West, many of whom shamelessly flaunt their admiration for him. We need look no further than the white supremacist rally in Charlottesville, Virginia, in August 2017, during which a self-described neo-Nazi rammed his car into a crowd, killing a young woman, while hundreds of others bore swastikas or the symbols of white nationalist groups such as Vanguard and the Ku Klux Klan and several were seen performing the Nazi salute. In so doing, today's neo-Nazis unwittingly expose themselves to a devastating charge: by any objective moral test, they are *more* repellent than the ordinary members of Hitler's movement, because today's Nazis go about the grisly business of demonizing whole 'races' and religions fully cognisant of the genocidal crimes committed by the man in whose name they act. The same cannot be said of most of the Nazi rank and file in the 1940s, who were ignorant of the existence or the full extent of the Final Solution.

Yet the facts of the Holocaust against the Jews, the death camps, the murder of homosexuals, the disabled and the mentally ill, the medical tests on prisoners and the millions killed in the Second World War on Hitler's orders don't seem to persuade the twenty-first century's Nazis to rethink their affiliation. On the contrary, they revel in it. From Warsaw to Washington, via Athens, Rome, Vienna, Dresden, Paris and London, the self-appointed heirs of National Socialism rally round their home-grown demagogues like hyenas round a carcass, recycling the crudest form of political opportunism, the scapegoat.

Of the many recent examples of violent neo-fascism, two stand out as exceptionally repugnant. Thomas Mair, the murderer of Jo Cox, a British MP and pro-Europe campaigner, drew his inspiration straight from the Nazis: obsessed with Hitler, he decked his home in Nazi memorabilia and shelves with books on SS race theory and white supremacy. On 16 June 2016, two weeks before Britain voted to leave the European Union, he stabbed Mrs Cox multiple times, then shot her three times in the head, while shouting 'Freedom for Britain' and 'Britain First'. A year earlier, on 17 June 2015, twenty-two-year-old Dylann Storm Roof entered the Emanuel African Methodist Episcopal Church in Charleston, South Carolina, and shot dead nine black worshippers. Roof, who fantasized about the canonization of Hitler and about a Confederate victory, believed he was launching a race war and fulfilling the work of the Ku Klux Klan and the Nazis, whose '*Heil Hitler!*' salute was encoded into his website.

Millions of people share the beliefs, if not the 'methods', of these murderers. Among them is America's National Socialist movement, a leading neo-Nazi group that disseminates 'violent anti-Jewish rhetoric'.[13] In 2016 this small but vocal group enjoyed the attention of a *New York Times* profile[14] and a public platform. Surprised, perhaps, by its sudden 'popularity', the group's members decided to replace the swastika worn on their uniforms with a Norse rune, an 'Aryan' symbol the Nazis approved of. It was a magnanimous gesture, in the circumstances, to public sensitivities. No such compromise is evident in the group's '25 points', a direct echo of Hitler's 1920 manifesto. Point 4, for example, states: 'Only those of pure White blood, whatever their creed, may be members of the nation . . . no Jew or homosexual may be a member of the nation.'[15]

Of course, America's Alt-Right (Alternative Right), France's Le Penists, the UK Independence Party, the Dutch Freedom Party, the Alternative for Germany (AfD), the Greek Golden Dawn, etc., should not be bundled up with the neo-Nazi movement. For while their policies amount to the crassest kind of 'racial nationalism', they have operated within the democratic system and not (yet) espoused a violent programme of lawless persecution. All were in the process of failing or unravelling at the time of writing. (Neo-fascist groups inflicted scores of 'unofficial' attacks on migrants in 2016, including ten a day in Germany by the AfD and other extremists.)

Insofar as they have any intellectual ballast, Steven Bannon, the former publisher of *Breitbart News* who was sacked as a senior adviser to US President Donald Trump in August 2017, is their anointed guru. Bannon and his followers at *Breitbart News* and other Alt-Right forums think themselves novel, but they stand in the long tradition of white nationalists whose ideas draw on the writing of 'Nazi racial theorists', such as de Gobineau, Chamberlain and Rosenberg, and boil down to a crude alloy of Social Darwinism and racial nationalism. Their twenty-first-century heirs are buttressed by Holocaust deniers such as David Irving – who lost his defamation case in 2000 against a US historian who had accused him of being one (a case brilliantly described in Richard Evans' book *Lying About Hitler: History, Holocaust and the*

David Irving Trial) – and by racial theories purporting to be scientific such as Richard Herrnstein and Charles Murray's *The Bell Curve: Intelligence and Class Structure in American Life*, which claims to find a genetic or 'racial' basis for intelligence but in fact finds none, according to a damning assessment by the American Psychological Association's Board of Scientific Affairs. Perhaps whites are simply more familiar with filling in IQ tests than blacks?[16]

There is something else insidious about Bannon. A neo-crusader and a prominent champion of the 'clash of civilizations' thesis, he believes the Christian armies of the West are destined to fight the mother of all battles against the Islamic world. He speaks like a man determined to avenge the West for the loss of Constantinople to the Ottoman Empire in 1453 and the Muslim siege of Vienna in 1529. In ushering in what we might call the age of 'Techno-Mediaevalism' (with apologies to the Middle Ages, which were more complex and enquiring than this crude atavism suggests), Bannon and his disciples would harness the pre-Enlightenment mind – of which he is perhaps today's most powerful exemplar – to America's twenty-first-century nuclear arsenal.

In the summer of 2014 Bannon laid out his 'global vision' to a conference held by the Human Dignity Institute in the Vatican. 'We're now, I believe,' he said, 'at the beginning stages of a global war against Islamic fascism.' It would be, he warned:

. . . a very brutal and bloody conflict, of which if the people in this room, the people in the church, do not bind together and really form what I feel is an aspect of the church militant to . . . fight for our beliefs against this new barbarity that's starting, [it] will completely eradicate everything that we've been bequeathed over the last two thousand [or] two thousand five hundred years.[17]

Like all blowhard catastrophists, Bannon resorts to conjuring tricks, rustling up an apocalypse like a magician to terrify the faint-hearted and summon another crusade. It is Bannon and his ilk who are frightened, who are reeling from terror. And his kind of thinking plays straight into the hands of jihadists who think in the same apocalyptic terms, rejoice in what they see as the decline of the West and clamour for exactly the kind of global 'holy war' that Bannon sounds eager to give them. At any other time he would have been seen as a 'holy fool' or court jester, but for a brief period he had to be taken seriously because of his influence in the White House.

In this light, it is painful to witness the contortions of the credible media as they attempt to report on phenomena they clearly detest. *The Economist* magazine recently expressed its disgust at having to cover Bannon's Alt-Right as though it were part of normal discourse, which at the time it clearly was. 'First an apology, or rather a regret,' the old liberal magazine confided, '*The Economist* would prefer not to advertise the rantings of racists and cranks. Unfortunately, and somewhat astonishingly, the Alt-Right – the misleading name for a ragtag but consistently repulsive movement that hitherto has flourished only on the internet – has insinuated itself, unignorably, into American politics.' The movement championed 'a neo-segregationist "race realism",' the magazine reported, 'which, of course, is really just old-fashioned white supremacism in skimpy camouflage.'[18]

This time around, people of the Muslim religion are the targets of far-right hatred, in America and Europe, stoked by the atrocious crimes of a small number of Islamic extremists. Demonizing an entire faith, the more poisonous commentators carelessly invoke Hitler's example. Katie Hopkins, the British media personality and newspaper columnist, tweeted after the Manchester terrorist attack in May 2017: 'We need a final solution.' On any other day Hopkins' opinions would be treated as another passing venom-spill in the great swim of history, but her tweets have catapulted her into the annals of infamy. According to a report by the Brookings Institution, a leading think tank, in December 2016, '[T]o those who consider minority faiths to be a threat, Jews have been eclipsed by Muslims, who, in the popular imagination, threaten to destroy the white Christian West physically with terrorism and immigration and culturally with alien laws.'[19]

While Brookings' statement lazily conflates *Mein Kampf* with

Samuel P. Huntington's *The Clash of Civilisations*, it captures a sense of the *psychological and tactical* similarities between the Nazis of the 1920s and the Alt-Right of 2017–18, who seek to project the abhorrent crimes of a small minority of jihadists on to a religion of more than 1.6 billion people. Indeed, extremists on both sides seem determined to accelerate the confrontation, fragmenting our benighted world and drawing us closer to the 'holy war' of the jihadist and neo-fascist fantasy.

Hopefully, this story of Hitler's youth has answered, to some degree, that often asked question, 'How could Hitler have happened?' These days, we see how easily it could happen again. And this raises a second question: 'What can we do to stop another Hitler?' How can Western governments act to avoid the social and economic chaos that would spawn another genocidal dictator?

The simple answer – but extremely difficult task – is to prevent another global conflagration and economic depression. Hitler was the bastard child of the First World War and the economic and social chaos that followed. In this respect, Western society has little in common with Weimar Germany in the 1920s. In its *effect*, the Great Recession of 2008–11 bears no comparison to the Great Depression of 1929–31, when millions lost their jobs and life savings. None of us has suffered the hyperinflation of the early 1920s. Our society is, by comparison, prosperous and productive; and most of us are fed, housed, educated and tend to live by the rule of law.

Yet we see signs everywhere of splintering, of a terrible rupture; we hear cries of profound anguish. The obscene division between rich and poor, the social isolation of the chronically jobless, the prolifer-ation of online hysteria, the complacency of Western governments (and indifference towards the disdain in which they're held) have envenomed large sections of the West against itself, fomenting the politics of hatred and self-loathing.

The solution to these ills does not lie in surrendering to 'popu-lism', the grotesquely misnamed 'movement' that merely exploits the misery of those it claims to defend. The solution has nothing to do with blaming foreigners, be they Mexicans or Moroccans. Islam will not defeat us by 'out-breeding' us, once the economy strengthens and political stability returns. Nor should we yield to the fearmongering of excited catastrophists such as Douglas Murray (author of *The Strange Death of Europe*), who ache for a non-existent golden age of Christian purity rid of non-whites, and who believe 'Europe is committing suicide' because we've abandoned our 'Judeo-Christian values'. No doubt the European Union is in serious need of reform (but that's another story). Yet Murray seems determined to ignore inconvenient truths, such as the fact that the nations of 'Europe' have forged a remarkable peace since the Second World War, enjoyed astonishing post-war economic growth and demonstrated great and unique Christian altruism (i.e. the expression of our 'values', as he concedes) towards desperate people. It is striking that London, Paris, Manchester and Berlin, the cities most tormented by terrorists in 2016–17 and which, in Murray's telling, are plagued by migrants (especially Muslims), voted overwhelmingly *for* Europe and rejected 'populism' in the 2017 elections, and showed extraordinary solidarity across ethnic and religious divides during and after the terrorist attacks.

Western civilization is not about to crumble to a few crazed, straggle-bearded, sexually stunted young men strapped to nail bombs and the seats of trucks. Europeans will be revelling in 'Western values', dancing the tango on the banks of the Seine, arguing over flat whites in Borough Market, baptizing their children in cathedrals, applauding concerts in the Bataclan and thronging the gay bars of Soho long after Bannon, Murray and their fellow apocalypticians fade away and people realize that the real threat to our society emanates not from 'foreigners' or our 'Godless decadence' or populist fearmongering, but from our own chronic economic dysfunction and social injustice.

The solution has everything to do with economic and social policy. It means accepting that 'trickle-down' economics championed in recent decades hasn't worked as hoped or promised, and that large sections of Western society are economically and socially destitute even as the world's richest echelons concentrate wealth in their hands on a scale not seen since before the outbreak of war in 1914. You only have to glance at French economist Thomas Piketty's extraordinary research to see how society has reverted to pre-First World War levels of inequity. Social and economic injustice, not the presence of a proportionately small number of asylum-seekers and migrants, lay at the root of the outrage that fuelled the 2016–17 elections. That hard truth was lost in the utterly unscrupulous scapegoating of refugees by politicians and journalists, the Fifth Horsemen of the 'populist elite'.[20]

The solution means realizing, and investing for the benefit of all, the treasures of regulated competition and free and fair trade; and rejecting the politics of bigotry towards women, ethnic minorities and people of different faiths.

It means launching, in parallel and in cohesion with other governments and religious organizations, the firmest and most carefully thought-through plan of cooperative vigilance and, when necessary, coordinated military action, against those who seek to harm us.

The solution means reaffirming the Enlightened spirit of scientific enquiry, political reform and creative brilliance that energized the past 300 years and has been so gravely undermined, respectively, by the rejection of evolution and the denial of climate change; the stifling of political thought and ideas; and the slow demise of academic and artistic excellence. It means being able to distinguish value from volume, and experienced insight from the wilful ignorance of the trolletariat. It means reinforcing the Western (or, if you prefer, Judeo-Christian) values of charity, community and compassion, hidden and demeaned in a world in which obscene avarice and egomaniacal individualism are treated as virtues.

The solution, in sum, means finding Western leaders and governments of quiet strength, honesty and surpassing vision who are determined to preserve 'our way of life' by reinforcing, not merely defending, the Enlightenment values of freedom of thought and speech, so often maligned or misunderstood, and the great democratic traditions of true liberalism and openness, so often taken for granted or twisted to the point that common decency is mistaken for a malign form of political correctness. It means controlling immigration, of course, not slamming the door; reforming not crushing our institutions; building not destroying our communities (a start might be to revitalize the town hall as a place to meet and dance and debate); and recognizing our shared story in that beautiful and terrible, ingenious and slovenly, chaotic and orderly, brutal and compassionate, and always delicious realm of humanity, Europe.

Without this combined emphasis on enjoying while affirming our values and freedoms, the West will continue to slide into a kind of pre-Enlightened, superstitious gloom, a state of nuclear-armed techno-medievalism, ruled by unread men in gilded houses and ex-bankers dreaming of holy war.[21] In such circumstances, extremists may one day find a genuine 'Führer' to lead them, from among the cartoonish thugs and blonde cranks who have hitherto held the job.

In the meantime, the far-right excrescences of the early twenty-first century will probably suppurate for a while, causing a lot of grief and damage, before sinking back into oblivion (they are dying as I write this, contrary to the apocalypticians' warnings) . . . until a fresh parade of demagogues arrives to exploit another financial crisis or terrorist attack by promising 'the people' that their future happiness depends on slamming the door on the wretched, or vilifying 'Muslims' or 'Jews' or 'Mexicans' or another minority group – and all the while failing to deal with the deep economic trauma that is the true scourge of the West.

Indeed, it is a short mental leap to imagine today's fashionable young fascists signing up for another experiment in organized oppression. Their disciples will presumably be 'social media experts', or trolls, rather than beer-hall thugs, but they will do the same job, in effect: rubber-stamping a new programme of savage persecution of innocent people in the name of their late, beloved Führer.

Young Hitler would have been proud of them.

The German National Socialist '25-point Programme'

Adolf Hitler announced the '25-point Programme' of the National Socialist German Workers' Party (NSDAP) before about 2,000 people in the Hofbräuhaus in Munich on 24 February 1920. The party's manifesto became an 'unalterable expression' of its philosophy and mission, and would be adopted, in part, by the nationalist socialist movements in America and fascist organizations in other countries in the twenty-first century. In essence a prescription for state tyranny, it contains several points that find an echo in right- and left-wing policy programmes today.

1. We demand the unification of all Germans in the Greater Germany on the basis of the people's right to self-determination.
2. We demand equality of rights for the German people in respect to the other nations; abrogation of the peace treaties of Versailles and St. Germain.
3. We demand land and territory (colonies) for the sustenance of our people, and colonization for our surplus population.
4. Only a member of the race can be a citizen. A member of the race can only be one who is of German blood, without consideration of creed. Consequently, no Jew can be a member of the race.
5. Whoever has no citizenship is to be able to live in Germany only

as a guest, and must be under the authority of legislation for foreigners.

6. The right to determine matters concerning administration and law belongs only to the citizen. Therefore, we demand that every public office, of any sort whatsoever, whether in the Reich, the county or municipality, be filled only by citizens. We combat the corrupting parliamentary economy, office-holding only according to party inclinations without consideration of character or abilities.

7. We demand that the state be charged first with providing the opportunity for a livelihood and way of life for the citizens. If it is impossible to sustain the total population of the State, then the members of foreign nations (non-citizens) are to be expelled from the Reich.

8. Any further immigration of non-citizens is to be prevented. We demand that all non-Germans, who have immigrated to Germany since 2 August 1914, be forced immediately to leave the Reich.

9. All citizens must have equal rights and obligations.

10. The first obligation of every citizen must be to productively work mentally or physically. The activity of individuals is not to counteract the interests of the universality, but must have its result within the framework of the whole for the benefit of all. Consequently, we demand:

11. Abolition of unearned (work and labour) incomes. Breaking of debt (interest)-slavery.

12. In consideration of the monstrous sacrifice in property and blood that each war demands of the people, personal enrichment through a war must be designated as a crime against the people. Therefore, we demand the total confiscation of all war profits.

13. We demand the nationalisation of all (previous) associated industries (trusts).

14. We demand a division of profits of all heavy industries.

15. We demand an expansion on a large scale of old age welfare.

16. We demand the creation of a healthy middle class and its conservation, immediate communalization of the great warehouses and

their being leased at low cost to small firms, the utmost consideration of all small firms in contracts with the State, county or municipality.

17. We demand a land reform suitable to our needs, provision of a law for the free expropriation of land for the purposes of public utility, abolition of taxes on land and prevention of all speculation in land.

18. We demand struggle without consideration against those whose activity is injurious to the general interest. Common national criminals, usurers, profiteers and so forth are to be punished with death, without consideration of confession or race.

19. We demand substitution of a German common law in place of the Roman Law serving a materialistic world-order.

20. The state is to be responsible for a fundamental reconstruction of our whole national education program, to enable every capable and industrious German to obtain higher education and subsequently introduction into leading positions. The plans of instruction of all educational institutions are to conform with the experiences of practical life. The comprehension of the concept of the State must be striven for by the school [*Staatsbürgerkunde*] as early as the beginning of understanding. We demand the education at the expense of the State of outstanding intellectually gifted children of poor parents without consideration of position or profession.

21. The State is to care for the elevating national health by protecting the mother and child, by outlawing child-labor, by the encouragement of physical fitness, by means of the legal establishment of a gymnastic and sport obligation, by the utmost support of all organizations concerned with the physical instruction of the young.

22. We demand abolition of the mercenary troops and formation of a national army.

23. We demand legal opposition to known lies and their promulgation through the press. In order to enable the provision of a German press, we demand, that:

a. All writers and employees of the newspapers appearing in the German language be members of the race;

b. Non-German newspapers be required to have the express permission of the State to be published. They may not be printed in the German language;

c. Non-Germans are forbidden by law any financial interest in German publications, or any influence on them, and as punishment for violations the closing of such a publication as well as the immediate expulsion from the Reich of the non-German concerned. Publications which are counter to the general good are to be forbidden. We demand legal prosecution of artistic and literary forms which exert a destructive influence on our national life, and the closure of organizations opposing the above made demands.

24. We demand freedom of religion for all religious denominations within the state so long as they do not endanger its existence or oppose the moral senses of the Germanic race. The Party as such advocates the standpoint of a positive Christianity without binding itself confessionally to any one denomination. It combats the Jewish-materialistic spirit within and around us, and is convinced that a lasting recovery of our nation can only succeed from within on the framework: The common good before the individual good. [*Gemeinnutz geht vor Eigennutz* has also been translated as 'The good of the state before the good of the individual.']

25. For the execution of all of this we demand the formation of a strong central power in the Reich. Unlimited authority of the central parliament over the whole Reich and its organizations in general. The forming of state and profession chambers for the execution of the laws made by the Reich within the various states of the confederation. The leaders of the Party promise, if necessary by sacrificing their own lives, to support by the execution of the points set forth above without consideration.

SOURCES: German History in Documents and Images: http://german historydocs.ghi-dc.org/sub_document.cfm?document_id=3910; and Wikipedia: https://en.wikipedia.org/wiki/National_Socialist_Program

Notes and References

Unless otherwise noted, quotations from Hitler's *Mein Kampf* are taken from the translation by Ralph Mannheim.

Prologue: A little context . . .

1 Kershaw, *Hitler 1889–1936: Hubris*, p. 80.
2 The finest biographies of Hitler – Ullrich, *Hitler: Ascent, 1889–1939*; Kershaw; Fest, *Hitler;* Bullock, *Hitler: A Study in Tyranny* – tend to give less emphasis to the role of the First World War in shaping Hitler's character than it deserves. Three well-researched books assess Hitler's record in the Great War: Carruthers, *Private Hitler's War 1914–1918*; Weber, *Hitler's First War: Adolf Hitler, the Men of the List Regiment, and the First World War*; and Williams, *Corporal Hitler and the Great War 1914–1918: The List Regiment.* Jetzinger's *Hitler's Youth* traces Hitler's life from childhood to his early political career (but is dated and unfairly discredits August Kubizek, Hitler's boyhood friend). Several 'psycho-histories' attempt to diagnose Hitler's post-war mental state, implying that war trauma led to the Holocaust: Bromberg and Small, *Hitler's Psychopathology*; Dorpat, *Wounded Monster: Hitler's Path from Trauma to Malevolence*; Waite, *The Psychopathic God: Adolf Hitler*; Hiden and Farquharson, *Explaining Hitler's Germany: Historians and the Third Reich*, pp. 13–32. For a view of the US war-time secret service (OSS), see Murray, 'Analysis of the Personality of Adolf Hitler, with Predictions for his Future Behavior and Suggestions for Dealing With Him Now and After Germany's Surrender', OSS Archives, October 1943.
3 See Piketty, *Capital in the Twenty-First Century.* For online data, see: http://piketty.pse.ens.fr/files/capital21c/en/pdf/F10.6.pdf *and* http://piketty.pse.ens.fr/files/capital21c/en/pdf/F12.4.pdf
4 Pakenham, *The Scramble for Africa: The White Man's Conquest of the Dark Continent from 1876 to 1912*, p. xxi.
5 Ham, *1914: The Year the World Ended*, pp. 399–413.
6 See Mitchell, *The Great Train Race: Railways and the Franco-German Rivalry, 1815–1914*; Feuchtwanger, *Imperial Germany, 1850–1918*, Table 1, p. 199.
7 See Hennock, *The Origin of the Welfare State in England and Germany, 1850–1914.*
8 See BBC debate, 'The Necessary War', 4 June 2014: http://www.bbc.co.uk/programmes/b03wtmz6

9   Ham, pp. 575–600.
10   Ibid., pp. 22–35.
11   Brook-Shepherd, *The Austrians: A Thousand-Year Odyssey*, pp. 95–6; Kolmer (ed.), 'The Linz Program', *Parlament und Verfassung in Österreich* [Parliament and Constitution in Austria], Vol. 3, pp. 212–14: https://www.mtholyoke.edu/acad/intrel/FacultyInformation/jking/linz_pro[1].htm

1 'At the time I thought everything should be blown up'

1   Kershaw, *Hitler 1889–1936: Hubris*, p. 11.
2   Hamann, *Hitler's Vienna: A Portrait of the Tyrant as a Young Man*, p. 7.
3   Bloch, 'My Patient Hitler', *Collier's Weekly*, 15 March 1941, p. 35.
4   Hitler, *Mein Kampf*, p. 20.
5   Bloch, p. 36.
6   Kubizek, *The Young Hitler I Knew: The Memoirs of Hitler's Childhood Friend*, p. 21.
7   Quoted in Grafton, 'Mein Buch', *New Republic*, 24 December 2008.
8   Bromberg and Small, *Hitler's Psychopathology*, p. 41.
9   *Mein Kampf*, p. 17.
10   Shirer, *The Rise and Fall of the Third Reich*, pp. 13–14.
11   Bromberg and Small, p. 44; see also Waite, *The Psychopathic God: Adolf Hitler*.
12   *Mein Kampf*, p. 8.
13   Ibid., p. 9.
14   Ibid., p. 10.
15   Kershaw, p. 18.
16   Kubizek, p. 25.
17   'Interview with Hitler's Sister on 5th June 1946', Modern Military Records, US National Archives.
18   *Mein Kampf*, p. 10.
19   Jetzinger, *Hitler's Youth*, pp. 105–6.
20   Goebbels, *The Goebbels Diaries*, p. 331.
21   Quoted in Hamann, op. cit, p. 19.
22   Ibid.
23   Ullrich, *Hitler: Ascent, 1889–1939*, p. 19.
24   Fest, *Hitler*, p. 21.
25   Kubizek, pp. 6–10; Jetzinger, pp. 166–8.

2 'At home I do not remember having heard the word Jew'

1   Kubizek, *The Young Hitler I Knew: The Memoirs of Hitler's Childhood Friend*, p. 6.
2   As Ian Kershaw, Brigitte Hamann, Hugh Trevor-Roper and other historians attest.
3   Bromberg and Small, *Hitler's Psychopathology*, p. 51.
4   Kubizek, p. 13.
5   Ibid., p. 8.
6   Ibid., p. 10.
7   Ibid., p. 26.

8   Hitler, *Mein Kampf*, p. 51.
9   Richter, *Historical Dictionary of Wittgenstein's Philosophy*, p. 98.
10 *Mein Kampf*, p. 51.
11 'The Making of Adolf Hitler', *Timewatch*, BBC documentary, 4 January 2002.
12 Kubizek, p. 32.
13 Hanfstaengl, *Zwischen Weissem und Braunem Haus: Memoiren eines politischen Aussenseiters* [Between the White and Brown House: Memoirs of a Political Outsider], p. 174.
14 Kubizek, p. 34.
15 'The Making of Adolf Hitler'.

3 'I had honoured my father, but my mother I had loved'

1   Vaget, 'Syberberg's "Our Hitler": Wagnerianism and Alienation', *Massachusetts Review*, Vol. 23, No. 4, Winter 1982, pp. 593–612.
2   Kubizek, *The Young Hitler I Knew: The Memoirs of Hitler's Childhood Friend*, p. 53.
3   Hamann, *Hitler's Vienna: A Portrait of the Tyrant as a Young Man*, p. 24.
4   Vaget, pp. 597–98.
5   Kubizek, p. 145.
6   Hamann, *Hitlers Edeljude*, p. 81.
7   Hamann, *Hitler's Vienna*, p. 28.
8   Hitler, *Mein Kampf*, p. 20.
9   Ibid.
10 Ibid.
11 Bloch, 'My Patient Hitler', *Collier's Weekly*, 15 March 1941, p. 39; Jetzinger, *Hitler's Youth*, pp. 176–81.
12 Kubizek, p. 166ff.; Hamann, *Hitler's Vienna*, p. 54.
13 Macleod, 'Mrs Hitler and Her Doctor', *Australasian Psychiatry*, 13 (4), December 2005, pp. 412–14.
14 Ibid.
15 *Mein Kampf*, p. 19.
16 Bloch, p. 39.
17 Carruthers, *Private Hitler's War 1914–1918*, p. 66.
18 See Cocks, 'The Hitler Controversy': reviews of *Adolf Hitler* by John Toland, *Hitler's War* by David Irving, *The Psychopathic God: Adolf Hitler* by Robert G. L. Waite, *Hitler among the Germans* by Rudolph Binion, in *Political Psychology*, Vol. 1, No. 2, Autumn 1979, pp. 67–81. See also Macleod.
19 Cocks, 'The Hitler Controversy', pp. 72–3.
20 Hamann, *Hitler's Vienna*, p. 69.
21 Macleod.

4 'The whole academy should be dynamited'

1   Hitler, *Mein Kampf*, p. 20.
2   Quoted in Carruthers, *Private Hitler's War 1914–1918*, p. 73.
3   See Hašek, *The Good Soldier Švejk and his Fortunes in the World War*.

4   *Mein Kampf*, p. 77.
5   Ibid.
6   Kershaw, *Hitler 1889–1936: Hubris*, p. 31.
7   Ibid., p. 32.
8   See Hamann, *Hitler's Vienna: A Portrait of the Tyrant as a Young Man*, pp. 78–82, and also her 'Jews in Vienna', Porges Family site: http://www.porges.net/JewsInVienna/1HistoricalBackground.html
9   Hamann, pp. 59–62.
10   Kubizek, *The Young Hitler I Knew: The Memoirs of Hitler's Childhood Friend*, p. 199ff.
11   Fest, *Hitler*, p. 31.
12   Kubizek, pp. 126 and 210–20.
13   *Mein Kampf*, p. 24; Kubizek, p. 202.
14   Fest, pp. 32–4.
15   Quoted in Hamann, p. 136.
16   *Mein Kampf*, p. 41.
17   Quoted in Hamann, p. 137.
18   Kubizek, p. 123.
19   Heiden, *The Führer: Hitler's Rise to Power*, pp. 43–50. For his condition, see also Smith, *Adolf Hitler: His Family, Childhood, and Youth*, p. 127; Fest, p. 45.
20   *Mein Kampf*, pp. 40–2; Hamann, pp. 206–11.
21   *Mein Kampf*, p. 40.
22   Bromberg and Small, *Hitler's Psychopathology*, p. 71.
23   Ibid.
24   Hanisch, 'I was Hitler's Buddy', *New Republic*, 5 April 1939, pp. 239–300. See also Carruthers, *Hitler's Violent Youth: How Trench Warfare and Street Fighting Moulded Hitler*, Chapter 5: 'The Jewish Question'.
25   Hanisch, pp. 239–300.
26   Quoted in Hamann, p. 379.
27   Fest, p. 47.

5 'Is this a German?'

1   Fest, *Hitler*, p. 52.
2   Kubizek, *The Young Hitler I Knew: The Memoirs of Hitler's Childhood Friend*, p. 275.
3   Hitler, *Hitler's Table Talk 1941–1944*, p. 230ff.
4   Waite, *The Psychopathic God: Adolf Hitler*, p. 51; see also Fuchs, *The Limits of Ferocity: Sexual Aggression and Modern Literary Rebellion*, p. 123.
5   Kubizek, p. 120.
6   Kershaw, *Hitler 1889–1936: Hubris*, p. 44ff.
7   Taylor, *The Habsburg Monarchy, 1809–1918: A History of the Austrian Empire and Austria–Hungary*, p. 9.
8   Kubizek, p. 9.
9   Hitler, *Mein Kampf*, p. 35; Ryback, *Hitler's Private Library: The Books That Shaped His Life*.
10   Hitler, *Mein Kampf* (trans. Roberto), p. 15.
11   Hamann, *Hitler's Vienna: A Portrait of the Tyrant as a Young Man*, pp. 74–8.

12 Ibid., pp. 230–3.
13 *Mein Kampf*, Chapter 2.
14 Ibid., p. 69.
15 Ullrich, *Hitler: Ascent, 1889–1939*, p. 43; see also Hamann, pp. 239–42; Kershaw, pp. 60–7; and Toland, *Adolf Hitler*, Vol. 1, p. 48ff.
16 *Mein Kampf*, p. 56.
17 Ibid., pp. 60–61.
18 Ibid., p. 58.
19 Hanisch, 'I was Hitler's Buddy', *New Republic*, 5 April 1939, pp. 239–300. See also Hamann, pp. 166 and 347–59.
20 Hamann, pp. 164–6.
21 Hanisch.
22 Ibid.
23 Quoted in Hamann, p. 498.
24 *Mein Kampf*, p. 52.
25 Boyer, 'Karl Lueger and the Viennese Jews', *Leo Baeck Institute Yearbook*, Vol. 26, Issue 1, 1981.
26 Hamann, p. 286.
27 Ibid.
28 Kershaw, p. 35.
29 Turner, 'To Hitler via Two Men', *American Scholar*, Vol. 6, No. 1, Winter 1937, p. 9.
30 *Mein Kampf*, p. 107.
31 Quoted in Lukacs, *The Hitler of History*, p. 71.
32 Ibid.

6 'I fell down on my knees and thanked Heaven'

1 Hitler, *Mein Kampf*, p. 123.
2 Ibid.
3 Hitler, *Hitler's Table Talk 1941–1944*, p. 115.
4 *Mein Kampf*, pp. 123–4.
5 Ibid., p. 126.
6 Ibid., p. 127.
7 Kershaw, *Hitler 1889–1936: Hubris*, p. 82.
8 Heinz, *Germany's Hitler*, p. 51.
9 Payne, *The Life and Death of Adolf Hitler*, pp. 100 and 102.
10 Fest, *Hitler*, p. 62; see also Jetzinger, *Hitler's Youth*, p. 253ff.
11 Jetzinger, p. 265; Carruthers, *Private Hitler's War 1914–1918*, p. 104.
12 *Mein Kampf*, p. 128.
13 Ibid., p. 158.
14 Ibid., p. 161.
15 Ibid.
16 Ibid.
17 Ferguson, *The Pity of War: Explaining World War I*, pp. 28–30.
18 Weber, *Hitler's First War: Adolf Hitler, the Men of the List Regiment, and the First World War*, p. 17.
19 *Mein Kampf*, p. 162.

7 'I passionately loved soldiering'

1   Asquith, *Memories and Reflections 1914–1927*, Vol. II, p. 195.
2   Grey, *Twenty-Five Years, 1892–1916*, p. 20.
3   'Report of a speech delivered by Herr von Bethmann-Hollweg, German Imperial Chancellor, on 4 August 1914', Appendix to 'Germany's Reasons for War with Russia', *German White Book*, World War I Document Archive: https://wwi.lib.byu.edu/index.php/The_German_White_Book
4   Ibid.
5   Bethmann-Hollweg, *Reflections on the World War*, p. 147.
6   'Report of a speech delivered by Herr von Bethmann-Hollweg'.
7   Ibid.
8   Tirpitz, *My Memoirs*, Vol. I, pp. 279–80.
9   Hitler, *Hitler's Table Talk 1941–1944*, p. 43.
10 Hitler, *Mein Kampf*, p. 163.
11 Williams, *Corporal Hitler and the Great War 1914–1918: The List Regiment*, p. 9.
12 Weber, *Hitler's First War: Adolf Hitler, the Men of the List Regiment, and the First World War*, p. 24.
13 Ibid., p. 20.
14 Ibid., p. 18.
15 Hitler, *Sämtliche Aufzeichnungen 1905–1924* [Complete Notes 1905–1924], No. 24, p. 59.
16 *Mein Kampf*, p. 165.

8 'Louvain was a heap of rubble'

1   Tuchman, *The Guns of August*, p. 164.
2   German soldiers' song, printed in *Daheim*, the army field newspaper, No. 50, August–September 1914, p. 442, Heidelberg Historical Records.
3   'The Martyrdom of Belgium: Official Report of Massacres of Peaceable Citizens, Women and Children by the German Army'.
4   Kluck, *The March on Paris: The Memoirs of Alexander von Kluck, 1914–1918*, p. 26.
5   'The Martyrdom of Belgium', p. 5.
6   Ibid., p. 13.
7   Ibid., p. 8.
8   Ibid., p. 9.
9   Ibid., p. 17.
10 Quoted in Tuchman, p. 321.
11 'The Martyrdom of Belgium', p. 1.
12 Quoted in Gilbert, *The First World War: A Complete History*, p. 88.
13 'The Martyrdom of Belgium', p. 19.
14 Hitler, *Sämtliche Aufzeichnungen 1905–1924* [Complete Notes 1905–1924], No. 26, p. 60.
15 Solleder (ed.), *Vier Jahre Westfront, Geschichte des Regiments List R.I.R. 16* [Four Years on the Western Front, History of the List Regiment, 16th R.I.R.], p. 325.
16 Hitler (ed. Jochmann), *Monologues at Hitler's Headquarters from 1941 to 1944*, p. 407ff.

17   Williams, *Corporal Hitler and the Great War 1914–1918: The List Regiment*, p. 41.
18   *Sämtliche Aufzeichnungen*, No. 30, p. 68ff. Hitler's 'Hepp Letter' is published in full in English in several books and websites. See Carruthers, *Private Hitler's War 1914–1918*, p. 34.
19   Maser, *Hitler's Letters and Notes*, p. 50.
20   Quoted in Weber, *Hitler's First War: Adolf Hitler, the Men of the List Regiment, and the First World War*, p. 32.
21   Williams, p. 49; Maser, p. 53.
22   Quoted in Heiden, *The Führer: Hitler's Rise to Power*, pp. 68–75.
23   Ibid.
24   Ibid.

9 'I was right out in front, ahead of everyone'

1   Beckett, *Ypres: The First Battle 1914*, p. 60.
2   Foch, *The Memoirs of Marshal Foch*, p. 169.
3   Beckett, p. 58.
4   Ibid.
5   Keegan, *The First World War*, p. 143.
6   Hitler, *Mein Kampf*, pp. 164–5.
7   For detailed accounts of the battle at Langemarck, see Sheldon and Cave, *Ypres 1914: Langemarck*; and Beckett.
8   *Mein Kampf*, p. 165.
9   Mend, *Adolf Hitler im Felde, 1914–1918* [Adolf Hitler in the Field, 1914–1918], pp. 19–20; Williams, *Corporal Hitler and the Great War 1914–1918: The List Regiment*, p. 58.
10   Quoted in Carruthers, *Private Hitler's War 1914–1918*, pp. 125–9; see other translations in Heiden, *The Führer: Hitler's Rise to Power*, pp. 70–71; and Williams, p. 57.
11   Carruthers, pp. 125–9.
12   Ibid.
13   Geoffrey, review of *Blut und Paukboden. Eine Geschichte der Burschenschaften* [Blood and Duelling Lofts, A History of Student Societies] by Heither et al., in *German Studies Review*, Vol. 22, No. 1, February 1999, pp. 141–2.
14   Heiden, p. 71.
15   Keegan, p. 144.
16   Quoted in Beckett, p. 103.
17   Ibid.
18   Heiden, p. 71.
19   Bromberg and Small, *Hitler's Psychopathology*, p. 77.
20   Quoted in Williams, p. 54.
21   Quoted in Weber, *Hitler's First War: Adolf Hitler, the Men of the List Regiment, and the First World War*, p. 48.
22   *Mein Kampf*, p. 145.
23   Weiskopf, 'Penetrating the "Intellectual Gas Mask"', *Books Abroad*, Vol. 17, No. 1, Winter 1943, pp. 9–12.
24   Baird, review of *The Attractions of Fascism: Social Psychology and Aesthetics of the*

'*Triumph of the Right*', ed. John Milfull, *German Studies Review*, Vol. 15, No. 1, February 1992, pp. 169–170.

25 Ibid.

10 'You will hear much more about me'

1 Ryback, *Hitler's Private Library: The Books That Shaped his Life*, p. 4.
2 Ibid.
3 Quoted in Maser, *Hitler's Letters and Notes*, p. 54.
4 Ryback, p. 5; Williams, *Corporal Hitler and the Great War 1914–1918: The List Regiment*, p. 11.
5 Quoted in Williams, p. 14.
6 Carruthers, *Private Hitler's War 1914–1918*, p. 139.
7 Weber, *Hitler's First War: Adolf Hitler, the Men of the List Regiment, and the First World War*, p. 78.
8 Quoted in Carruthers, p. 149.
9 Quoted in Weber, p. 98; Meyer, *Mit Adolf Hitler im Bayerischen-Reserve-Infanterie-Regiment 16 List* [With Adolf Hitler in the 16th Bavarian Reserve Infantry Regiment List], p. 35. See also: Calvin College, German Propaganda Archive, Michigan State University Press.
10 Quoted in Flood, *Hitler: The Path to Power*, p. 16.
11 Lloyd-Burch, private papers, IWM.
12 Quoted in Williams, p. 81.
13 Carruthers, p. 141.
14 Diver, 'Journal reveals Hitler's dysfunctional family', *Guardian*, 4 August 2005.
15 Mend, *Adolf Hitler im Felde, 1914–1918* [Adolf Hitler in the Field, 1914–1918], pp. 47–51.
16 Quoted in Carruthers, p. 145.
17 Ibid., p. 141.
18 Hitler, *Hitler's Table Talk 1941–1944*, pp. 232–3.
19 Quoted in Carruthers, p. 155.
20 *Hitler's Table Talk 1941–1944*, p. 76.
21 'Wannsee Conference and the "Final Solution"', United States Holocaust Memorial Museum.
22 Ham, *Passchendaele: Requiem for Doomed Youth*, p. 413 and Appendix 8, p. 477.
23 Quoted in Kershaw, *Hitler 1889–1936: Hubris*, p. 94; Heiden, *The Führer: Hitler's Rise to Power*, pp. 68–75; Maser, pp. 73–6; Mend, p. 163.
24 Mend, pp. 61–2.
25 Ibid.
26 Williams, p. 134.
27 Toland, *Adolf Hitler*, p. 70; Cocks, reviews of Toland, *Adolf Hitler*; Irving, *Hitler's War*; Waite, *The Psychopathic God: Adolf Hitler*; Binion, *Hitler among the Germans, Political Psychology*, Vol. 1, No. 2, Autumn 1979, pp. 67–81.
28 Heiden, p. 72.
29 Quoted in Carruthers, p. 152.
30 Brandmayer, *Meldegänger Hitler* [Hitler the Messenger], p. 36; Toland, p. 64; Williams, p. 13.

31 Brandmayer, pp. 136–40.
32 Fest, *Hitler*, p. 70.

11 'At last my will was undisputed master'
 1 Quoted in Williams, *Corporal Hitler and the Great War 1914–1918: The List Regiment*, p. 104; Mend, *Adolf Hitler im Felde, 1914–1918* [Adolf Hitler in the Field, 1914–1918], pp. 85–95.
 2 Williams, p. 111.
 3 Kershaw, *Hitler 1889–1936: Hubris*, p. 92; Brandmayer, *Meldegänger Hitler* [Hitler the Messenger], pp. 52–6.
 4 Carruthers, *Private Hitler's War 1914–1918*, p. 158.
 5 Dorpat, *Wounded Monster*, p. 86; Flood, *Hitler: The Path to Power*, p. 16.
 6 Quoted in Holmes, *The Western Front*, p. 37.
 7 Harris, *Douglas Haig and the First World War*, pp. 153–77.
 8 Ryback, *Hitler's Private Library: The Books That Shaped His Life*, pp. 9–11.
 9 Osborn, 'The Beginning of the End of German Jewry', 25 January 1933, Jewish Museum, Berlin.
10 Hitler, *Mein Kampf*, p. 165.
11 Quoted in Carruthers, p. 150.
12 Ryback, p. 13.
13 Mend, p. 186; Brandmayer, pp. 48–58.
14 Sheffield, *Forgotten Victory: The First World War – Myths and Realities*, p. 190.
15 Solleder (ed,), *Vier Jahre Westfront, Geschichte des Regiments List R.I.R. 16* [Four Years on the Western Front, History of the List Regiment, 16th R.I.R.], p. 241.
16 Brandmayer, pp. 62–5.
17 Quoted in Williams, pp. 156–7.
18 *Mein Kampf*, p. 192.
19 Vincent, *The Politics of Hunger: The Allied Blockade of Germany, 1915–1919*, pp. 21–2.
20 Ibid.
21 Quoted in Vincent, p. 45.
22 Herwig, *The First World War: Germany and Austria–Hungary, 1914–1918*, p. 280.
23 Ibid., p. 291.
24 *Mein Kampf*, p. 192.
25 Ibid., pp. 192–3.
26 'Project find postcard from Hitler', Europeana 1914–18, an archival project partnered by Oxford University and the British Library, University of Oxford.
27 Weber, *Hitler's First War: Adolf Hitler, the Men of the List Regiment, and the First World War*, p. 173.
28 *Mein Kampf*, pp. 193–4.
29 Williams, p. 95; Mend, p. 78.
30 Weber, p. 144.

12 'For the last time the Lord's grace smiled on His ungrateful children'

1   Williams, *Corporal Hitler and the Great War 1914–1918: The List Regiment*, p. 161.

2   Weber, *Hitler's First War: Adolf Hitler, the Men of the List Regiment, and the First World War*, p. 165.

3   Wiedemann, *Der Mann, der Feldherr werden wollte* [The Man Who Wanted to Be Commander], p. 30.

4   Ullrich, *Hitler: Ascent, 1889–1939*, p. 60.

5   Solleder (ed.), *Vier Jahre Westfront, Geschichte des Regiments List R.I.R. 16* [Four Years on the Western Front, History of the List Regiment, 16th R.I.R.], p. 284.

6   Quoted in Sheldon, *The German Army at Passchendaele*, p. 43.

7   Ibid., p. 59.

8   Beumelburg, *Flandern 1917*, p. 10.

9   Bostyn (ed.), *Passchendaele 1917: The Story of the Fallen and Tyne Cot Cemetery*, p. 15.

10 Beumelburg, p. 10.

11 Kuhl, *Der Weltkrieg 1914–1918: Dem Deutschen Volke dargestellt* [The World War, 1914–1918, For the German People], pp. 121–2.

12 Ham, *1914: The Year the World Ended*, p. 589.

13 Ham, *Passchendaele: Requiem for Doomed Youth*, Appendix 1 'Casualty Figures', pp. 447–8.

14 Ibid., pp. 411–12.

15 Williams, p. 173.

16 Hitler, *Hitler's Table Talk 1941–1944*, p. 94.

17 Quoted in Kershaw, *Hitler 1889–1936: Hubris*, p. 93.

18 Herwig, *The First World War: Germany and Austria–Hungary, 1914–1918*, p. 284.

19 Ibid., p. 254.

20 Ibid., p. 332.

21 Ibid., p. 273.

22 Ibid., p. 292.

23 'Spotlights on History: The Blockade of Germany', National Archives, United Kingdom. See also Osborne, *Britain's Economic Blockade of Germany, 1914–1919*; and Grebler and Winkler, *The Cost of the World War to Germany and to Austria-Hungary*, p. 78.

24 'Spotlights on History'.

25 Maser, *Hitler's Letters and Notes*, p. 96; also quoted in Weber, p. 202.

26 Rupprecht, *My War Diary*, 3 November 1917.

27 Hitler, *Mein Kampf*, p. 198.

13 'Since the day I stood at my mother's grave, I had not wept'

1   Sheffield, *Forgotten Victory: The First World War – Myths and Realities*, p. 100.

2   Edmonds, *Official History of the Great War: Military Operations France and Belgium 1917*, Vol. 2, p. 490.

3   Sheffield, p. 233.

4   'Sir Douglas Haig's "Backs to the Wall" Order, 11 April 1918': www.firstworldwar.com/source/backstothewall.htm

5 Quoted in Weber, *Hitler's First War: Adolf Hitler, the Men of the List Regiment, and the First World War*, p. 209.

6 Ibid., p. 210.

7 Quoted in Carruthers, *Private Hitler's War 1914–1918*, p. 166.

8 Beumelburg, *Flandern 1917*, p. 27.

9 Gibbs, *From Bapaume to Passchendaele 1917*, p. 139.

10 Quoted in Dorpat, *Wounded Monster: Hitler's Path from Trauma to Malevolence*, p. 86.

11 See Weber.

12 Quoted in Ullrich, *Hitler: Ascent, 1889–1939*, p. 59.

13 Ibid.

14 Quoted in Weber, p. 176.

15 Kershaw, *Hitler 1889–1936: Hubris*, p. 96.

16 Quoted in Carruthers, pp. 174–5.

17 Ibid., pp. 177–8.

18 Hitler, *Mein Kampf*, p. 93.

19 See 'Facts about Sulfur Mustard', Centers for Disease Control and Prevention: https://emergency.cdc.gov/agent/sulfurmustard/basics/facts.asp

20 See Weber, p. 221.

21 Ibid., pp. 220–21.

22 Armbruster, Jan, and Theiss-Abendroth, Peter, 'Deconstructing the myth of Pasewalk: Why Adolf Hitler's psychiatric treatment at the end of World War I bears no relevance', *Archives of Clinical Psychiatry (São Paulo)*, Vol. 43, No. 3, May/June 2016.

23 Kitchen, *The German Offensives of 1918*, p. 234.

24 Weldon Whalen, Robert, 'War Losses (Germany)', *International Encyclopedia of the First World War*: http://encyclopedia.1914-1918-online.net/article/war_losses_germany

25 Sheffield, p. 263.

26 *Mein Kampf*, p. 204.

14 'What was all the pain in my eyes compared to this misery?'

1 Wheeler-Bennett, 'Ludendorff: The Soldier and the Politician', *Virginia Quarterly Review*, 14 (2), Spring 1938, pp. 187–202; see also Shirer, *The Rise and Fall of the Third Reich*, p. 31.

2 Churchill, *History of the Second World War*, Vol. I: *The Gathering Storm*, pp. 47–8.

3 Hitler, *Mein Kampf*, pp. 205–6.

4 Kershaw, *Hitler 1889–1936: Hubris*, p. 104.

5 Herwig, 'Clio Deceived: Patriotic self-censorship in Germany after the Great War', *International Security*, 12 (2), Autumn 1987, p. 9.

6 Quoted in Ullrich, *Hitler: Ascent, 1889–1939*, p. 76.

7 Quoted in Williams, *Corporal Hitler and the Great War 1914–1918: The List Regiment*, p. 162.

8 *Mein Kampf*, p. 200.

9 Quoted in Kershaw, p. 122.

15 'I could speak!'

1   Quoted in Ullrich, *Hitler: Ascent, 1889–1939*, p. 80.
2   Kellogg, *The Russian Roots of Nazism: White Émigrés and the Making of National Socialism, 1917–1945*, p. 278.
3   Steigmann-Gall, *The Holy Reich: Nazi Conceptions of Christianity, 1919–1945*, p. 16.
4   Müller, *Mars und Venus: Erinnerungen 1914–1918* [Mars and Venus: Memories 1914–1918], p. 338.
5   Ibid., p. 338ff.
6   Bromberg and Small, *Hitler's Psychopathology*, p. 84.
7   Ullrich, p. 83.
8   See: http://en.wikipedia.org/wiki/Article_231_of_the_Treaty_of_Versailles; and https://en.wikisource.org/wiki/Treaty_of_Versailles. For the best book on the treaty, see: MacMillan, *Paris 1919: Six Months that Changed the World*.
9   Keylor, *The Legacy of the Great War: Peacemaking, 1919*, p. 34.
10 Kolb, *The Weimar Republic*, p. 31; Burleigh, *The Third Reich: A New History*, p. 47.
11 *Völkischer Beobachter*, 6 April 1920.
12 Burleigh, p. 47.
13 Taylor, *The Origins of the Second World War*, p. 80.
14 Ullrich, p. 85.
15 Hitler, Letter to Herr Gemlich in 'Adolf Hitler: First Anti-Semitic Writing', 16 September 1919, Jewish Virtual Library: http://www.jewishvirtuallibrary.org/jsource/Holocaust/Adolf_Hitler's_First_Antisemitic_Writing.html
16 Quoted in Ullrich, p. 87. For several other records of this episode, see Kershaw, *Hitler 1889–1936: Hubris*, p. 107, fn79.
17 Phelps, 'Hitler and the Deutsche Arbeiterpartei', *American Historical Review*, Vol. 68, No. 4, July 1963, pp. 974–86.
18 Fest, *Hitler*, p. 119.
19 Hitler, *Mein Kampf*, p. 355.
20 Quoted in Ullrich, p. 88.
21 Hoffmann, *Hitler Was My Friend: The Memoirs of Hitler's Photographer*, p. 46.
22 Binchy, 'Adolf Hitler', *Studies: An Irish quarterly review of letters, philosophy and science*, Vol. 22, No. 85, March 1933, p. 29.
23 Schramm, *Hitler: The Man and the Military Leader*, p. 21.
24 *Völkischer Beobachter*, 22 April 1922.
25 Ibid.

16 'The movement was on the march'

1   Quoted in Fest, *Hitler*, p. 92.
2   Ibid. See also Hitler's speeches published in *Völkischer Beobachter* on 27 April 1920, 22 September 1920, 28 July 1922 and other dates.
3   'Program of the German Workers' Party (1920)', German History in Documents and Images (GHDI): http://germanhistorydocs.ghi-dc.org/sub_document.cfm?document_id=3910
4   Hitler, *Mein Kampf* (trans. Murphy), p. 160. (Mannheim, p. 370, translates

this dramatic moment: 'Thus slowly the hall emptied. The movement took its course.').

5   Phelps, 'Hitler and the Deutsche Arbeiterpartei', *American Historical Review*, Vol. 68, No. 4, July 1963, p. 985.
6   Kershaw, *Hitler 1889–1936: Hubris*, p. 132.
7   Redles, 'The Nazi Old Guard: Identity Formation During Apocalyptic Times', *Nova Religio: The Journal of Alternative and Emergent Religions*, Vol. 14, No. 1, August 2010, p. 35.
8   Ibid., p. 26.
9   *Mein Kampf* (trans. Murphy), p. 37.
10 Heiden, 'Hitler's Better Half', *Foreign Affairs*, Vol. 20, No. 1, October 1941, p. 75.
11 Ibid., p. 74.
12 Ibid., p. 73.
13 Ibid., p. 85.
14 Ibid., p. 75.
15 Hitler, *Hitler's Table Talk 1941–1944*, p. 168.
16 Orlow, 'The Organizational History and Structure of the NSDAP, 1919–23', *Journal of Modern History*, Vol. 37, No. 2, June 1965, p. 216.
17 Ibid., p. 208.
18 Ibid., p. 226.
19 Heiden, p. 77.
20 Kershaw, p. viii.
21 Heiden, p. 73.
22 Orlow, p. 218.
23 Ibid., p. 210.
24 Lukacs, *The Hitler of History*, p. 67.
25 Bromberg and Small, *Hitler's Psychopathology*, p. 90.
26 Ibid.

17 'The world of the woman is the man'

1   Schramm, *Hitler: The Man and the Military Leader*, pp. 17–18.
2   Palmer, 'Did Hitler Invent the Hitler Mustache?', *Slate*, 30 May 2013.
3   Hanfstaengl, *Zwischen Weissem und Braunem Haus: Memoiren eines politischen Aussenseiters* [Between the White and Brown House: Memoirs of a Political Outsider], p. 69.
4   Moorhouse, 'On Hitler's Teeth – or, the Death of a Dictator', *historian at large* (personal blog), 25 March 2015, http://historian-at-large.blogspot.fr/2015/03/on-hitlers-teeth-or-death-of-dictator.html
5   Kershaw, *Hitler 1889–1936: Hubris*, p. 162.
6   Bullock, *Hitler: A Study in Tyranny*, p. 68. See also Bullock, *Hitler and Stalin: Parallel Lives*.
7   Schramm, p. 126.
8   Bullock, *Hitler: A Study in Tyranny*, p. 68.
9   Hiden and Farquharson, *Explaining Hitler's Germany: Historians and the Third Reich*, p. 26.
10 Schramm, pp. 10–11.

11 Ibid., p. 12.
12 Ibid., p. 30.
13 Ibid., p. 93.
14 Hanfstaengl, pp. 123–4; Bromberg and Small, *Hitler's Psychopathology*, p. 92.
15 Schramm, p. 36.
16 Neumann and Eberle, *Was Hitler Ill?: A Final Diagnosis*, p. 29.
17 Ibid., p. 31.
18 Kershaw, p. 220.
19 For a sample of the range of speculation about Hitler's sexuality, see Bromberg and Small; Ullrich, *Hitler: Ascent, 1889–1939*; Kershaw; Neumann and Eberle; Hayman, *Hitler and Geli*; Heiden, *Hitler: A Biography*; Langer, 'A Psychological Analysis of Adolph Hitler, His Life and Legend'; Waite, *The Psychopathic God: Adolf Hitler*; and Dorpat, *Wounded Monster: Hitler's Path from Trauma to Malevolence*. The most reliable conclusions are those of Ullrich, Kershaw, and Neumann and Eberle.
20 Schramm, p. 39.
21 Ibid., p. 122.
22 Lukacs, *The Hitler of History*, p. 43.
23 Murray, 'Analysis of the Personality of Adolf Hitler', OSS Archives, October 1943.
24 For a sample of the range of speculation about Hitler's 'psychological disorders', see Bromberg and Small; Ullrich; Kershaw; Neumann and Eberle; Hayman; Heiden; Langer; Waite; and Dorpat. The most reliable conclusions are those of Ullrich, Kershaw and Neumann and Eberle.
25 Kaplan, 'Was Hitler Ill? A Reply to Eberle and Neumann', *German Politics and Society*, 33 (3), 1 September 2015, pp. 70–9.
26 Ohler, *Blitzed: Drugs in Nazi Germany*; see also the review by Evans, 'Blitzed: Drugs in Nazi Germany – a crass and dangerously inaccurate account', *Guardian*, 16 November 2016.
27 Neumann and Eberle, p. 189.
28 Ensor, 'Who Hitler Is', *Oxford Pamphlets on World Affairs*, No. 20, p. 31.
29 Neumann and Eberle, p. 186.
30 Ibid., p. 190.
31 Schramm, p. 35.
32 Ibid., p. 34.
33 Ensor, p. 30.
34 Hitler, *Mein Kampf*, p. 322.
35 Dolibois, *Pattern of Circles: An Ambassador's Story*, p. 114.
36 Heiden, p. 99; Bromberg and Small, p. 93.

18 'You must fight with me – or die with me!'

1 Ensor, 'Who Hitler Is', *Oxford Pamphlets on World Affairs*, No. 20, p. 28.
2 Hitler, *Mein Kampf*, p. 544.
3 Steinert, *Hitler*, p. 125.
4 Hanfstaengl, *Zwischen Weissem und Braunem Haus: Memoiren eines politischen Aussenseiters* [Between the White and Brown House: Memoirs of a Political Outsider], p. 84.

5   Redles, *Hitler's Millennial Reich: Apocalyptic Belief and the Search for Salvation*, p. 24.
6   Burleigh, *The Third Reich: A New History*, pp. 77–8.
7   *Mein Kampf*, p. 496.
8   Hitler, *Samtliche Aufzeichnungen 1905–1924* [Complete Notes 1905–1924], No. 101, 19 May 1920, p. 134.
9   Redles, p. 24.
10 Ibid.
11 Quoted in Ullrich, *Hitler: Ascent, 1889–1939*, p. 142.
12 Kershaw, *Hitler 1889–1936: Hubris*, p. 128.
13 Quoted in Fest, *Hitler*, p. 183.
14 Ibid; see a different translation in Ullrich, p. 149.
15 Quoted in Ullrich, p. 150.
16 Quoted in Kershaw, p. 129.
17 Ibid.
18 Ibid.
19 Fest, p. 185.
20 Quoted in Kershaw, p. 128.
21 Quoted in Fest, p. 187.
22 Ibid.
23 Ibid., p. 192.
24 Landauer, 'The Bavarian Problem in the Weimar Republic: Part II', *Journal of Modern History*, 16 (3), September 1944, p. 222.
25 Quoted in Shirer, *The Rise and Fall of the Third Reich*, pp. 76–8; Fest, p. 193. See also Hess, *Briefe 1908–1933* [Letters 1908–1933], p. 317.
26 Ullrich, p. 162.
27 Fest, p, 195.

19 'If fifteen thousand of these Hebrew corrupters had been held under poison gas . . .'

1   Fest, *Hitler*, p. 199.
2   See Fleischman, *Hitler als Häftling in Landsberg am Lech 1923/25* [Hitler as a Prisoner in Landsberg am Lech 1923/25].
3   Hanfstaengl, *Zwischen Weissem und Braunem Haus: Memoiren eines politischen Aussenseiters* [Between the White and Brown House: Memoirs of a Political Outsider], p. 157.
4   Ibid., p. 164. Other accounts suggest that Hitler began a strict vegetarian diet after the death of his niece, Geli Raubal.
5   Hanfstaengl, p. 164.
6   Hitler, *Hitler's Table Talk 1941–1944*, p. 218.
7   Quoted in Ullrich, *Hitler: Ascent, 1889–1939*, p. 165.
8   *Hitler's Table Talk 1941–1944*, p. 262.
9   Hess, *Briefe 1908–1933* [Letters 1908–1933], p. 338.
10 Quoted in Fest, p. 200, from Goethe's play *Torquato Tasso*.
11 Hitler, *Mein Kampf*, p. 662.
12 Hiden and Farquharson, *Explaining Hitler's Germany: Historians and the Third Reich*, p. 16.

13 Fest, p. 204.
14 Schopenhauer, in *Parerga and Paralipomena*, had written: '. . . the Jews were at all times and by all nations loathed and despised. This may be due partly to the fact that they were the only people on earth who did not credit man with any existence beyond this life and were, therefore, regarded as cattle, as the dregs of humanity, but as past masters in telling lies.'
15 Hitler, *The Racial Conception of the World*, p. 17.
16 *Mein Kampf*, p. 198.
17 *Mein Kampf* (trans. Murphy), p. 42.
18 *Mein Kampf*, p. 562 – one of many such references to the Jews.
19 Prange (ed.), *Hitler's Words: Two Decades of National Socialism, 1923–1943*, p. 68.
20 *Mein Kampf*, p. 169.
21 Lukacs, *The Hitler of History*, p. 183.
22 *Mein Kampf* (trans. Murphy), p. 35.
23 *Mein Kampf*, p. 65.
24 Prange, p. 68.
25 *Mein Kampf* (trans. Murphy), p. 60.
26 Luther, *The Jews and Their Lies*.
27 Luther, 'That Jesus Christ Was Born a Jew'.
28 Luther, *The Jews and Their Lies*, p. 267. On the 500th anniversary of the Reformation in 2017, the official organizing body of the commemorations issued a paper on Luther's stance on the Jews – 'The Reformation and the Jews: an Orientation' – on behalf of the Scientific Advisory Board for the Reformation Jubilee 2017 (www.luther2017.de). It concluded: '[T]he unfathomable crime of the "Final Solution" cannot be traced back to *The Jews and Their Lies*, for the final objective of Luther's treatise was not mass murder but expulsion, and its arguments were not racial politics but religious. Hence, that Nazis and German Christians made appeals to its text is beside the point. On the other hand, *The Jews and Their Lies* was useful for Nazi propaganda because it, too, demonizes the Jews and insists that governments should create lands without them. An anniversary of the Reformation which reflects on the full range of the heritage left by this historical turning point cannot keep silent about such a burdensome legacy.' This statement is rich in euphemism and understatement. Luther was more than 'useful' to the Nazis, and the fiery monk surely would have been aware of the historical impact of his writing. It is hardly 'beside the point' that, regardless of what Luther said or meant to say, the Nazis did find inspiration in his words and promoted this in pamphlets and propaganda: https://www.luther2017.de/fileadmin/luther2017/material/grundlagen/Die_Reformation_und_die_Juden_Engl.pdf
29 Prange, pp. 3–5.
30 Ibid., p. 10; *Mein Kampf*, pp. 372 and 422.
31 Prange, p. 4.
32 Ibid., p. 3.
33 *Mein Kampf*, p. 452.
34 'Jewish Communities of Pre-War Germany', Holocaust Encyclopaedia http://www.ushmm.org/wlc/en/article.php?ModuleId=10007052
35 Lukacs, p. 183.

36 *Mein Kampf*, p. 284.
37 'New Fossils from Jebel, Irhoud, Morocco and the pan-African origin of *Homo sapiens*', *Nature*, No. 546, 8 June 2017, pp. 289–92, Macmillan, New York, 2017.
38 Harari, *Sapiens: A Brief History of Humankind*.
39 Prange, p. 5.
40 'Persecution of Homosexuals in the Third Reich', Holocaust Encyclopaedia: https://www.ushmm.org/wlc/en/article.php?ModuleId=10005261
41 *Mein Kampf*, p. 679.
42 Ibid., p. 302.
43 Ibid., p. 170.
44 Hitler, *The Racial Conception of the World*.
45 *New York Times*, 21 December 1924.
46 Goebbels, *The Goebbels Diaries*, Part 1, Vol. 1/1, p. 375.
47 Ibid., Vol. 1/2, p. 96.

Epilogue: The making of the Führer

1   Zweig, *The World of Yesterday*, p. 361.
2   Prochnik, 'When it's too late to stop fascism, according to Stefan Zweig', *New Yorker*, 6 February 2017: http://www.newyorker.com/books/page-turner/when-its-too-late-to-stop-fascism-according-to-stefan-zweig
3   Churchill, broadcast, 16 November 1934, in *Never give in!: Winston Churchill's Finest Speeches*, p. 89.
4   Churchill, 'Full transcript of notes of a speech by Winston Churchill broadcast on BBC radio, 10pm, 15 November 1934', UK Government Parliamentary Archives: http://www.winstonchurchill.org/resources/speeches/1930-1938-the-wilderness/the-threat-of-nazi-germany
5   Fest, *Hitler*, p. 12.
6   For the rigorous debate about the involvement of the German people and soldiers in the Nazis' crimes against humanity, see: Browning, *Ordinary Men: Reserve Police Battalion 101 and the Final Solution in Poland*; Goldhagen, *Hitler's Willing Executioners: Ordinary Germans and the Holocaust*; and Kershaw, *Popular Opinion and Public Dissent in the Third Reich: Bavaria 1933–1945*: https://www.jstor.org/stable/3788269?seq=1#page_scan_tab_contents. For a fascinating examination of the psychopaths in our midst, see: Hare, *Without Conscience: The Disturbing World of the Psychopaths Among Us*.
7   Fest, p. 7.
8   Williams, *Corporal Hitler and the Great War 1914–1918: The List Regiment*, p. 3.
9   Hitler, *Mein Kampf*, p. 92.
10 Ibid., p. 220.
11 Ullrich, *Hitler: Ascent, 1889–1939*, p. 104.
12 Goldhagen.
13 'The National Socialist Movement', Southern Poverty Law Center: https://www.splcenter.org/fighting-hate/extremist-files/group/national-socialist-movement
14 Kovaleski et al., 'An Alt-Right Makeover Shrouds the Swastikas', *New York*

Times, 10 December 2016: http://www.nytimes.com/2016/12/10/us/alt-right-national-socialist-movement-white-supremacy.html?emc=edit_th_20161211&nl=todaysheadlines&nlid=55326310

15 '25 Points of American National Socialism', National Socialist Movement, http://www.nsm88.org/25points/25pointsengl.html

16 Herrnstein and Murray, *The Bell Curve: Intelligence and Class Structure in American Life*. Concerning the authors' claims of a link between intelligence and genes, the American Psychological Association's Board of Scientific Affairs concluded: 'There is certainly no such support for a genetic interpretation. It is sometimes suggested that the Black/White differential in psychometric intelligence is partly due to genetic differences. There is not much direct evidence on this point, but what little there is fails to support the genetic hypothesis.' Concerning other explanations for 'racial' differences in IQ test results, the APA stated: 'The differential between the mean intelligence test scores of Blacks and Whites (about one standard deviation, although it may be diminishing) does not result from any obvious biases in test construction and administration, nor does it simply reflect differences in socio-economic status. Explanations based on factors of caste and culture may be appropriate, but so far have little direct empirical support. There is certainly no such support for a genetic interpretation. At present, no one knows what causes this differential.' http://www.intelltheory.com/apa96.shtml
Many scientists have more strongly criticized the findings of *The Bell Curve*. See: Gould, 'Curveball', *New Yorker*, 28 November 1994.

17 'This is How Steve Bannon Sees the Entire World', *Buzzfeed* (full transcript), 15 November 2016: https://www.buzzfeed.com/lesterfeder/this-is-how-steve-bannon-sees-the-entire-world?utm_term=.sbKXO21Wb#.jjzp4LjNX

18 'Pepe and the Stormtroopers: How Donald Trump ushered a hateful fringe movement into the mainstream', *The Economist*, 17 September 2016: http://www.economist.com/news/united-states/21707201-how-donald-trump-ushered-hateful-fringe-movement-mainstream-pepe-and?cid1=cust/ednew/n/bl/n/20160915n/owned/n/n/nwl/n/n/n/n

19 McCants, 'The implications of Donald Trump's sharp contrast from Obama and Bush on Islam', 15 December 2016, Brookings Institution: https://www.brookings.edu/blog/markaz/2016/12/15/the-implications-of-donald-trumps-sharp-contrast-from-obama-and-bush-on-islam/?utm_campaign=Brookings+Brief&utm_source=hs_email&utm_medium=email&utm_content=39427467

20 See Piketty, *Capital in the Twenty-First Century*.

21 For more on Steve Bannon's medieval world view, see Green, *Devil's Bargain: Steve Bannon, Donald Trump, and the Storming of the Presidency*. The seriousness of Bannon's vision needs to be set against his personal motto, 'honey badger don't give a shit', a reference to the creature's anarchic habits, as seen on a popular YouTube video, and Bannon's Leninist conviction that the established world order must be destroyed.

Select Bibliography

Books

Albertini, Luigi, *The Origins of the War of 1914* (3 vols), Enigma Press, New York, 2005

Asquith, Herbert H., *Memories and Reflections 1914–1927*, Vols I and II, Albion Press, London, 2016

Banks, Arthur, *A Military Atlas of the First World War*, Pen & Sword, Barnsley, South Yorkshire, 2001

Baynes, H. G., *Germany Possessed*, Cape, London, 1941

Beckett, Ian, *Ypres: The First Battle 1914*, Routledge, New York, 2006

Bernhardi, General Friedrich von, *Germany and the Next War*, Edward Arnold, London, 1914

Bethmann-Hollweg, Theobald von, *Reflections on the World War* (trans. George Young), Cornell University Library, New York, 1920

Beumelburg, Werner von, *Flandern 1917*, Gerhard Stalling, Berlin, 1928

Binion, Rudolph, *Hitler Among the Germans*, Northern Illinois University Press, DeKalb, Illinois, 1984

Bloch, Ivan, *Is War Now Impossible? Being an Abridgment of: The War of the Future in Its Technical, Economic & Political Relations*, Richards, London, 1899

Bostyn, Franky (ed.), *Passchendaele 1917: The Story of the Fallen and Tyne Cot Cemetery*, Pen & Sword, Barnsley, South Yorkshire, 2007

Brandmayer, Balthasar, *Meldegänger Hitler* [Hitler the Messenger], Franz Walter, Überlingen, 1933

Bromberg, Norbert, and Small, Verna Volz, *Hitler's Psychopathology*, International Universities Press, Inc., New York, 1984

Brook-Shepherd, Gordon, *The Austrians: A Thousand-Year Odyssey*, Carroll & Graf, Inc., New York, 1997

Browning, Christopher, *Ordinary Men: Reserve Police Battalion 101 and the Final Solution in Poland*, Harper Perennial, New York, 1998

Bukey, Evan Burr, *Hitler's Hometown: Linz, Austria, 1908–1945*, Indiana University Press, Bloomington, Indiana, 1986

Bullock, Alan, *Hitler: A Study in Tyranny*, Harper & Row, New York, 1964

—, *Hitler and Stalin: Parallel Lives*, Vintage Books, New York, 1993

Burleigh, Michael, *The Third Reich: A New History*, Pan Books, London, 2012

Carr, William, *Hitler: a Study in Personality and Politics*, Edward Arnold, London, 1978

Carruthers, Bob, *Private Hitler's War 1914–1918*, Pen & Sword, Barnsley, South Yorkshire, 2014

—, *Hitler's Violent Youth: How Trench Warfare and Street Fighting Moulded Hitler*, Pen & Sword, Barnsley, South Yorkshire, 2015

Churchill, Winston, *The World Crisis* (Vols 1–4), Thornton Butterworth, London, 1927

—, *History of the Second World War*, Vol. I: *The Gathering Storm*, Mariner Books, Boston, 1986

—, *Never give in!: Winston Churchill's Finest Speeches*, Pimlico, London, 2007

Clark, Christopher, *Iron Kingdom: The Rise and Downfall of Prussia, 1600–1947*, Harvard University Press, Cambridge, Massachusetts, 2006

Dell, Robert, *Germany Unmasked*, Hopkinson, London, 1934

Deuerlein, Ernst, *Der Hitler-Putsch: Bayerische Dokuments von 8./9. November 1923*, Deutsche Verlags, Munich, 1962

Dolibois, John, *Pattern of Circles: An Ambassador's Story*, Kent State University Press, Kent, Ohio, 2000

Dorpat, Theodore L., *Wounded Monster: Hitler's Path from Trauma to Malevolence*, University Press of America, Lanham, Maryland, 2002

Eberle, Henrik (ed.), *Letters to Hitler* (trans. Steven Rendall), Polity Press, Cambridge, 2012

—, and Uhl, Matthias (eds), *The Hitler Book: The Secret Dossier Prepared for Stalin from the Interrogations of Hitler's Personal Aides* (trans. Giles MacDonogh), PublicAffairs, New York, 2005

Edmonds, Brigadier General James E., *Official History of the Great War: Military Operations France and Belgium 1917*, Vol. 2, Naval & Military Press, Uckfield, East Sussex, 2013

Ellis, John, *Eye-Deep in Hell: Trench Warfare in World War I*, Johns Hopkins University Press, Baltimore, Maryland, 1989

Essen, Léon van der, *The Invasion and the War in Belgium from Liège to the Yser*, T. Fisher Unwin, London, 1917

Evans, Richard, *Lying About Hitler, History, Holocaust, and the David Irving Trial*, Basic Books, New York, 2002

—, *The Coming of the Third Reich*, Penguin Books, London, 2005

—, *The Third Reich in History and Memory*, Oxford University Press, Oxford, 2015

Ferguson, Niall, *The Pity of War: Explaining World War I*, Basic Books, New York, 1999

Fest, Joachim, *Hitler*, Mariner Books, Boston, 2002

Feuchtwanger, Edgar, *From Weimar to Hitler: Germany, 1918–33*, Macmillan, London, 1993

—, *Imperial Germany 1850–1918*, Routledge, New York, 2001

Fischer, Fritz, *Germany's Aims in the Great War*, Chatto & Windus, London, 1967

Fleischmann, Peter, *Hitler als Häftling in Landsberg am Lech 1923/25* [Hitler as a Prisoner in Landsberg am Lech 1923/25], Schmidt Philipp, Neustadt an der Aisch, 2015

Flood, Charles, *Hitler: The Path to Power*, Houghton Mifflin, Boston, 1989

Foch, Ferdinand, *The Memoirs of Marshal Foch* (trans. T. Bentley Mott), Doubleday, New York, 1931

Frank, Tibor (ed.), *Discussing Hitler: Advisors of US Diplomacy in Central Europe 1934–41*, Central European University Press, Budapest, 2003

Friedman, Tuviah (ed.), *Long Dark Nazi Years: Forty Years After the Collapse of the Third Reich, 1945–1985: A Record of Documents and Photographs of Adolf Hitler's Final Solution*, Documentation Centre, Institute of Documentation in Israel for the Investigation of Nazi War Crimes, Haifa, 1999

Fuchs, Daniel von, *The Limits of Ferocity: Sexual Aggression and Modern Literary Rebellion*, Duke University Press, Durham, North Carolina, 2011

Geiss, Imanuel, *July 1914: The Outbreak of the First World War: Selected Documents*, Charles Scribner's Sons, New York, 1967

German General Staff, *Ypres: An Unofficial Account*, Constable, London, 1919

Gibbs, Philip, *From Bapaume to Passchendaele 1917*, William Heinemann, London, 1918

—, *The Realities of War*, William Heinemann, London, 1918

Gilbert, Martin, *The First World War: A Complete History*, Holt Paperbacks, New York, 2004

Goebbels, Joseph, *The Goebbels Diaries*, Penguin Books, London, 1984

Goldhagen, Daniel Jonah, *Hitler's Willing Executioners: Ordinary Germans and the Holocaust*, Vintage, New York, 1997

Gordon, Harold, *Hitler and the Beer Hall Putsch*, Princeton University Press, New Jersey, 1972

Grebler, Leo, and Winkler, Wilhelm, *The Cost of the World War to Germany and to Austria-Hungary*, Yale University Press, New Haven, Connecticut, 1940

Green, Joshua, *Devil's Bargain: Steve Bannon, Donald Trump, and the Storming of the Presidency*, Penguin Press, New York, 2017

Grey, Sir Edward, *Twenty-Five Years, 1892–1916*, Hodder & Stoughton, New York, 1925

Grosshans, Henry, *Hitler and the Artists*, Holmes & Meier, New York, 1983

Gulbenkian, Edward Vahé, *The European Intellectual Background to Hitler's Racial Policy*, Harq Publications, London, 1994

Haig, Douglas, *The Private Papers of Douglas Haig, 1914–1919: being selections from the private diary and correspondence of Field-Marshal the Earl Haig of Bemersyde*, Eyre & Spottiswoode, London, 1952

—, *War Diaries & Letters, 1914–18*, Weidenfeld & Nicolson, London, 2005

Ham, Paul, *The Rape of Belgium*, Random House Short Cuts, Sydney, 2014

—, *1914: The Year the World Ended*, Random House, Sydney and London, 2013/14

—, *Passchendaele: Requiem for Doomed Youth*, Penguin Random House, Sydney and London, 2016/17

Hamann, Brigitte, *Winifred Wagner: A Life at the Heart of Hitler's Bayreuth* (trans. Alan Bance), Granta, London, 2005

—, *Hitlers Edeljude: Das Leben des Armenarztes Eduard Bloch* [The Life of the Armenian Eduard Bloch], Piper Verlag, Munich, 2008

—, *Hitler's Vienna: A Portrait of the Tyrant as a Young Man*, Tauris Parke Paperbacks, London, 2010

Hanfstaengl, Ernst, *Zwischen Weissem und Braunem Haus: Memoiren eines politischen Aussenseiters* [Between the White and Brown House: Memoirs of a Political Outsider], Piper Verlag, Munich, 1970

Harari, Yuval Noah, *Sapiens: A Brief History of Humankind*, Random House, New York, 2015

Hare, Robert, *Without Conscience: The Disturbing World of the Psychopaths Among Us*, Guilford Press, New York, 1999

Harris, John P., *Douglas Haig and the First World War*, Cambridge University Press, Cambridge, 2009

Hašek, Jaroslav, *The Good Soldier Švejk and his Fortunes in the World War* (trans. Cecil Parrott), Penguin Classics, London, 2005

Hayman, Ronald, *Hitler and Geli*, Bloomsbury USA, New York, 1999

Heiden, Konrad, *Hitler: A Biography*, A. A. Knopf, New York, 1936

—, *The Führer: Hitler's Rise to Power* (trans. Ralph Mannheim and Norbert Guterman), Beacon Press, Boston, 1999

Heinz, Heinz A., *Germany's Hitler*, Liberty Bell Publications, Reedy, West Virginia, 2004

Hennock, E. P., *The Origin of the Welfare State in England and Germany, 1850–1914: Social Policies Compared*, Cambridge University Press, Cambridge, 2007

Herrnstein, Richard, and Murray, Charles, *The Bell Curve: Intelligence and Class Structure in American Life*, Free Press, New York, 1996

Herwig, Holger, *The First World War: Germany and Austria–Hungary, 1914–1918*, Bloomsbury, London, 2014

Hess, Rudolph, *Briefe 1908–1933* [Letters 1908–1933], Langen Müller, Munich, 1987

Hiden, John, and Farquharson, John, *Explaining Hitler's Germany: Historians and the Third Reich*, Batsford Academic and Educational, London, 1983

Hitler, Adolf, *Mein Kampf* (trans. Ralph Mannheim), Houghton Mifflin, Boston, 1998

—, *Mein Kampf* (trans. James Murphy), Kindle edn, Amazon Digital Services, 2016

—, *Mein Kampf* (trans. Marco Roberto), Ebook, Amazon Digital Services, 2017

—, *Sämtliche Aufzeichnungen 1905–1924* [Complete Notes 1905–1924] (eds Eberhard Jäckel and Axel Kuhn), Deutsche Verlags-Anstalt, Munich, 1986

—, *Hitler's Second Book: The Unpublished Sequel to Mein Kampf* (ed. Gerhard Weinberg; trans. Krista Smith), Enigma Books, Oxford, 2003

—, *Monologues in the Führer's Headquarters*, 1941 to 1944 (ed. Werner Jochmann), Albrecht Knaus, Hamburg, 1980

—, *The Racial Conception of the World* (*Friends of Europe* series), reissued by Kessinger Publishing, Whitefish, Montana, 2005

—, *The Nazi Party, the State and Religion* (*Friends of Europe* series), reissued by Kessinger Publishing, Whitefish, Montana, 2005

—, *Hitler's Table Talk 1941–1944: Secret Conversations* (ed. Hugh Trevor-Roper), Enigma Books, Oxford, 2007

—, *The Complete Hitler: Speeches and Proclamations, 1932–1945: The Chronicle of a Dictatorship* (ed. Max Domarus), Vols 1–4, Amazon Media, 2016

Hoffmann, Heinrich, *Hitler Was My Friend: The Memoirs of Hitler's Photographer*, Frontline Books, Barnsley, South Yorkshire, 2014

Holmes, Richard, *The Western Front*, BBC Books, London, 2009

Horstmann, Bernhard, *Hitler in Pasewalk*, Droste Verlag, Düsseldorf, 2004

Hötzendorf, Conrad von, *Aus meiner Dienstzeit, 1906–1918* [My Service, 1906–1918], University of Michigan Library, Ann Arbor, 1921

Jenks, William, *Vienna and the Young Hitler*, Columbia University Press, New York, 1960

Jetzinger, Franz, *Hitler's Youth*, Praeger, West Port, Connecticut, 1977

Joll, James, *Europe Since 1870: An International History*, Penguin, London, 1990

Keegan, John, *The First World War*, Vintage, London, 2000

Kellogg, Michael, *The Russian Roots of Nazism: White Émigrés and the Making of National Socialism, 1917–1945*, Cambridge University Press, Cambridge, 2005

Kennedy, Paul, *The Rise of the Anglo-German Antagonism, 1860–1914*, Humanity Books, New York, 1987

Kershaw, Ian, *Hitler 1889–1936: Hubris*, Penguin Books, London, 1998

—, *Hitler 1936–1945: Nemesis*, Penguin Books, London, 2001

—, *Popular Opinion and Public Dissent in the Third Reich: Bavaria 1933–1945*, Oxford University Press, Oxford, 2002

Keylor, William R., *The Legacy of the Great War: Peacemaking, 1919*, Houghton Mifflin, Boston, 2003

Kitchen, Martin, *The German Offensives of 1918*, Tempus Publishing, Stroud, Gloucestershire, 2001

Kluck, Alexander von, *The March on Paris: The Memoirs of Alexander von Kluck, 1914–1918*, Frontline Books, Barnsley, South Yorkshire, 2012

Kolb, Eberhard, *The Weimar Republic*, Routledge, Abingdon, Oxfordshire, 2004

Kubizek, August, *The Young Hitler I Knew: The Memoirs of Hitler's Childhood Friend*, Frontline Books, Barnsley, South Yorkshire, 2014 (references also sourced to PDFs available online, under websites below)

Kuhl, Hermann von, *Der Weltkrieg 1914–1918: Dem Deutschen Volke dargestellt* [The World War, 1914–1918: For the German People], Wilhelm Kolk, Berlin, 1929

Langer, Walter, *A Psychological Analysis of Adolf Hitler*, CreateSpace Independent Publishing Platform, 2012

Lentin, Anthony, *Lloyd George and the Lost Peace: From Versailles to Hitler, 1919–1940*, Palgrave Macmillan, London, 2001

Lukacs, John, *The Hitler of History*, Vintage, New York, 1998

Luther, Martin, *Luther's Works* (trans. Martin Bertram), Fortress Press, Philadelphia, 1971

—, *The Jews and their Lies*, Jewish Virtual Library: http://www.jewishvirtual-library.org/jsource/anti-semitism/Luther_on_Jews.html

Lynch, Edward, *Somme Mud: The War Experiences of an Infantryman in France, 1916–1919*, Random House Australia, Sydney, 2008

MacMillan, Margaret, *Paris 1919: Six Months that Changed the World*, Random House, London, 2003

Madden, Paul, *Adolf Hitler and the Nazi Epoch: An Annotated Bibliography of English-language Works on the Origins, Nature, and Structure of the Nazi State*, Salem Press, Pasadena, California, 1998

Maser, Werner, *Hitler: Legend, Myth and Reality*, Harper & Row, New York, 1973

—, *Hitler's Letters and Notes*, Bantam, New York, 1974

McElligott, Anthony, and Kirk, Tim (eds), *Working Towards the Führer: Essays in Honour of Sir Ian Kershaw*, Manchester University Press, Manchester, 2004

McRandle, James, *The Track of the Wolf: Essays on National Socialism and its Leader, Adolf Hitler*, Northwestern University Press, Evanston, Illinois, 1965

Mend, Hans, *Adolf Hitler im Felde, 1914–1918* [Adolf Hitler in the Field, 1914–1918], Huber, Munich, 1931

Meredith, Martin, *The State of Africa: A History of Fifty Years of Independence*, Simon & Schuster, New York, 2007

Meyer, Adolf, *Mit Adolf Hitler im Bayerischen Reserve Infanterie-Regiment 16 List* [With Adolf Hitler in the 16th Bavarian Reserve Infantry Regiment List], Georg Aupperle Verlag, Neustadt an der Aisch, 1934

Milfull, John (ed.), *Attractions of Fascism: Social Psychology and Aesthetics of the 'Triumph of the Right'*, Bloomsbury Academic, New York, 1990

Miller, Steven, et al. (eds), *Military Strategy and the Origins of the First World War: An International Security Reader*, Princeton University Press, New Jersey, 1991

Mitchell, Allan, *The Great Train Race: Railways and the Franco-German Rivalry, 1815–1914*, Berghahn Books, New York, 2000

Moltke, Helmuth von, *Essays, Speeches, and Memoirs of Field Marshal Count Helmuth von Moltke*, Vol. 1, Forgotten Books, Hong Kong, 2012

Mombauer, Annika, *Origins of the First World War: Controversies and Consensus*, Routledge, Abingdon, Oxfordshire, 2002

—, *Helmuth von Moltke and the Origins of the First World War*, Cambridge University Press, Cambridge, 2005

Müller, Karl Alexander von, *Mars und Venus: Erinnerungen 1914–1918* [Mars and Venus: Memories 1914–1918], G. Kilpper, Stuttgart, 1954

Murray, Williamson, et al. (eds), *The Making of Strategy: Rulers, States and War*, Cambridge University Press, Cambridge, 1996

Neillands, Robin, *The Death of Glory: Western Front 1915*, John Murray, London, 2006

Neumann, Hans-Joachim, and Eberle, Henrik, *Was Hitler Ill? A Final Diagnosis*, Polity, Cambridge, 2012

Neumann, Sigmund, *The Future in Perspective*, G. P. Putnam's Sons, New York, 1946

Niewyk, Donald L., *The Jews in Weimar Germany*, Routledge, New York, 2000

Ohler, Norman, *Blitzed: Drugs in Nazi Germany* (trans. Shaun Whiteside), Houghton Mifflin Harcourt, Boston, 2016

Osborne, Eric, *Britain's Economic Blockade of Germany, 1914–1919*, Routledge, Abingdon, Oxfordshire, 2004

Overy, Richard, *Goering: Hitler's Iron Knight*, I. B. Tauris, London, 2012

Pakenham, Thomas, *The Scramble for Africa: The White Man's Conquest of the Dark Continent from 1876 to 1912*, Avon Books, New York, 1992

Payne, Robert, *The Life and Death of Adolf Hitler*, Dorset Press, Dorchester, 1995

Pick, Daniel, *The Pursuit of the Nazi Mind: Hitler, Hess and the Analysts*, Oxford University Press, Oxford, 2014

Piketty, Thomas, *Capital in the Twenty-First Century* (trans. Arthur Goldhammer), Belknap Press, Cambridge, Massachussets, 2014

Prange, George (ed.), *Hitler's Words: Two Decades of National Socialism, 1923–1943*, American Council on Public Affairs, Washington, 1944

Redles, David, *Hitler's Millennial Reich: Apocalyptic Belief and the Search for Salvation*, New York University Press, New York, 2008

Redlich, Fritz, *Hitler: Diagnosis of a Destructive Prophet*, Oxford University Press, Oxford, 2000

Richter, Duncan, *Historical Dictionary of Wittgenstein's Philosophy*, Rowman & Littlefield, Lanham, Maryland, 2014

Rosenbaum, Ron, *Explaining Hitler: The Search for the Origins of his Evil*, Da Capo, Boston, 2014

Rosenfeld, Alvin, *Imagining Hitler*, Indiana University Press, Bloomington, 1985

Rosenfeld, Gavriel, *Hi Hitler!: How the Nazi Past is Being Normalized in Contemporary Culture*, Cambridge University Press, Cambridge, 2015

Rumbold, Horace, *The War Crisis in Berlin: July–August 1914*, Constable, London, 1940

Rupprecht, Crown Prince, *My War Diary*, Deutscher National Verlag, Munich, 1929

Ryback, Timothy, *Hitler's Private Library: The Books That Shaped His Life*, Vintage, London, 2010

Schopenhauer, Arthur, *The World as Will and Representation*, Vol. 1, Dover Publications, Mineola, New York, 2012

—, *Parerga and Paralipomena: Short Philosophical Essays*, Vol. 1, Cambridge Edition of the Works of Schopenhauer, Cambridge University Press, Cambridge, 2014

Schramm, Percy Ernst, *Hitler: The Man and the Military Leader* (ed. & trans. Donald Detwiler), Academy Chicago Publishers, Chicago, 1999

Sheffield, Gary, *The Somme – A New History*, Cassell, London, 2003

—, *Forgotten Victory: The First World War – Myths and Realities*, Endeavour Press, London, 2014

Sheldon, Jack, *The German Army at Passchendaele*, Pen & Sword, Barnsley, South Yorkshire, 2007

—, and Cave, Nigel, *Ypres 1914: Langemarck*, Casemate, Oxford, 2014

Shirer, William, *The Rise and Fall of the Third Reich*, Simon & Schuster, New York, 2011

Showalter, Walter, *Tannenberg: Clash of Empires 1914*, Potomac Books, Dulles, Virginia, 2004

Smith, Bradley, *Adolf Hitler: His Family, Childhood and Youth*, Hoover Institution Press, Stanford, California, 1967

Solleder, Fridolin (ed.), *Vier Jahre Westfront, Geschichte des Regiments List R.I.R. 16* [Four Years on the Western Front, History of the List Regiment, 16th R.I.R.], Max Schick, Munich, 1932

Stachura, Peter, *The Weimar Era and Hitler, 1918–1933: a Critical Bibliography*, Clio Press, Oxford, 1977

Steigmann-Gall, Richard, *The Holy Reich: Nazi Conceptions of Christianity, 1919–1945*, Cambridge University Press, New York, 2003

Steinert, Marlis, *Hitler's War and the Germans: Public Mood and Attitude During the Second World War*, Ohio University Press, Athens, Ohio, 1977

—, *Hitler*, W. W. Norton, London, 1991

Stevenson, David, *1914–1918: The History of the First World War*, Penguin, London, 2005

Strachan, Hew, *The First World War*, Vol. I: *To Arms*, Penguin Books, London, 2001

Stratigakos, Despina, *Hitler at Home*, Yale University Press, New Haven, Connecticut, 2015

Taylor, A. J. P., *The Habsburg Monarchy, 1809–1918: A History of the Austrian Empire and Austria–Hungary*, University of Chicago Press, Chicago, 1976

—, *The Origins of the Second World War*, Folio Society, London, 2009

—, *War by Timetable: How the First World War Began*, Endeavour Press, London, 2013

Taylor, Simon, *Germany, 1918–1933: Revolution, Counter-Revolution and the Rise of Hitler*, G. Dudeworth, London, 1983

Terrain, John, *The Western Front, 1914–1918*, Pen & Sword, Barnsley, South Yorkshire, 1960

Thomas, Nigel, and Embleton, Gerry, *The German Army in World War One: 1914–15*, Osprey Publishing, Oxford, 2003

Tirpitz, Alfred von, *My Memoirs*, Nabu Press, Charleston, South Carolina, 2010

Toland, John, *Adolf Hitler*, Wordsworth Editions, Ware, Hertfordshire, 1997

Trevor-Roper, Hugh, *The Last Days of Hitler*, Pan Macmillan, London, 2013

Tuchman, Barbara, *The Guns of August*, Presidio Press, New York, 2004

Ullrich, Volker, *Hitler: Ascent, 1889–1939* (trans. Jefferson Chase), Bodley Head, London, 2016

Vincent, Paul, *The Politics of Hunger: The Allied Blockade of Germany, 1915–1919*, Ohio University Press, Athens, Ohio, 1985

Waite, Robert G. L., *The Psychopathic God: Adolf Hitler*, New American Library, New York, 1977

Wall, Richard, and Winter, Jay, *The Upheaval of War: Family, Work and Welfare in Europe, 1914–1918*, Cambridge University Press, Cambridge, 1988

Weber, Thomas, *Hitler's First War: Adolf Hitler, the Men of the List Regiment, and the First World War*, Oxford University Press, Oxford, 2011

Wiedemann, Fritz, *Der Mann, der Feldherr werden wollte* [The Man Who Wanted to Be Commander], Blick und Bilde, Dortmund, 1964

Williams, John F., *Corporal Hitler and the Great War 1914–1918: The List Regiment*, Cass Military Studies, Routledge, New York, 2005

Zitelmann, Rainer, *Hitler: The Policies of Seduction*, Allison & Busby, London, 2000

Zweig, Stefan, *The World of Yesterday: Memories of a European*, Pushkin Press, London, 2009

Essays, papers and articles

Alsfeld, Richard, and Hitler, Adolf, 'Adolf Hitler's Letter to the Editor: A Note on Hitler's Message to "The Nation"', *International Social Science Review*, Vol. 61, No. 3, Summer 1986, pp. 123–7, Pi Gamma Mu, International Honor Society in Social Sciences

Armbruster, Jan, and Theiss-Abendroth, Peter, 'Deconstructing the myth of Pasewalk: Why Adolf Hitler's psychiatric treatment at the end of World War I bears no relevance', *Archives of Clinical Psychiatry (São Paulo)*, Vol. 43, No. 3, May/June 2016: http://www.scielo.br/pdf/rpc/v43n3/0101-6083-rpc-43-3-0056.pdf

Baird, Jay, 'Hitler's Muse: The Political Aesthetics of the Poet and Playwright Eberhard Wolfgang Möller', *German Studies Review*, Vol. 17, No. 2, May 1994, pp. 269–85, Johns Hopkins University Press on behalf of the German Studies Association

—, review of *The Attractions of Fascism: Social Psychology and Aesthetics of the 'Triumph of the Right'*, ed. John Milfull, *German Studies Review*, Vol. 15, No. 1, February 1992, Johns Hopkins University Press on behalf of the German Studies Association

Bannon, Steve, 'This is How Steve Bannon Sees the Entire World', *Buzzfeed* (full transcript), 15 November 2016: https://www.buzzfeed.com/lesterfeder/this-is-how-steve-bannon-sees-the-entire-world?utm_term=.sbKXO21Wb#.jjzp4LjNX

Binchy, Daniel, 'Adolf Hitler', *Studies: An Irish quarterly review of letters, philosophy and science*, Vol. 22, No. 85, March 1933, Irish Province of the Society of Jesus

Binion, Rudolph, 'Foam on the Hitler Wave', *Journal of Modern History*, Vol. 46, No. 3, September 1974, pp. 522–8, University of Chicago Press

Bloch, Eduard, 'My Patient Hitler', *Collier's Weekly*, 15 March 1941, pp. 11 and 35–9, and 22 March 1941, pp. 69–73

Bookbinder, Paul, 'Carl Schmitt, "Der Leviathan", and the Jews', *International Social Science Review*, Vol. 66, No. 3, Summer 1991, pp. 99–109, Pi Gamma Mu, International Honor Society in Social Sciences

Boyer, J. W., 'Karl Lueger and the Viennese Jews', *Leo Baeck Institute Yearbook*, Vol. 26, Issue 1, 1981

Carrier, Richard, ' "Hitler's Table Talk": Troubling Finds', *German Studies Review*, Vol. 26, No. 3 (October 2003), pp. 561–76, Johns Hopkins University Press on behalf of the German Studies Association

Churchill, Winston, 'Full transcript of notes of a speech by Winston Churchill broadcast on BBC radio, 10pm, 15 November 1934', UK Government Parliamentary Archives: http://www.winstonchurchill.org/resources/speeches/1930-1938-the-wilderness/the-threat-of-nazi-germany

Cocks, Geoffrey, 'The Hitler Controversy', reviews of *Adolf Hitler* by John Toland; *Hitler's War* by David Irving; *The Psychopathic God: Adolf Hitler* by Robert G. L. Waite; *Hitler among the Germans* by Rudolph Binion, in *Political Psychology*, Vol. 1, No. 2, Autumn 1979, pp. 67–81, International Society of Political Psychology

Cohan, A. S., 'Politics and Psychoanalysis: The Sources of Hitler's Political Behaviour', *British Journal of International Studies*, Vol. 1, No. 2, July 1975, pp. 160–75, Cambridge University Press

Diver, Krysia, 'Journal reveals Hitler's dysfunctional family', *Guardian*, 4 August 2005: https://www.theguardian.com/world/2005/aug/04/research.secondworldwar

Economist, The, 'Pepe and the Stormtroopers: How Donald Trump ushered a hateful fringe movement into the mainstream', *The Economist*, 17 September 2016: http://www.economist.com/news/united-states/21707201-how-donald-trump-ushered-hateful-fringe-movement-mainstream-pepe-and?cid1=cust/ednew/n/bl/n/20160915n/owned/n/n/nwl/n/n/n/n

Ensor, Robert, 'Who Hitler Is', *Oxford Pamphlets on World Affairs*, No. 20, Clarendon Press, Oxford, 1939

—,' Mein Kampf: Herr Hitler's Self Disclosure in Mein Kampf', *Oxford Pamphlets on World Affairs*, No. 3, Clarendon Press, Oxford, 1939

Evans, Richard, 'Blitzed: Drugs in Nazi Germany by Norman Ohler – a crass and dangerously inaccurate account', *Guardian*, 16 November 2016: https://www.theguardian.com/books/2016/nov/16/blitzed-drugs-in-nazi-germany-by-norman-ohler-review

Ferrell, Donald, 'The Unmourned Wound: Reflections on the Psychology of Adolf Hitler', *Journal of Religion and Health*, Vol. 34, No. 3, Fall 1995, pp. 175–97, Springer

Gatzke, Hans, 'Hitler and Psychohistory', *American Historical Review*, Vol. 78, No. 2, April 1973, pp. 394–401, Oxford University Press on behalf of the American Historical Association

Geoffrey, Giles, review of *Blut und Paukboden. Eine Geschichte der Burschenschaften* [Blood and Duelling Lofts, A History of Student Societies] by Dietrich Heither et al., *German Studies Review*, Vol. 22, No. 1, February 1999, pp. 141–2, Johns Hopkins University Press on behalf of the German Studies Association

Gould, Stephen Jay, 'Curveball', *New Yorker*, 28 November 1994: http://www.dartmouth.edu/~chance/course/topics/curveball.html

Grafton, Anthony, 'Mein Buch', review of *Hitler's Private Library: The Books That Shaped His Life* by Timothy Ryback, *New Republic*, 24 December 2008

Hale, Oron James, 'Adolf Hitler: Taxpayer', *American Historical Review*, Vol. 60, No. 4, July 1955, pp. 830–42, Oxford University Press on behalf of the American Historical Association

Hall, Walter, review of *The Future in Perspective* by Sigmund Neumann, *American Historical Review*, Vol. 52, No. 3, April 1947, p. 494

Hancock, Eleanor, ' "Only the Real, the True, the Masculine Held Its Value": Ernst Röhm, Masculinity, and Male Homosexuality', *Journal of the History of Sexuality*, Vol. 8, No. 4, April 1998, pp. 616–41, University of Texas Press

Heiden, Konrad, 'Hitler's Better Half', *Foreign Affairs*, Vol. 20, No. 1, October 1941, pp. 73–86, Council on Foreign Relations

Herwig, Holgar, 'Clio Deceived: Patriotic Self-Censorship in Germany After the Great War', *International Security*, 12 (2), Autumn 1987

Hitler, Adolf, Letter to Herr Gemlich, in 'Adolf Hitler: First Anti-Semitic Writing', 16 September 1919, Jewish Virtual Library: http://www.jewish virtuallibrary.org/jsource/Holocaust/Adolf_Hitler's_First_Antisemitic _Writing.html

Hüppauf, Bernd, 'Langemarck, Verdun and the Myth of the New Man in Germany After the Great War', *War & Society*, Vol. 6, No. 2, September 1988

Kaltenborn, Hans, and Hitler, Adolf, 'An Interview with Hitler, August 17, 1932', *Wisconsin Magazine of History*, Vol. 50, No. 4, unpublished documents on Nazi Germany from the Mass Communications History Center, Summer 1967, pp. 283–90, Wisconsin Historical Society

Kaplan, Robert, 'Was Hitler Ill? A Reply to Eberle and Neumann', *German Politics and Society*, 33 (3), 1 September 2015

Kasher, Steven, 'The Art of Hitler', *October*, Vol. 59, Winter 1992, pp. 48–85, MIT Press

Keegan, John, 'There's Rosemary for Remembrance', *American Scholar*, Vol. 66, No. 3, Summer 1997, pp. 335–48, Phi Beta Kappa Society

Kellerhoff, Sven Felix, 'Adolf Hitler war im Ersten Weltkrieg ein Feigling' ['Adolf Hitler was a coward in the First World War'], Welt 24: https://www.welt.de/kultur/article9673138/adolf-hitler-war-im-ersten-weltkrieg-ein-feigling.html

Kittler, Wolf, 'From Gestalt to Ge-Stell: Martin Heidegger Reads Ernst Jünger', Cultural Critique, No. 69: Radical Conservative Thought in Transition: Martin Heidegger, Ernst Jünger and Carl Schmitt, 1940–1960, Spring 2008, pp. 79–97, University of Minnesota Press

Kolmer, Gustave (ed.), 'The Linz Program' (trans. Jeremy King and Rachel Coll), Parlament und Verfassung in Österreich [Parliament and Constitution in Austria], Vol. 3, Wien: k.u.k. Hof-Buchdruckerei, 1905, pp. 212–14, 2001

Kovaleski, Serge, et al., 'An Alt-Right Makeover Shrouds the Swastikas', New York Times, 10 December 2016: http://www.nytimes.com/2016/12/10/us/alt-right-national-socialist-movement-white-supremacy.html?emc=edit_th_20161211&nl=todaysheadlines&nlid=55326310

Landauer, Carl, 'The Bavarian Problem in the Weimar Republic: Part II', Journal of Modern History, 16 (3), September 1944, pp. 205–23, University of Chicago Press

Langer, Walter, 'A Psychological Analysis of Adolph Hitler, His Life and Legend', The Nizkor Project, Office of Strategic Studies, Washington 1991–2012: http://www.nizkor.org/hweb/people/h/hitler-adolf/oss-papers/text/profile-index.html

Lavik, Nils Johan, 'A Psychiatrist Who Confronted Nazism', Political Psychology, Vol. 10, No. 4, December 1989, pp. 757–65, International Society of Political Psychology

Lukacs, John, 'Historiography: Hitler Becomes a Man', American Scholar, Vol. 51, No. 3, Summer 1982, pp. 391–5, Phi Beta Kappa Society

Luther, Martin, 'That Jesus Christ Was Born a Jew': https://www.uni-due.de/collcart/es/sem/s6/txt09_1.htm

Macleod, Professor Sandy, 'Mrs Hitler and Her Doctor', Australasian Psychiatry, 13 (4), December 2005: https://www.ncbi.nlm.nih.gov/pubmed/16403142?dopt=Abstract

McCants, William, 'The implications of Donald Trump's sharp contrast from Obama and Bush on Islam', 15 December 2016, Brookings Institution: https://www.brookings.edu/blog/markaz/2016/12/15/the-implications-of-donald-trumps-sharp-contrast-from-obama-and-bush-on-islam/?utm_campaign=Brookings+Brief&utm_source=hs_email&utm_medium=email&utm_content=39427467

Murray, Henry A., 'Analysis of the Personality of Adolf Hitler, with Predictions for his Future Behavior and Suggestions for Dealing With Him Now and After Germany's Surrender', OSS Archives, October 1943: https://www.cia.

gov/library/readingroom/docs/CIA-RDP78-02646R000100030002-2.
pdf

Orlow, Dietrich, 'The Organizational History and Structure of the NSDAP, 1919–23', *Journal of Modern History*, Vol. 37, No. 2, June 1965, pp. 208–26, University of Chicago Press

Osborn, Max, 'The Beginning of the End of German Jewry', Jewish Museum Berlin, 25 January 1933: https://www.jmberlin.de/1933/en/01_31_art-critic-max-osborns-response-to-a-letter-to-the-editor.php

Palmer, Brian, 'Did Hitler Invent the Hitler Mustache?', *Slate*, 30 May 2013: http://www.slate.com/articles/life/explainer/2013/05/the_hitler_mustache_was_it_ever_a_fashionable_style_of_facial_hair.html

Phelps, Ronald, 'Hitler and the Deutsche Arbeiterpartei', *American Historical Review*, Vol. 68, No. 4, July 1963, pp. 974–86, Oxford University Press on behalf of the American Historical Association

Prochnik, George, 'When it's too late to stop fascism, according to Stefan Zweig', *New Yorker*, 6 February 2017: http://www.newyorker.com/books/page-turner/when-its-too-late-to-stop-fascism-according-to-stefan-zweig

Redles, David, 'The Nazi Old Guard: Identity Formation During Apocalyptic Times', *Nova Religio: The Journal of Alternative and Emergent Religions*, Vol. 14, No. 1, August 2010, pp. 24–44, University of California Press

Reimann, Bruno, 'The Defeat of the German Universities 1933', *Historical Social Research/Historische Sozialforschung*, No. 39, July 1986, pp. 101–5, GESIS – Leibniz-Institute for the Social Sciences, Center for Historical Social Research

Smith, Arthur, 'Kurt Lüdecke: The Man Who Knew Hitler', *German Studies Review*, Vol. 26, No. 3, October 2003, pp. 597–606, Johns Hopkins University Press on behalf of the German Studies Association

Stachura, Peter, review of *To Die for Germany: Heroes in the Nazi Pantheon* by Jay W. Baird, in *English Historical Review*, Vol. 108, No. 429, October 1993, pp. 1078–9, Oxford University Press

Stiglitz, Joseph E., 'Trump's Rogue America', *Project Syndicate*, 2 June 2017

Trumpener, Ulrich, 'The Road to Ypres: The Beginnings of Gas Warfare in World War I', *Journal of Modern History*, Vol. 47, No. 3, September 1975, pp. 460–80, University of Chicago Press

Turner, Ewart Edmund, 'To Hitler via Two Men', *American Scholar*, Vol. 6, No. 1, Winter 1937, Phi Beta Kappa Society

Vaget, Hans, 'Syberberg's "Our Hitler": Wagnerianism and Alienation', *Massachusetts Review*, Vol. 23, No. 4, Winter 1982, pp. 593–612, Massachusetts Review, Inc.

Waite, Robert, 'Adolf Hitler's Guilt Feelings: A Problem in History and Psychology', *Journal of Interdisciplinary History*, Vol. 1, No. 2, Winter 1971, pp. 229–49, MIT Press

Watt, Roderick, '"Wanderer, kommst du nach Sparta": History Through Propaganda into Literary Commonplace', *Modern Language Review*, Vol. 80, No. 4, October 1985, pp. 871–83, Modern Humanities Research Association

Weinberg, Gerhard, review of *The Psychopathic God: Adolf Hitler* by Robert G. L. Waite, *American Historical Review*, Vol. 83, No. 3, June 1978, pp. 753–6, Oxford University Press on behalf of the American Historical Association

Weiskopf, F. C., 'Penetrating the "Intellectual Gas Mask"', *Books Abroad*, Vol. 17, No. 1, Winter 1943, pp. 9–12, Board of Regents of the University of Oklahoma

Weldon Whalen, Robert, 'War Losses (Germany)', *International Encyclopaedia of the First World War*: http://encyclopedia.1914-1918-online.net/article/war_losses_germany

Wheeler-Bennett, John, 'Ludendorff: The Soldier and the Politician', *Virginia Quarterly Review*, 14 (2), Spring 1938, pp. 187–202

Williams, Desmond, 'Adolf Hitler and the Historians', *University Review*, Vol. 1, No. 9, Summer 1956, pp. 37–51, Irish University Review

Private papers
British

Lloyd-Burch, David, Private Papers, Document 1423 87/26/1, Imperial War Museum, London

Naylor, Jim, Private Papers, Document 2352 86/21/1, Imperial War Museum, London

German

Baumann, Hermann, 'War Diary, 1914–1916' (ed. Magdalena Huck; trans. Martha Grieswelle, *née* Baumann), Document 300,10/collection military history, number 177, Archive Bielefeld, North-Rhine Westphalia

Delius, Walter, '*Kriegserinnerungen* [War Memories] *1914–1918*', collated from letters and diary entries, Document 300,5/HgB, number 8, Archive Bielefeld, North-Rhine Westphalia

Unknown soldier, extract, 'Battle of Ypres [1914]', Diary, Document 300,10/collection military history, number 231, Archive Bielefeld, North-Rhine Westphalia

Archives

Bayerisches Hauptstaatsarchiv, Kriegsarchiv [Bavarian National Archives, War Archives], Munich: http://www.gda.bayern.de/hauptstaatsarchiv/

Bielefeld City Archive, Bielefeld, North-Rhine Westphalia

Calvin College, German Propaganda Archive, Michigan State University Press: http://research.calvin.edu/german-propaganda-archive/

Europeana 1914–18, archival project partnered by Oxford University and the British Library, University of Oxford: http://www.europeana1914-1918. eu/en

FirstWorldWar.com – a multimedia history: http://www.firstworldwar.com/index.htm

German History in Documents and Images (GHDI): http://germanhistory docs.ghi-dc.org/

Heidelberger historische Bestände [Heidelberg Historical Records]: www. ub.uni-heidelberg.de/helios/digi/digilit.htm

Holocaust Encyclopaedia: https://www.ushmm.org/learn/holocaust-encyclopedia

Imperial War Museum, London: http://www.iwm.org.uk/

Jewish Museum, Berlin: https://www.jmberlin.de/en

National Archives, United Kingdom: http://www.nationalarchives.gov.uk/

Records of the Office of Strategic Services (OSS), 1943: https://www.archives. gov/iwg/declassified-records/rg-226-oss

Staatsarchiv Hamburg [National Archives, Hamburg]: http://www.ham burg.de/staatsarchiv/

United States Holocaust Memorial Museum: https://www.ushmm.org/

World War I Document Archive: https://wwi.lib.byu.edu/index.php/ Main_Page

Websites
'25 Points of American National Socialism', National Socialist Movement of America, http://www.nsm88.org/25points/25pointsengl.html

'Adolf Hitler wounded in British gas attack', *This Day in History*: http://www. history.com/this-day-in-history/adolf-hitler-wounded-in-british-gas-attack

Beatty, Brian (co-ordinator), 'The Bell Curve', responses to the book by members of the American Psychological Association: http://www.intell theory.com/bellcurve.shtml

'Documents: The Rise of the Nazis', German History in Documents and Images *(GHDI)*: http://germanhistorydocs.ghi-dc.org/sub_document. cfm?document_id=3910

'Facts About Sulfur Mustard', Centers for Disease Control and Prevention: https://emergency.cdc.gov/agent/sulfurmustard/basics/facts.asp

Haig, Sir Douglas, 'Sir Douglas Haig's "Backs to the Wall" Order, 11 April 1918', First World War.com: www.firstworldwar.com/source/backsto thewall.htm

Hamman, Brigitte, 'Hitler's Vienna: A Dictator's Apprenticeship: Jews in Vienna', Porges.net: http://www.porges.net/JewsInVienna/1Historical Background.html

Hitler Headquarters War Diaries and diarist's writings by Helmuth Greiner, Percy Ernst Schramm, and the Headquarters, United States Army Europe

Foreign Military Studies Branch, BACM Research – PaperlessArchives. com: http://www.paperlessarchives.com/hitler_headquarters_diary.html

'Interview with Hitler's Sister on 5th June 1946', Modern Military Records (NWCTM), Textual Archives Services Section, National Archives and Records Administration, Maryland: http://www.oradour.info/appendix/paulahit/paula01.htm

'Jewish Communities of Pre-War Germany', Holocaust Encyclopaedia: http://www.ushmm.org/wlc/en/article.php?ModuleId=10007052

Kubizek, August, *The Young Hitler I Knew*: https://archive.org/details/TheYoungHitlerIKnew
http://www.jrbooksonline.com/PDFs/The%20Young%20Hitler%20I%20Knew%20JR.pdf
http://scienceblogs.com/insolence/2006/04/17/mrs-hitler-and-her-doctor

Moorhouse, Roger, 'On Hitler's Teeth – or, the Death of a Dictator', *historian at large* (personal blog), 25 March 2015: http://historian-at-large.blogspot.fr/2015/03/on-hitlers-teeth-or-death-of-dictator.html

Macleod, Professor Sandy, 'Mrs Hitler and Her Doctor', *Australian Psychology*

'Persecution of Homosexuals in the Third Reich', *Holocaust Encyclopaedia*: https://www.ushmm.org/wlc/en/article.php?ModuleId=10005261

'Project find postcard from Hitler', Europeana 1914–18, an archival project partnered by Oxford University and the British Library, University of Oxford: http://www.ox.ac.uk/news/2012-05-02-project-finds-postcard-hitler

'Report of a speech delivered by Herr von Bethmann-Hollweg, German Imperial Chancellor, on 4 August 1914', Appendix to 'Germany's Reasons for War with Russia', *German White Book*, World War I Document Archive: https://wwi.lib.byu.edu/index.php/The_German_White_Book

'Spotlights on History: The Blockade of Germany', National Archives, United Kingdom: www.nationalarchives.gov.uk/pathways/firstworldwar/spotlights/blockade.htm

'The Beginning of the End of German Jewry', Jewish Museum, Berlin: https://www.jmberlin.de/1933/en/

'The Making of Adolf Hitler', *Timewatch*, BBC documentary, 4 January 2002: http://www.bbc.co.uk/programmes/b05tr19s

'The Martyrdom of Belgium: Official Report of Massacres of Peaceable Citizens, Women and Children by the German Army', World War I Document Archive, http://digicoll.library.wisc.edu/cgi-bin/History/History-idx?id=History.Martyrdom

'The Necessary War', BBC debate, 4 June 2014, http://www.bbc.co.uk/programmes/603ustm26

'The Reformation and the Jews: an Orientation', 500 Years Reformation Luther 2017, Scientific Advisory Board for the Reformation Jubilee 2017:

https://www.luther2017.de/fileadmin/luther2017/material/grundlagen/
Die_Reformation_und_die_Juden_Engl.pdf

'Treaty of Versailles' and 'Article 231 of the Treaty of Versailles', *Wikipedia*:
https://en.wikisource.org/wiki/Treaty_of_Versailles and http://en.wikipedia.
org/wiki/Article_231_of_the_Treaty_of_Versailles

'Wannsee Conference and the "Final Solution"', United States Holocaust
Memorial Museum, https://www.ushmm.org/wlc/en/article.php?Module
Id=10005477

Acknowledgements

I'd like to thank everybody involved in the production of *Young Hitler: The Making of the Führer*. What began as a short 'Kindle Single' has evolved into a full biography of Hitler's youth, thanks in particular to: Bill Scott-Kerr, Alison Urquhart, Nikki Christer, Matthew Lynn, Richard Foreman, Brenda Updegraff, Patsy Irwin, Darcy Nicholson, Jane Burridge and many other people working in publishing and in bookstores whom I have not met, but without whom books could not be designed, published and sold. Thank you.

Picture Acknowledgements

Page 1: Alois Hitler, father of Adolf Hitler, *c.* 1880: akg-images; Klara Hitler, mother of Adolf Hitler, *c.* 1890: akg-images; Orthodox Jews in a ghetto in Vienna, Austria, pre-1914: Chronicle / Alamy stock photo; Karl Leuger: akg images / Imagno; Georg Ritter von Schonerer: akg images / Pictures from History.

Page 2: Hitler among crowds in front of Feldhernhalle in Munich July 1914: akg-images; A watercolour of the ruins of Messines church, Flanders, by Adolf Hitler, *c.* 1914: © Illustrated London News Ltd/Mary Evans.

Page 3: Hitler as a soldier in the First World War in the 2nd Bavarian Reserve Infantry Regiment no 16: akg-images; Adolf Hitler dressed in his field uniform during the First World War, 1916: Bridgeman Images; German soldiers with gas masks in the trenches: akg-images.

Page 4: Karl Liebknecht holds a rally in Temton Park, Germany, 1918: akg-images / Fototeca Gilardi; Rosa Luxemburg addressing a meeting, after the second International Social Democratic Congress, Stuttgart, 1907: History Archive / REX / Shutterstock; Urban butter sales during inflation in Germany, 1922: © SZ Photo / Scherl / Bridgeman Images.

Page 5: Raffke types in Germany, *c.* 1923: private collection / © SZ Photo / Bridgeman Images; Hitler surrounded by members of the fledgling Nazi party, Munich Beer hall putsch, 1923: History Archive / REX / Shutterstock; Hitler giving a speech, *c.* 1925: Imagno / Getty Images; A rare edition of *Mein Kampf*: akg images / Interfoto.

Page 6: Hitler with Emil Maurice, Herman Kriebel, Rudolf Hess and Friedrich Weber in Landsberg Prison 1925,: Images / REX / Shutterstock; Anton Drexler: akg images / IAM; Eckart Dietrich: akg images / ullsteinbild; Julius Streicher, *c.* 1927: akg images / Interfoto / awkz.

Index